Garfield
THE BIG CHEESE

BY JIM DAVIS

Ballantine Books Trade Paperbacks • **New York**

A Ballantine Books Trade Paperback Original

Copyright © 2015 by PAWS, Inc. All Rights Reserved.
"GARFIELD" and the GARFIELD characters are trademarks of PAWS, Inc.

Published in the United States by Ballantine Books, an imprint of Random House,
a division of Random House LLC, a Penguin Random House Company, New York.

BALLANTINE and the HOUSE colophon are registered trademarks of Random House LLC.

ISBN 978-0-345-52604-5
eBook ISBN 978-0-8041-7733-7

Printed in the United States of America on acid-free paper

www.ballantinebooks.com

9 8 7 6 5 4 3 2 1

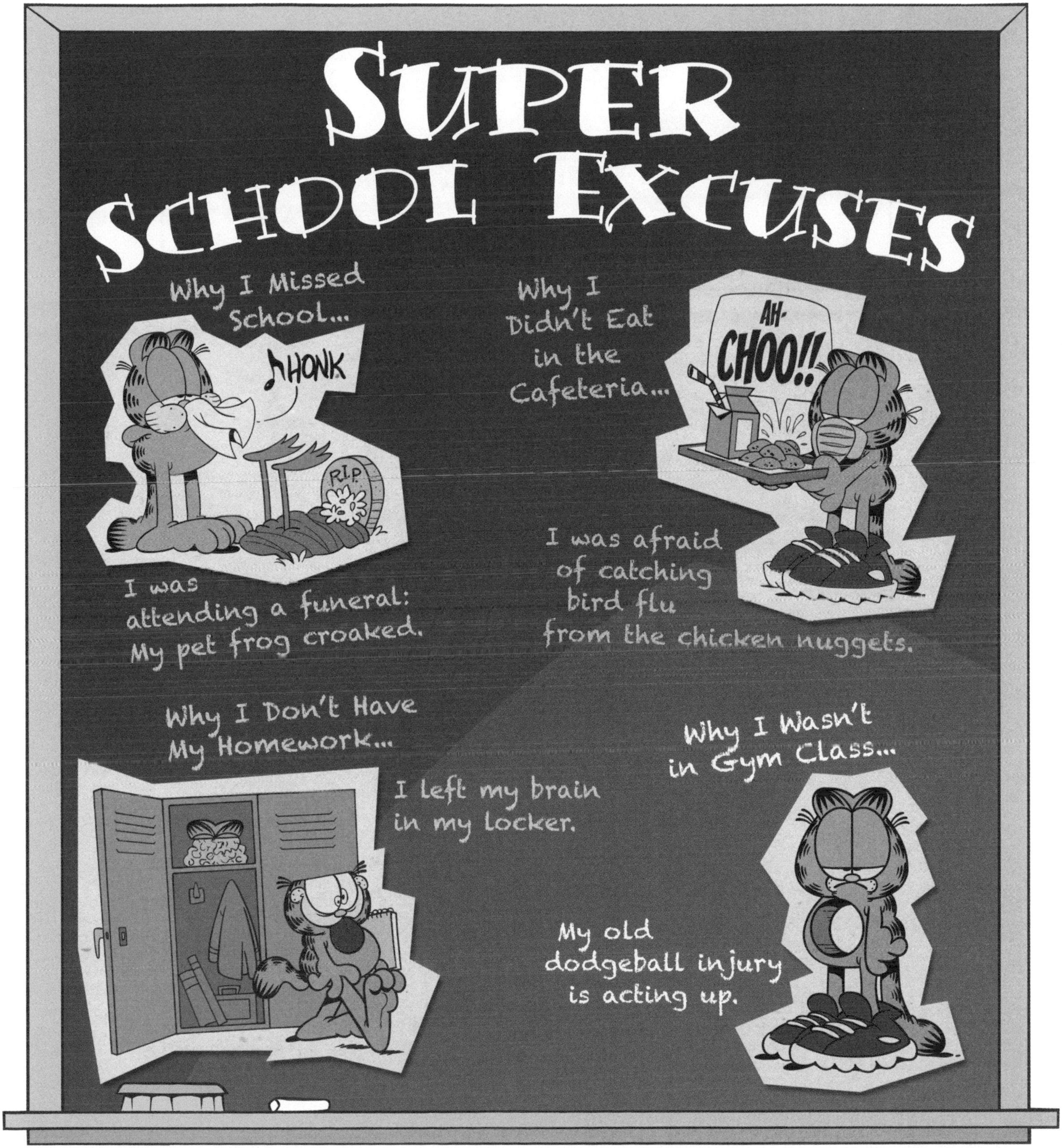
SUPER SCHOOL EXCUSES
Why I Missed School...
HONK
R.I.P.
I was attending a funeral: My pet frog croaked.
Why I Didn't Eat in the Cafeteria...
AH-CHOO!!
I was afraid of catching bird flu from the chicken nuggets.
Why I Don't Have My Homework...
I left my brain in my locker.
Why I Wasn't in Gym Class...
My old dodgeball injury is acting up.

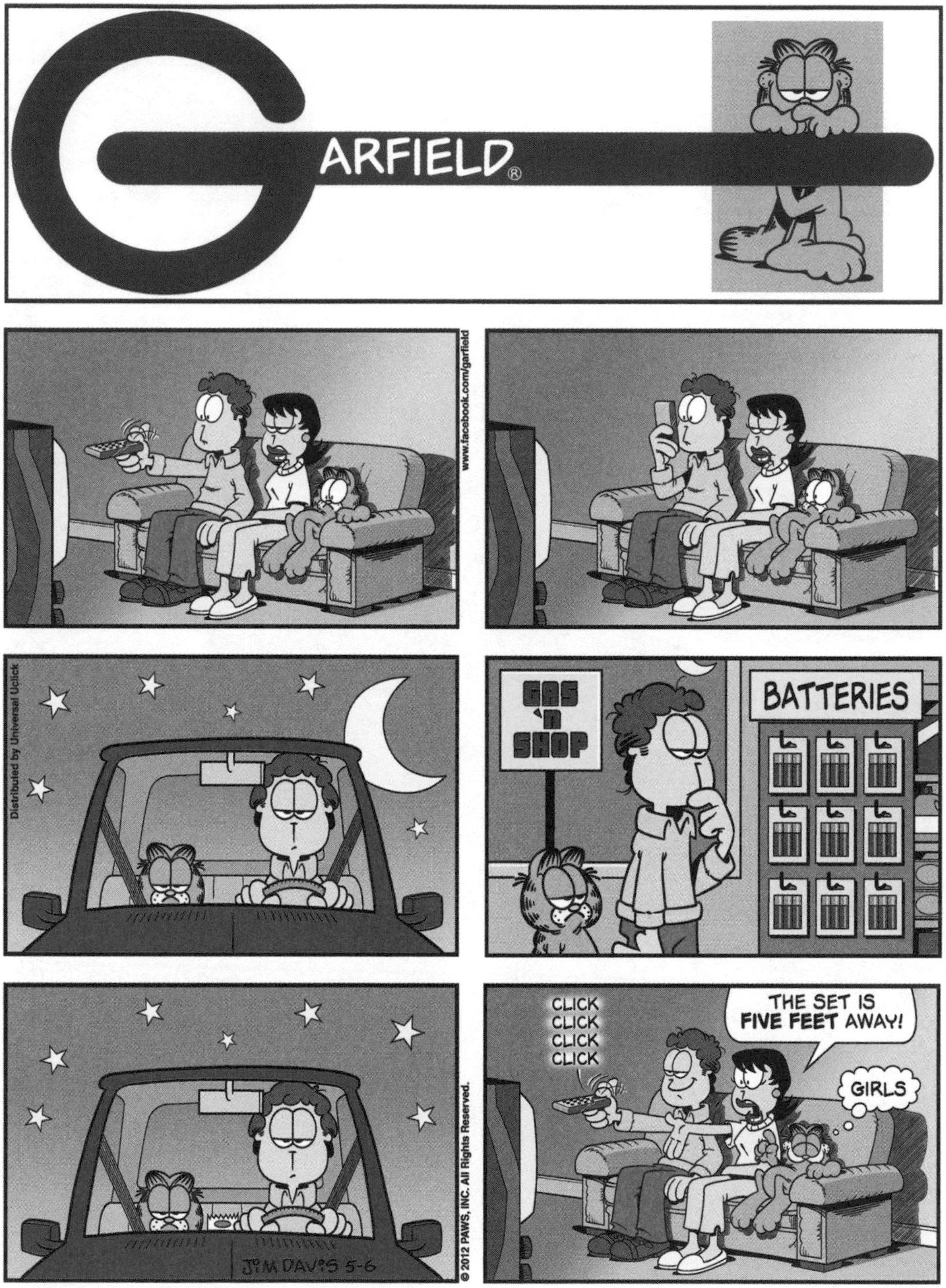
GARFIELD®
www.facebook.com/garfield
Distributed by Universal Uclick
GAS 'N SHOP
BATTERIES
CLICK
CLICK
CLICK
CLICK
THE SET IS FIVE FEET AWAY!
GIRLS
JIM DAVIS 5-6
© 2012 PAWS, INC. All Rights Reserved.

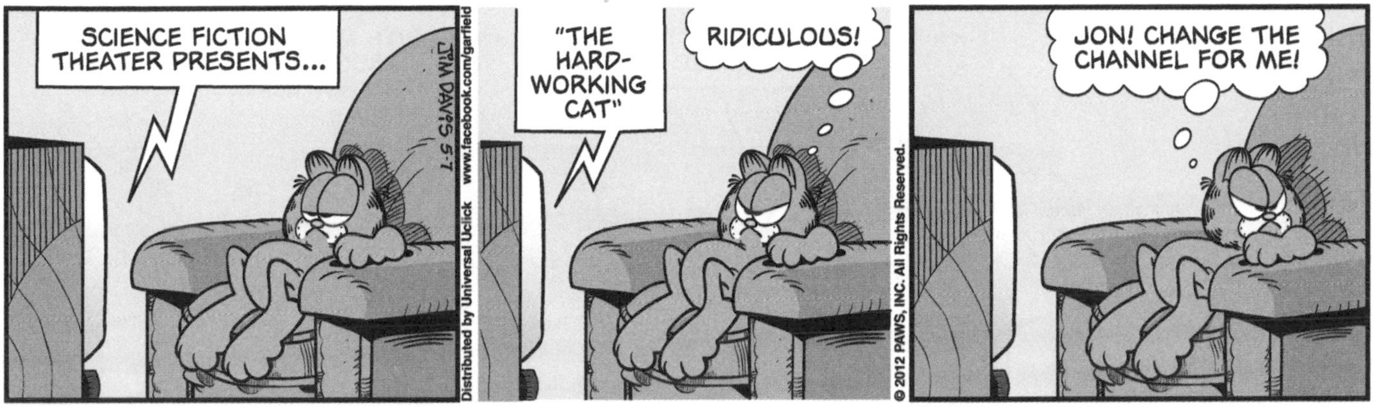
SCIENCE FICTION THEATER PRESENTS...
JIM DAVIS 5-7
www.facebook.com/garfield
Distributed by Universal Uclick
"THE HARD-WORKING CAT"
RIDICULOUS!
© 2012 PAWS, INC. All Rights Reserved.
JON! CHANGE THE CHANNEL FOR ME!

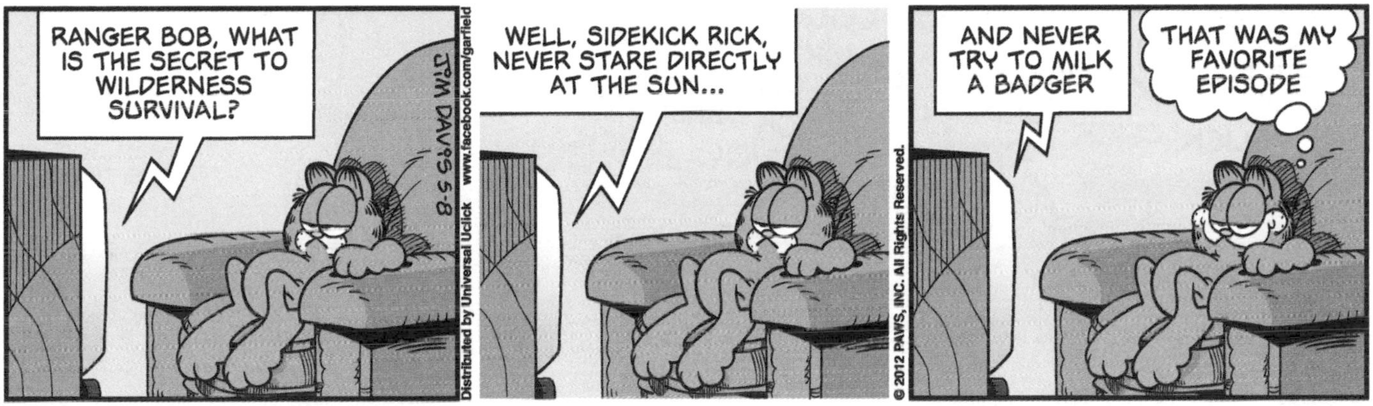
RANGER BOB, WHAT IS THE SECRET TO WILDERNESS SURVIVAL?
JIM DAVIS 5-8
www.facebook.com/garfield
Distributed by Universal Uclick
WELL, SIDEKICK RICK, NEVER STARE DIRECTLY AT THE SUN...
© 2012 PAWS, INC. All Rights Reserved.
AND NEVER TRY TO MILK A BADGER
THAT WAS MY FAVORITE EPISODE

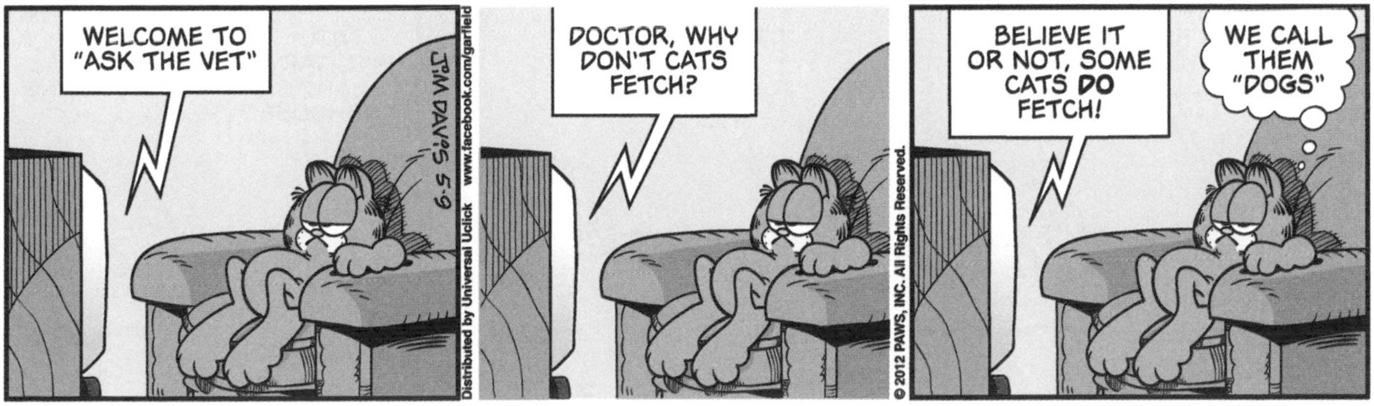
WELCOME TO "ASK THE VET"
JIM DAVIS 5-9
www.facebook.com/garfield
Distributed by Universal Uclick
DOCTOR, WHY DON'T CATS FETCH?
© 2012 PAWS, INC. All Rights Reserved.
BELIEVE IT OR NOT, SOME CATS **DO** FETCH!
WE CALL THEM "DOGS"

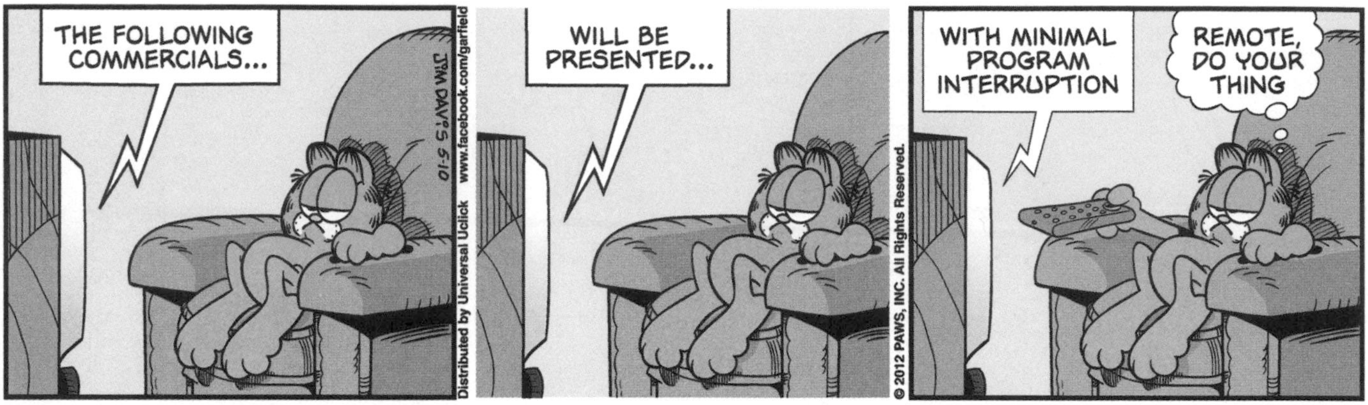
THE FOLLOWING COMMERCIALS...
JIM DAVIS 5-10
Distributed by Universal Uclick www.facebook.com/garfield
WILL BE PRESENTED...
© 2012 PAWS, INC. All Rights Reserved.
WITH MINIMAL PROGRAM INTERRUPTION
REMOTE, DO YOUR THING

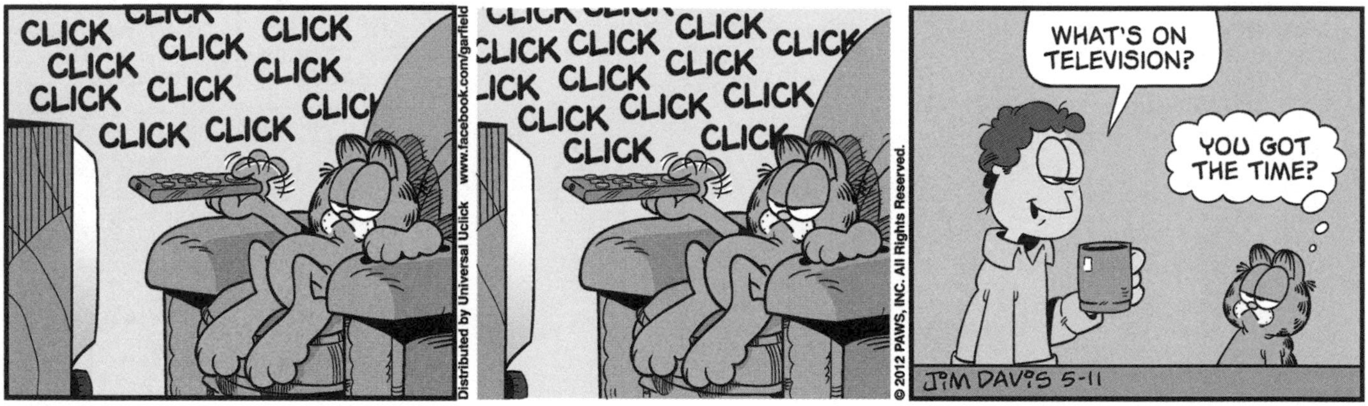
CLICK CLICK CLICK
CLICK CLICK CLICK
CLICK CLICK
CLICK CLICK
Distributed by Universal Uclick www.facebook.com/garfield
CLICK CLICK CLICK
CLICK CLICK CLICK
CLICK CLICK CLICK
CLICK
© 2012 PAWS, INC. All Rights Reserved.
WHAT'S ON TELEVISION?
YOU GOT THE TIME?
JIM DAVIS 5-11

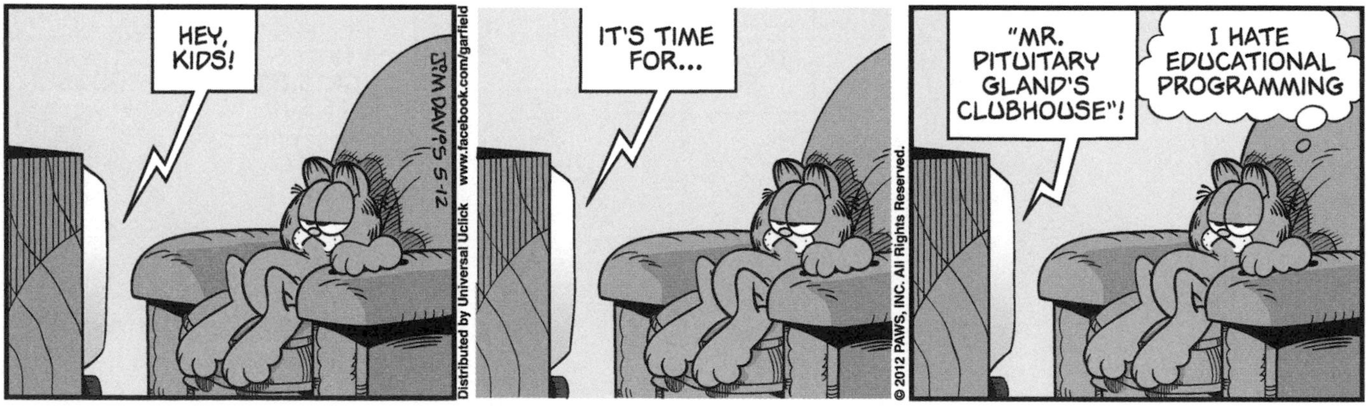
HEY, KIDS!
JIM DAVIS 5-12
Distributed by Universal Uclick www.facebook.com/garfield
IT'S TIME FOR...
© 2012 PAWS, INC. All Rights Reserved.
"MR. PITUITARY GLAND'S CLUBHOUSE"!
I HATE EDUCATIONAL PROGRAMMING

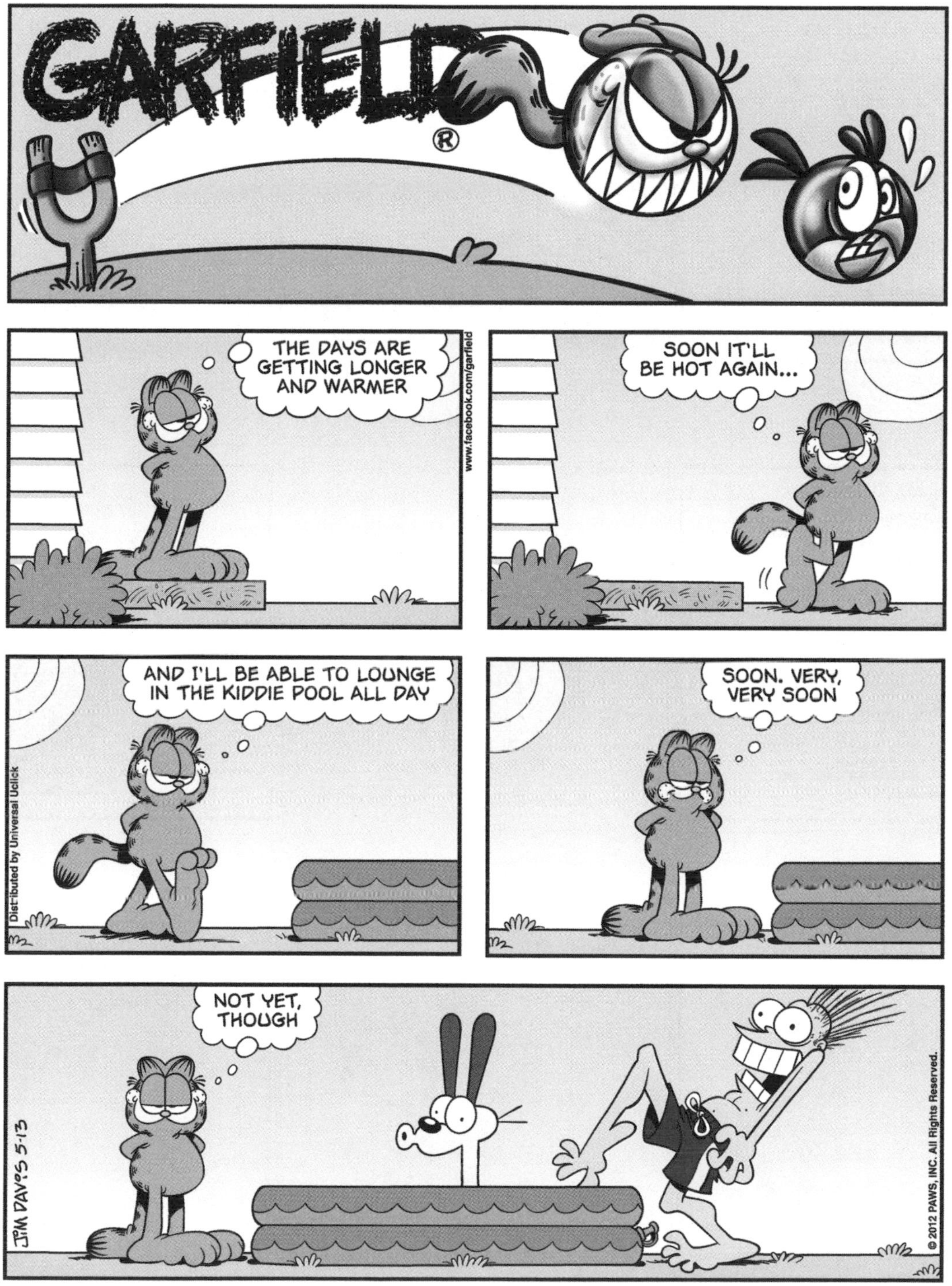
GARFIELD®
THE DAYS ARE GETTING LONGER AND WARMER
www.facebook.com/garfield
SOON IT'LL BE HOT AGAIN...
AND I'LL BE ABLE TO LOUNGE IN THE KIDDIE POOL ALL DAY
Distributed by Universal Uclick
SOON. VERY, VERY SOON
NOT YET, THOUGH
JIM DAVIS 5-13
© 2012 PAWS, INC. All Rights Reserved.

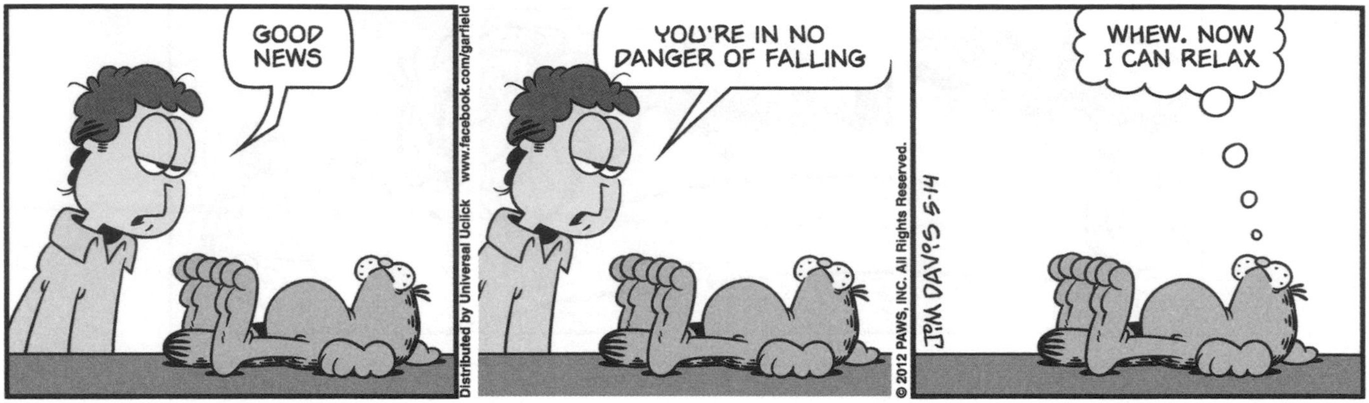
GOOD NEWS
YOU'RE IN NO DANGER OF FALLING
WHEW. NOW I CAN RELAX
Distributed by Universal Uclick www.facebook.com/garfield
© 2012 PAWS, INC. All Rights Reserved.
JIM DAVIS 5-14

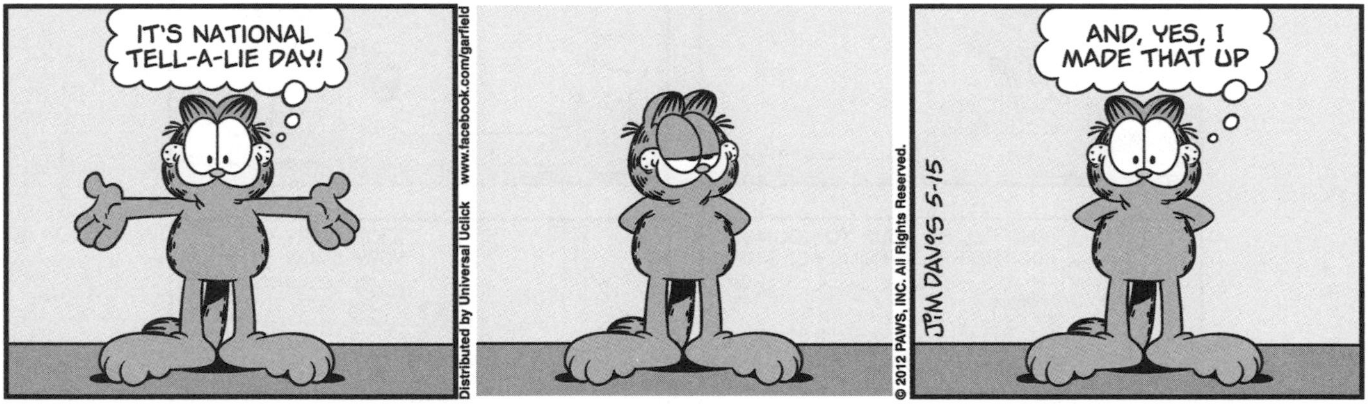
IT'S NATIONAL TELL-A-LIE DAY!
AND, YES, I MADE THAT UP
Distributed by Universal Uclick www.facebook.com/garfield
© 2012 PAWS, INC. All Rights Reserved.
JIM DAVIS 5-15

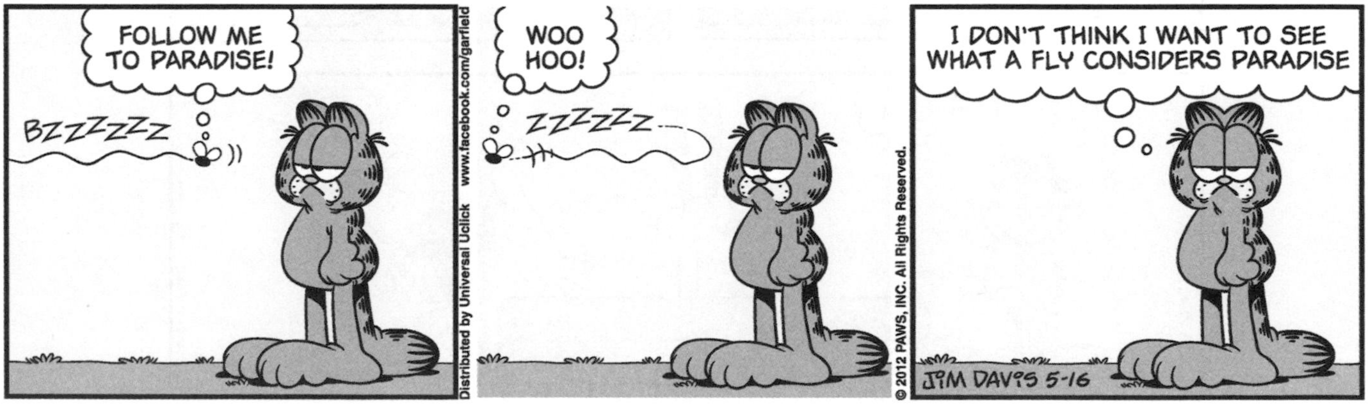
FOLLOW ME TO PARADISE!
BZZZZZZ
WOO HOO!
ZZZZZZ
I DON'T THINK I WANT TO SEE WHAT A FLY CONSIDERS PARADISE
Distributed by Universal Uclick www.facebook.com/garfield
© 2012 PAWS, INC. All Rights Reserved.
JIM DAVIS 5-16

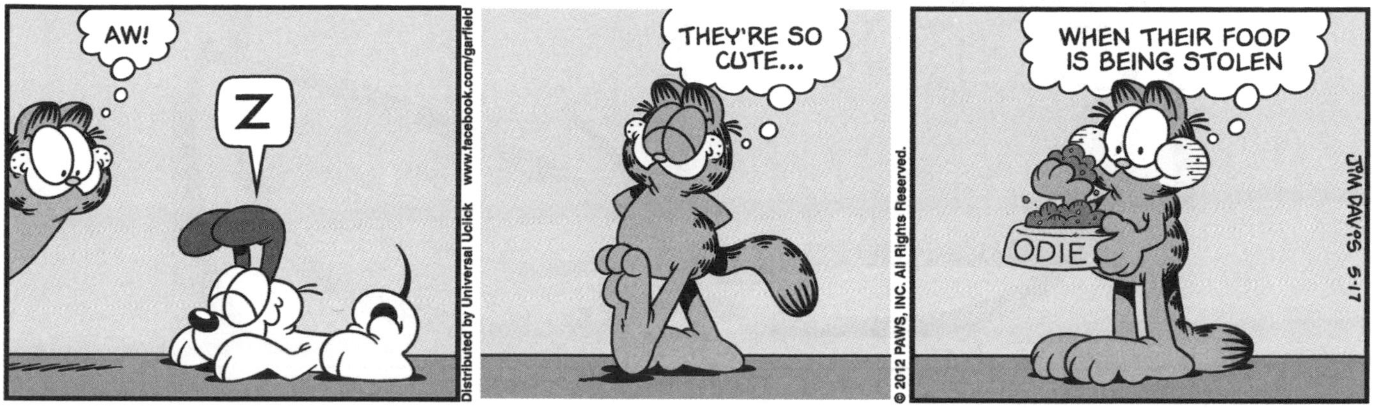
AW!
Z
THEY'RE SO CUTE...
WHEN THEIR FOOD IS BEING STOLEN
ODIE
JIM DAVIS 5-17
Distributed by Universal Uclick www.facebook.com/garfield
© 2012 PAWS, INC. All Rights Reserved.

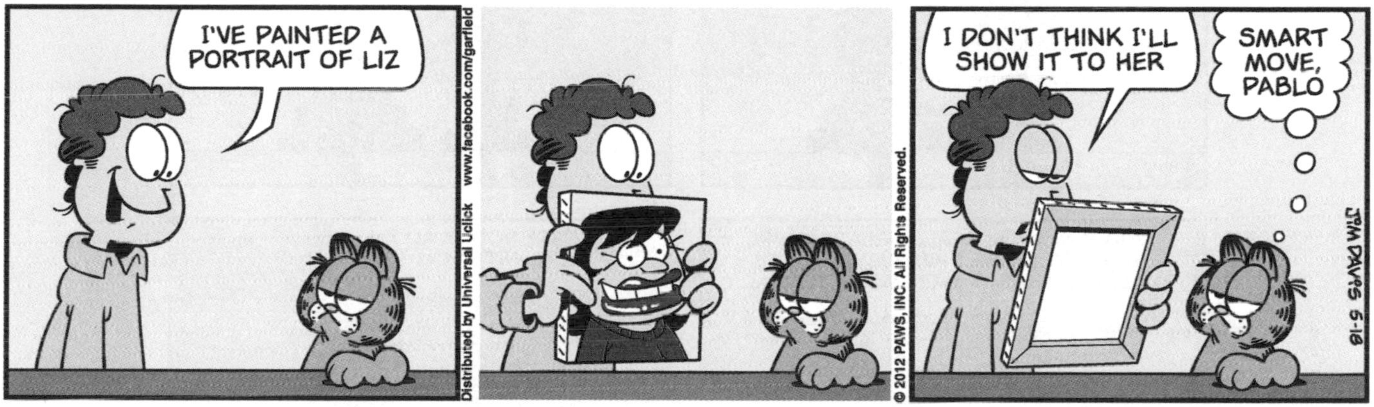
I'VE PAINTED A PORTRAIT OF LIZ
I DON'T THINK I'LL SHOW IT TO HER
SMART MOVE, PABLO
JIM DAVIS 5-18
Distributed by Universal Uclick www.facebook.com/garfield
© 2012 PAWS, INC. All Rights Reserved.

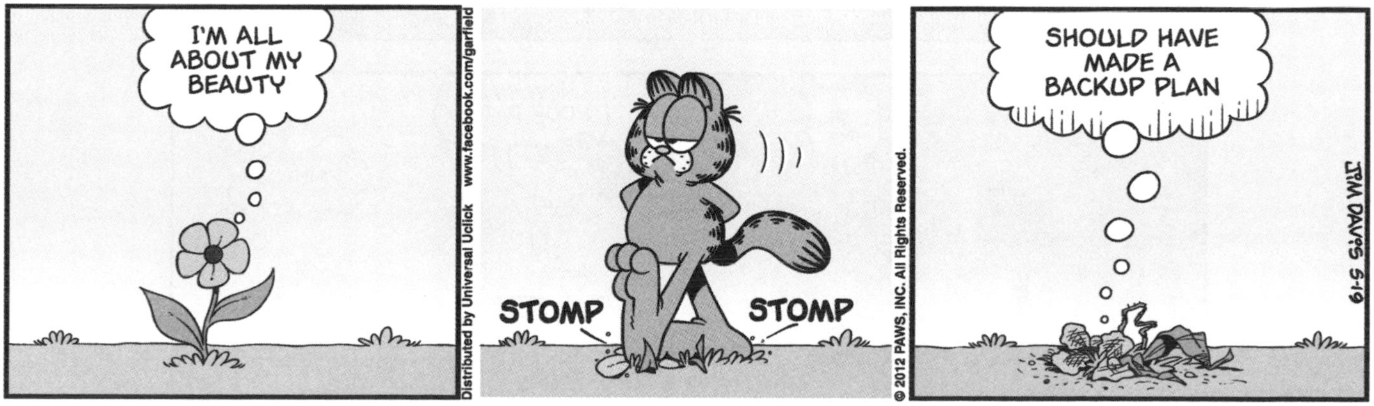
I'M ALL ABOUT MY BEAUTY
STOMP
STOMP
SHOULD HAVE MADE A BACKUP PLAN
JIM DAVIS 5-19
Distributed by Universal Uclick www.facebook.com/garfield
© 2012 PAWS, INC. All Rights Reserved.

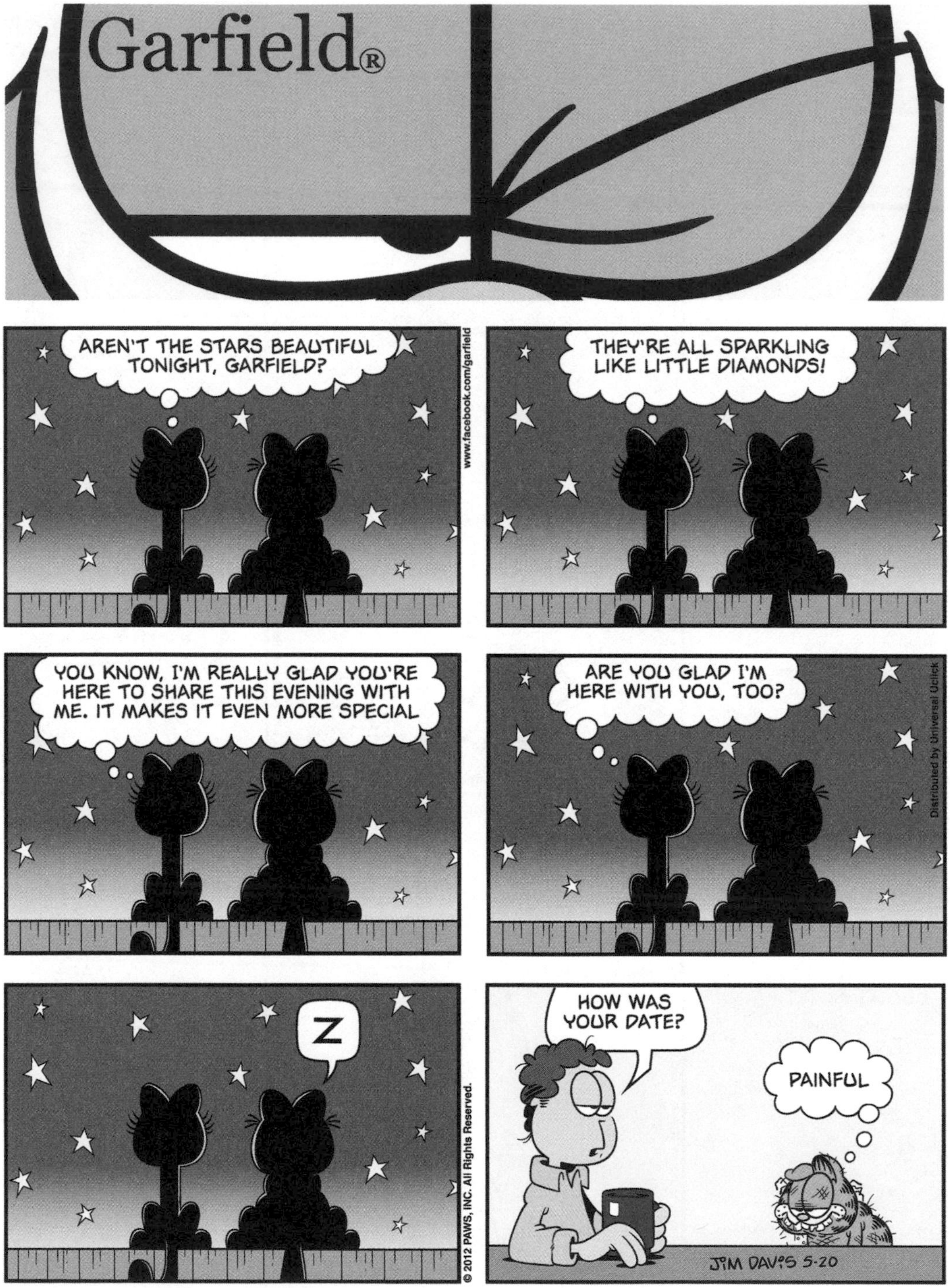
Garfield®
ARE'T THE STARS BEAUTIFUL TONIGHT, GARFIELD?
www.facebook.com/garfield
THEY'RE ALL SPARKLING LIKE LITTLE DIAMONDS!
YOU KNOW, I'M REALLY GLAD YOU'RE HERE TO SHARE THIS EVENING WITH ME. IT MAKES IT EVEN MORE SPECIAL
ARE YOU GLAD I'M HERE WITH YOU, TOO?
Distributed by Universal Uclick
Z
© 2012 PAWS, INC. All Rights Reserved.
HOW WAS YOUR DATE?
PAINFUL
JIM DAVIS 5-20

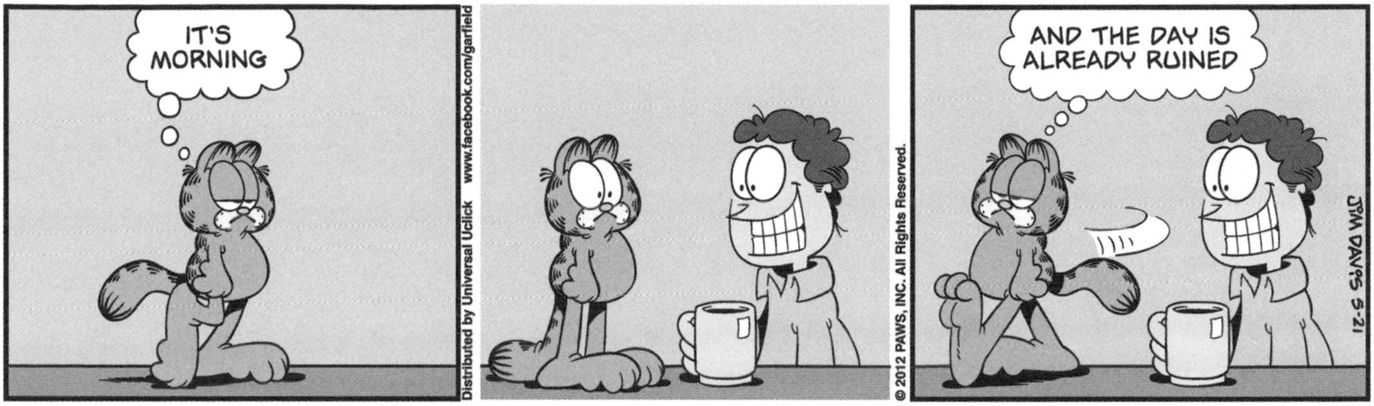
IT'S MORNING
Distributed by Universal Uclick www.facebook.com/garfield
© 2012 PAWS, INC. All Rights Reserved.
AND THE DAY IS ALREADY RUINED
JIM DAVIS 5-21

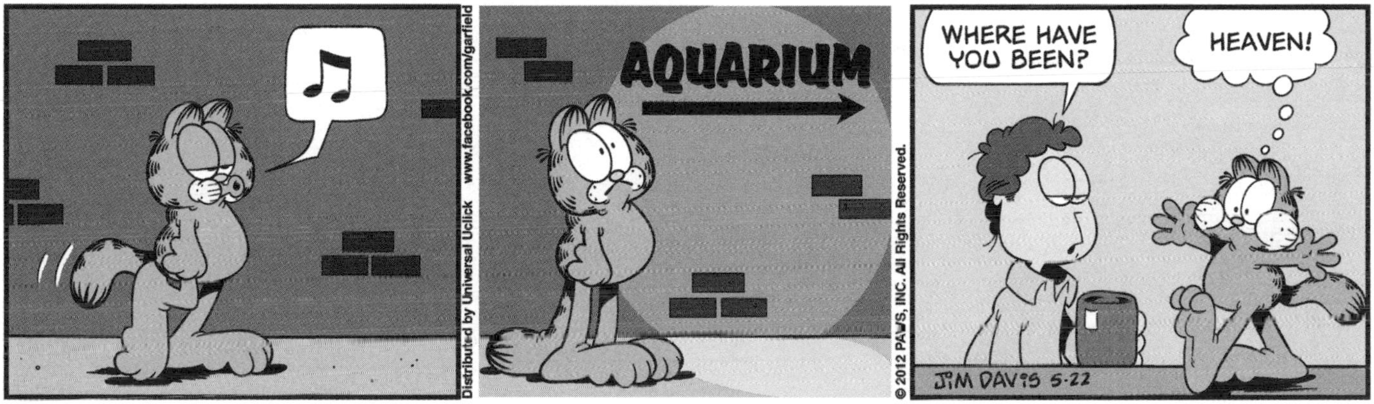
Distributed by Universal Uclick www.facebook.com/garfield
AQUARIUM
© 2012 PAWS, INC. All Rights Reserved.
WHERE HAVE YOU BEEN?
HEAVEN!
JIM DAVIS 5-22

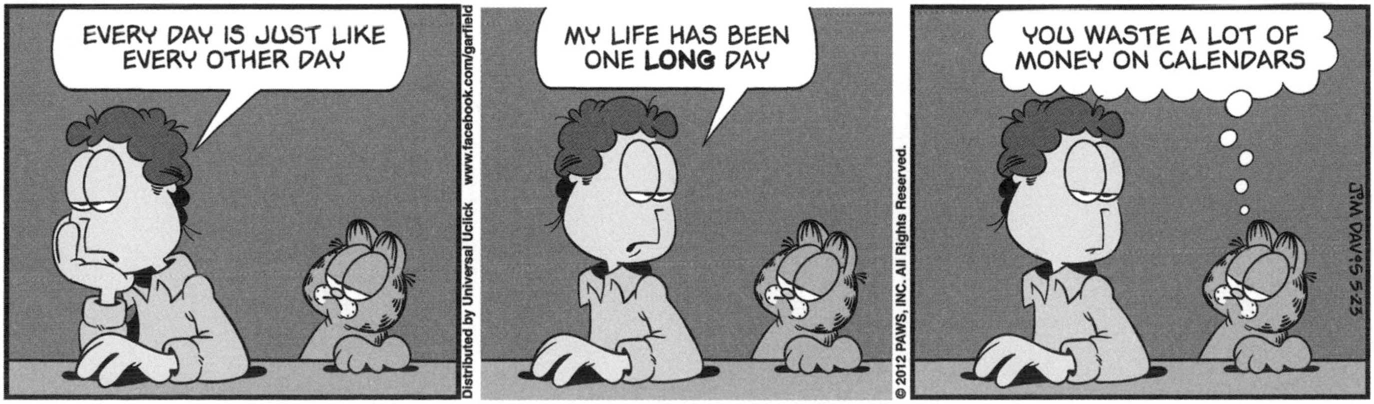
EVERY DAY IS JUST LIKE EVERY OTHER DAY
Distributed by Universal Uclick www.facebook.com/garfield
MY LIFE HAS BEEN ONE **LONG** DAY
© 2012 PAWS, INC. All Rights Reserved.
YOU WASTE A LOT OF MONEY ON CALENDARS
JIM DAVIS 5-23

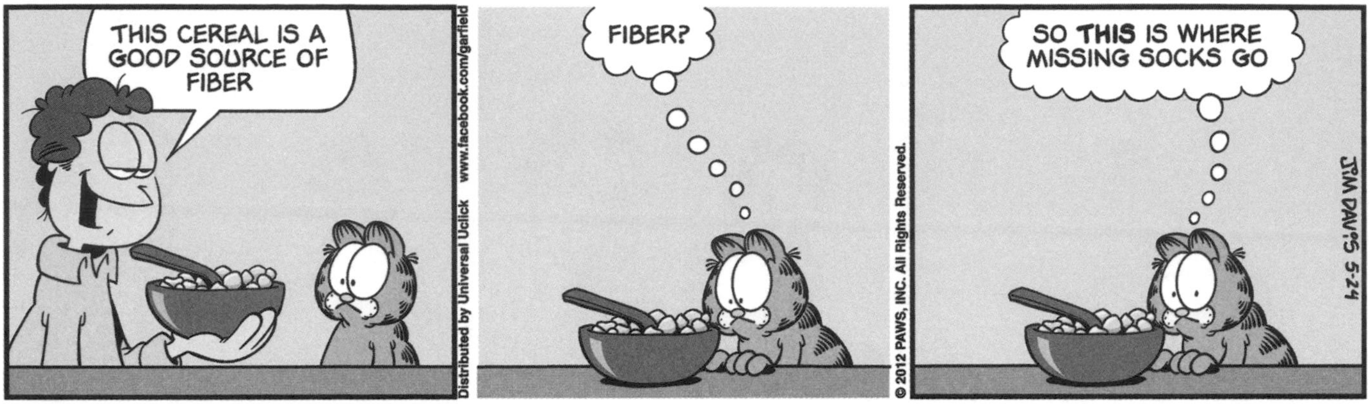
THIS CEREAL IS A GOOD SOURCE OF FIBER
Distributed by Universal Uclick www.facebook.com/garfield
FIBER?
© 2012 PAWS, INC. All Rights Reserved.
SO THIS IS WHERE MISSING SOCKS GO
JIM DAVIS 5-24

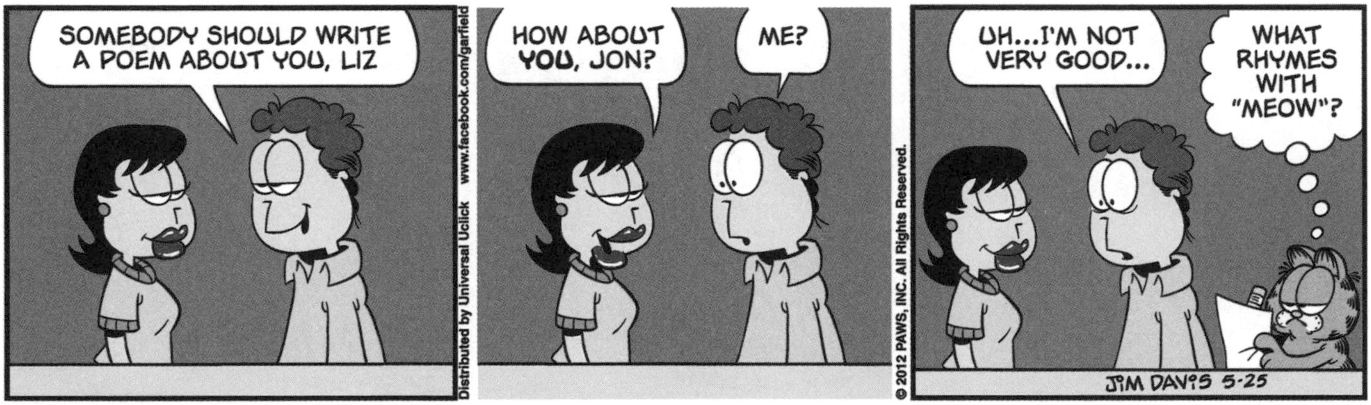
SOMEBODY SHOULD WRITE A POEM ABOUT YOU, LIZ
Distributed by Universal Uclick www.facebook.com/garfield
HOW ABOUT YOU, JON?
ME?
© 2012 PAWS, INC. All Rights Reserved.
UH...I'M NOT VERY GOOD...
WHAT RHYMES WITH "MEOW"?
JIM DAVIS 5-25

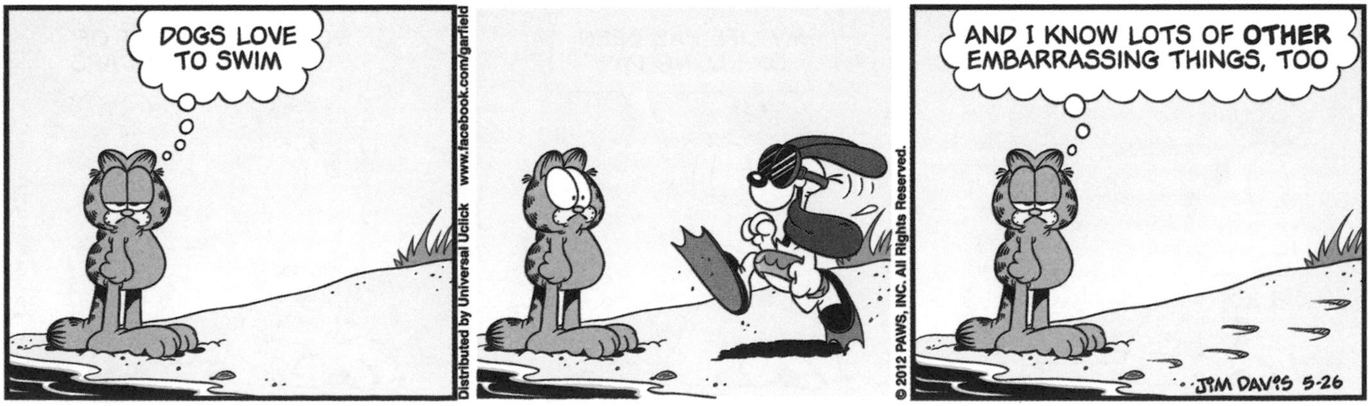
DOGS LOVE TO SWIM
Distributed by Universal Uclick www.facebook.com/garfield
© 2012 PAWS, INC. All Rights Reserved.
AND I KNOW LOTS OF OTHER EMBARRASSING THINGS, TOO
JIM DAVIS 5-26

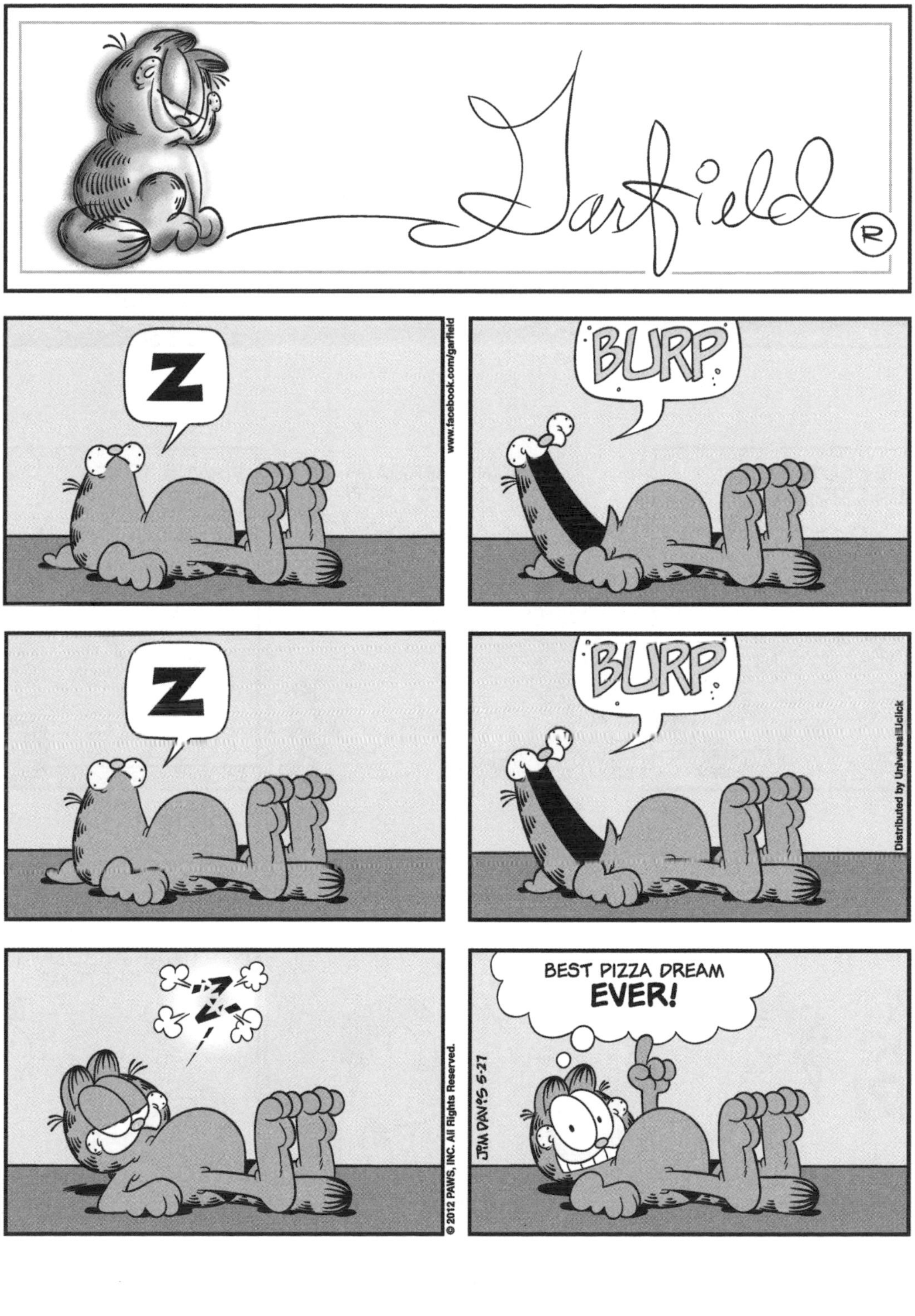
Garfield ®
www.facebook.com/garfield
Z
BURP
Z
BURP
Distributed by Universal Uclick
© 2012 PAWS, INC. All Rights Reserved.
JIM DAVIS 5-27
BEST PIZZA DREAM
EVER!

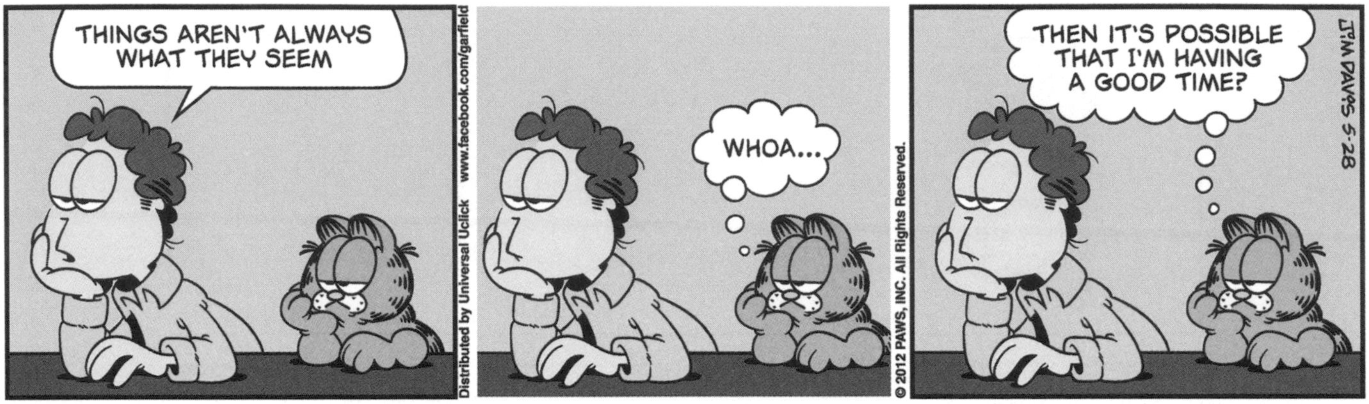
THINGS AREN'T ALWAYS WHAT THEY SEEM
Distributed by Universal Uclick www.facebook.com/garfield
WHOA...
© 2012 PAWS, INC. All Rights Reserved.
THEN IT'S POSSIBLE THAT I'M HAVING A GOOD TIME?
JIM DAVIS 5-28

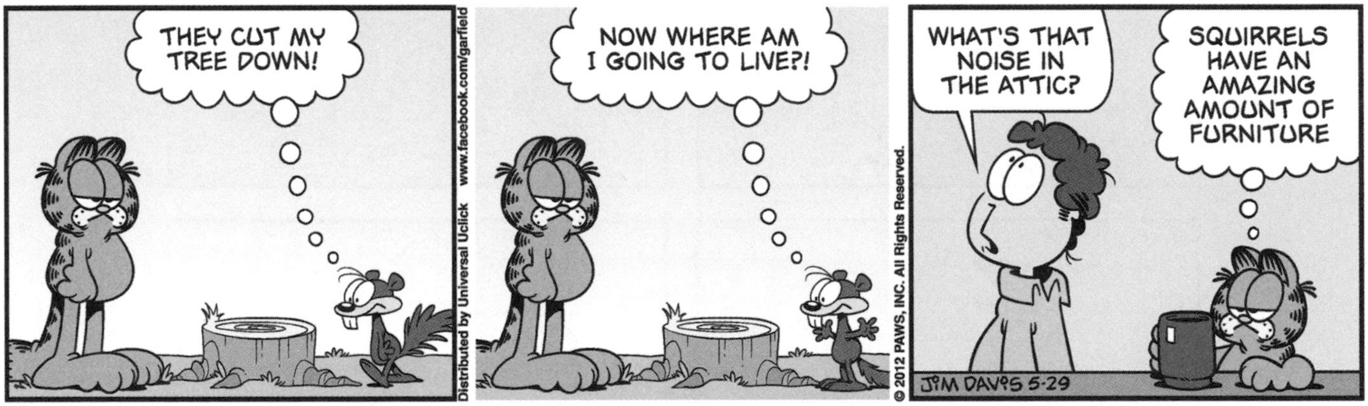
THEY CUT MY TREE DOWN!
Distributed by Universal Uclick www.facebook.com/garfield
NOW WHERE AM I GOING TO LIVE?!
© 2012 PAWS, INC. All Rights Reserved.
WHAT'S THAT NOISE IN THE ATTIC?
SQUIRRELS HAVE AN AMAZING AMOUNT OF FURNITURE
JIM DAVIS 5-29

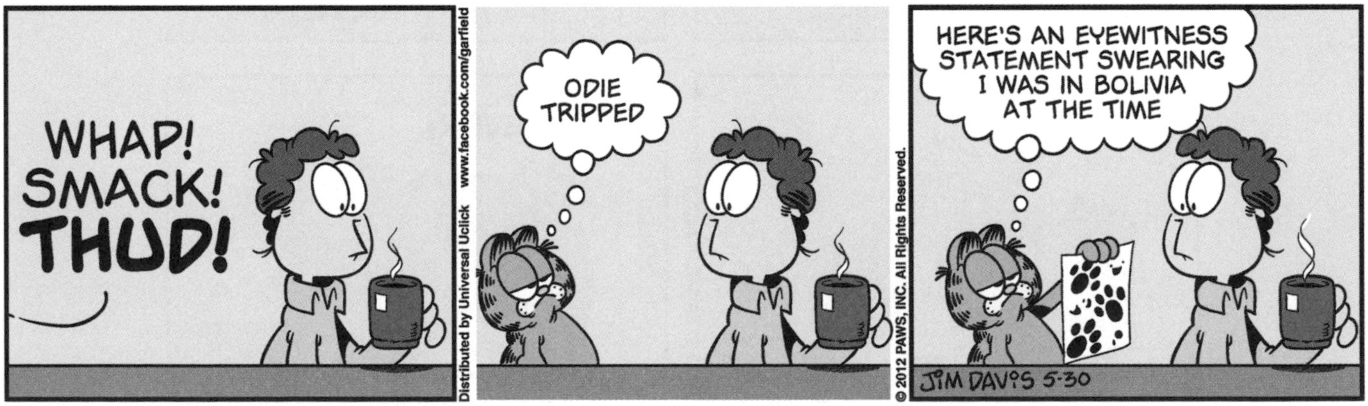
WHAP! SMACK! THUD!
Distributed by Universal Uclick www.facebook.com/garfield
ODIE TRIPPED
© 2012 PAWS, INC. All Rights Reserved.
HERE'S AN EYEWITNESS STATEMENT SWEARING I WAS IN BOLIVIA AT THE TIME
JIM DAVIS 5-30

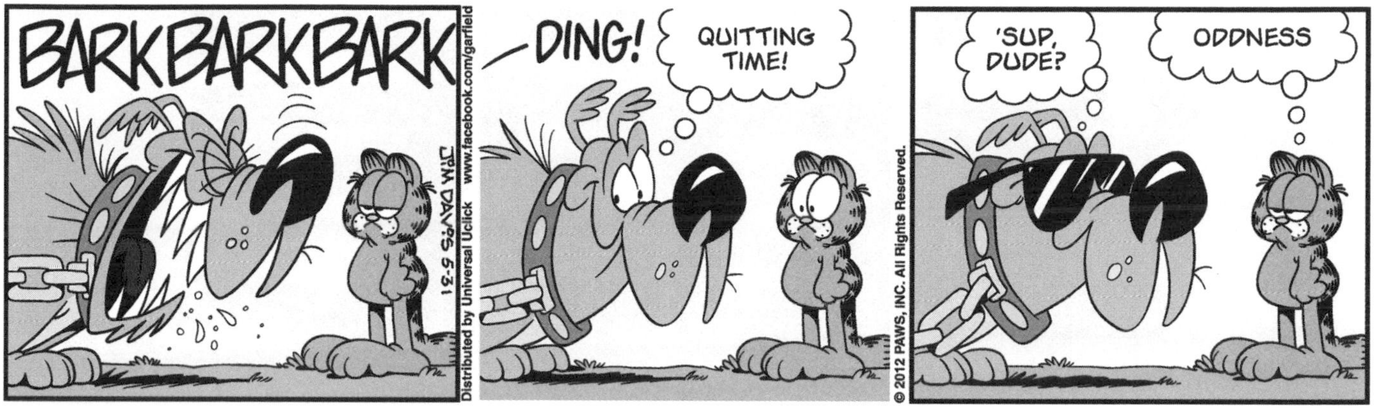
BARKBARKBARK
-DING!
QUITTING TIME!
'SUP, DUDE?
ODDNESS
JIM DAVIS 5-31
Distributed by Universal Uclick www.facebook.com/garfield
© 2012 PAWS, INC. All Rights Reserved.

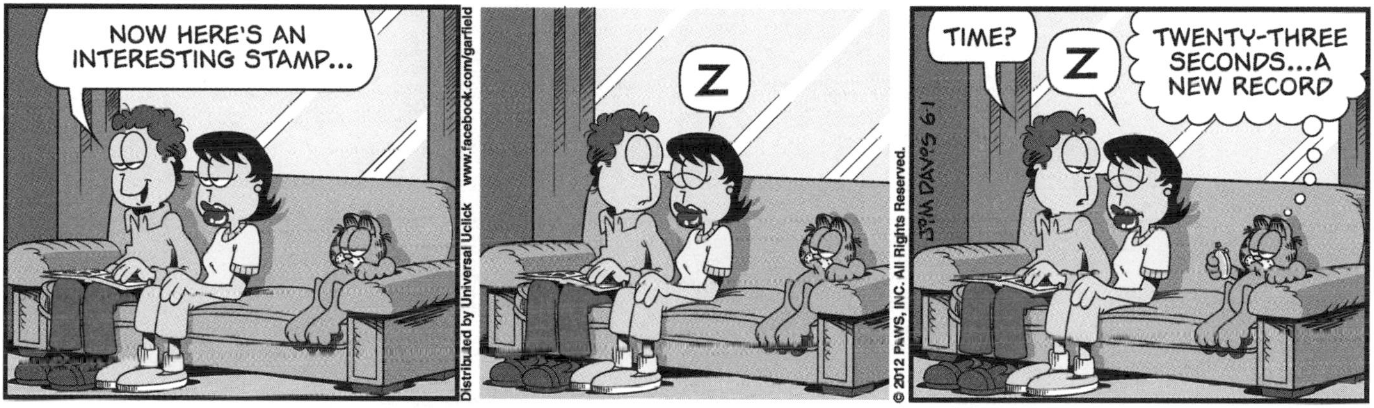
NOW HERE'S AN INTERESTING STAMP...
Z
TIME?
Z
TWENTY-THREE SECONDS...A NEW RECORD
JIM DAVIS 6-1
Distributed by Universal Uclick www.facebook.com/garfield
© 2012 PAWS, INC. All Rights Reserved.

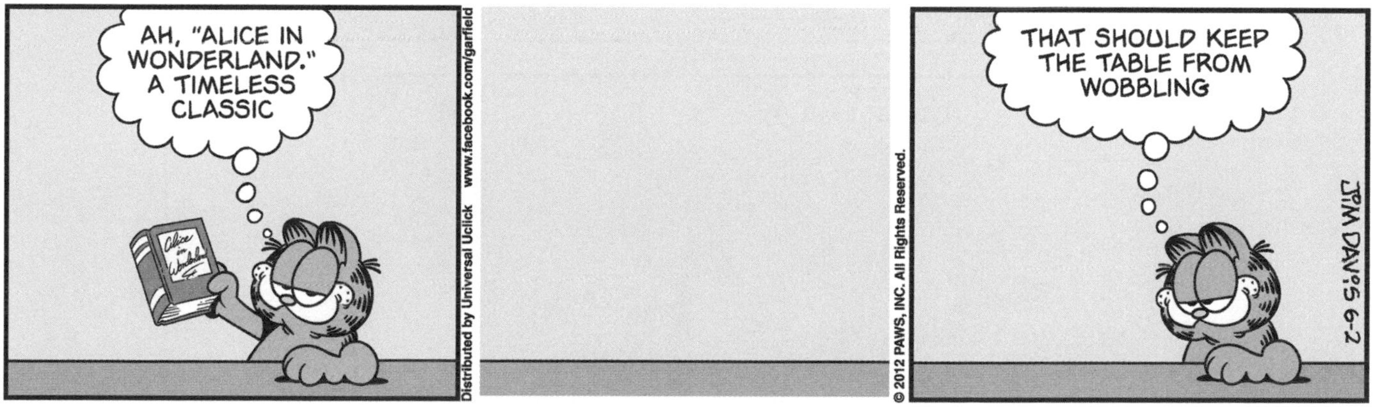
AH, "ALICE IN WONDERLAND." A TIMELESS CLASSIC
THAT SHOULD KEEP THE TABLE FROM WOBBLING
JIM DAVIS 6-2
Distributed by Universal Uclick www.facebook.com/garfield
© 2012 PAWS, INC. All Rights Reserved.

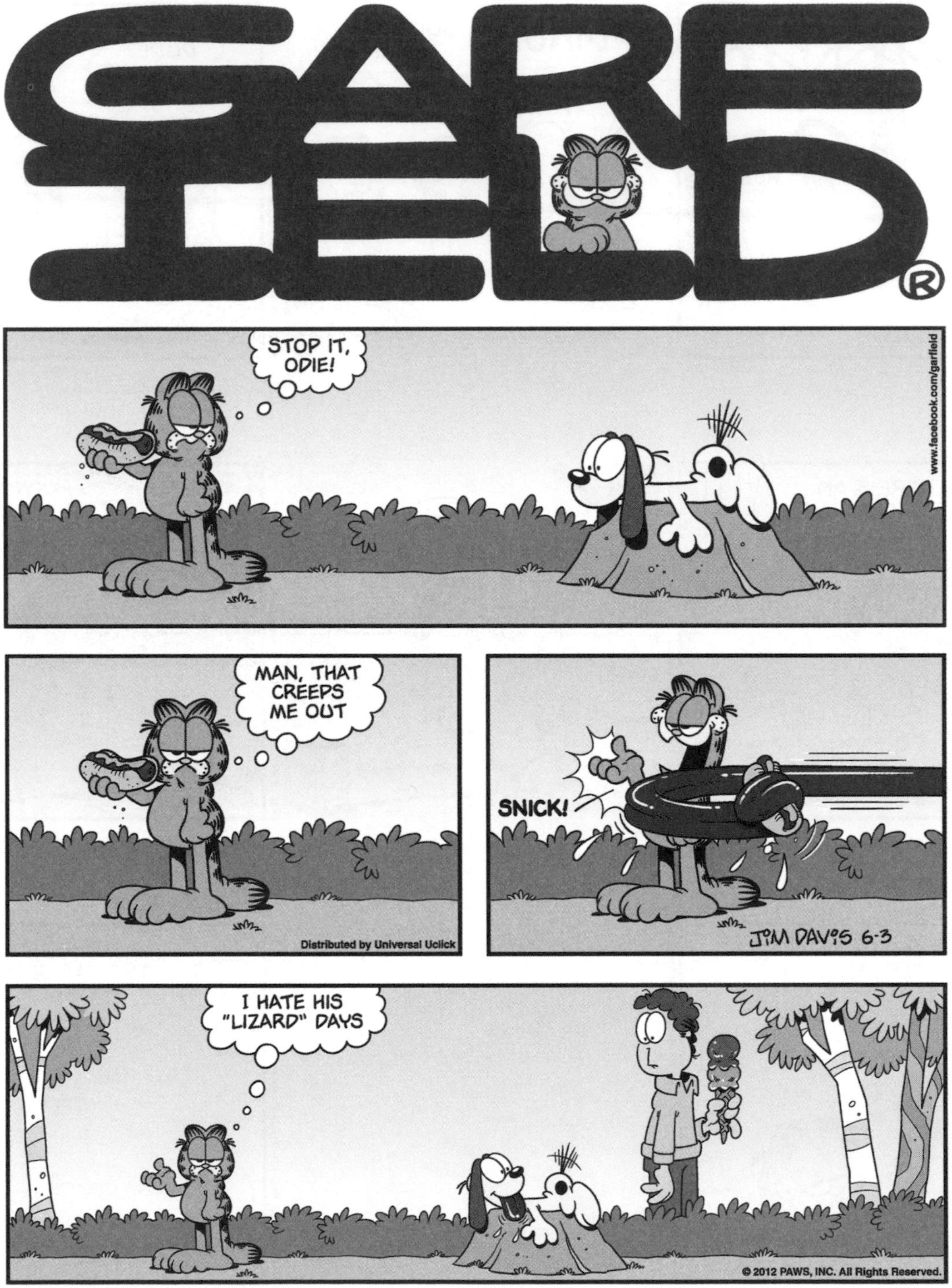
GARFIELD®
STOP IT, ODIE!
www.facebook.com/garfield
MAN, THAT CREEPS ME OUT
Distributed by Universal Uclick
SNICK!
JIM DAVIS 6-3
I HATE HIS "LIZARD" DAYS
© 2012 PAWS, INC. All Rights Reserved.

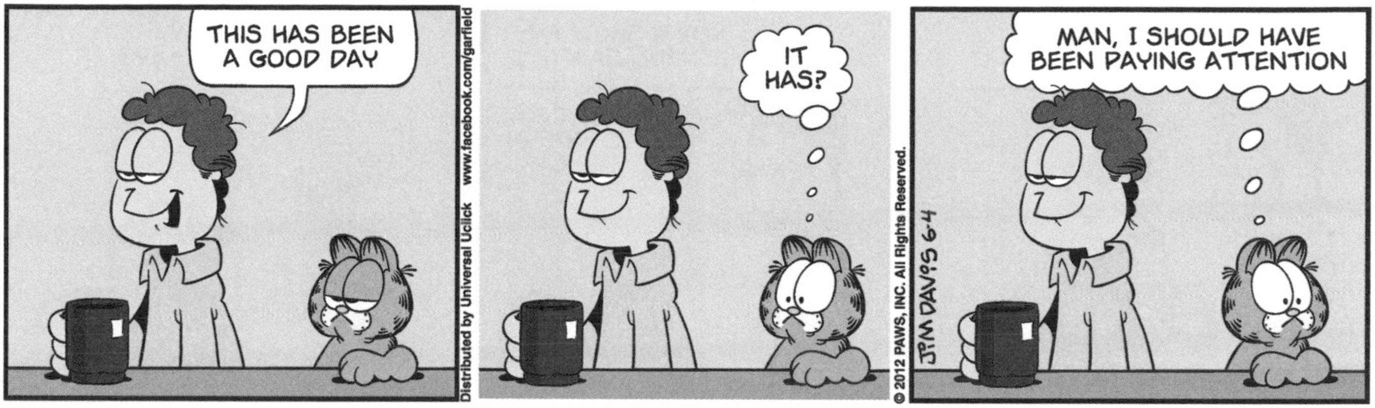
THIS HAS BEEN A GOOD DAY
Distributed by Universal Uclick www.facebook.com/garfield
IT HAS?
© 2012 PAWS, INC. All Rights Reserved.
JIM DAVIS 6-4
MAN, I SHOULD HAVE BEEN PAYING ATTENTION

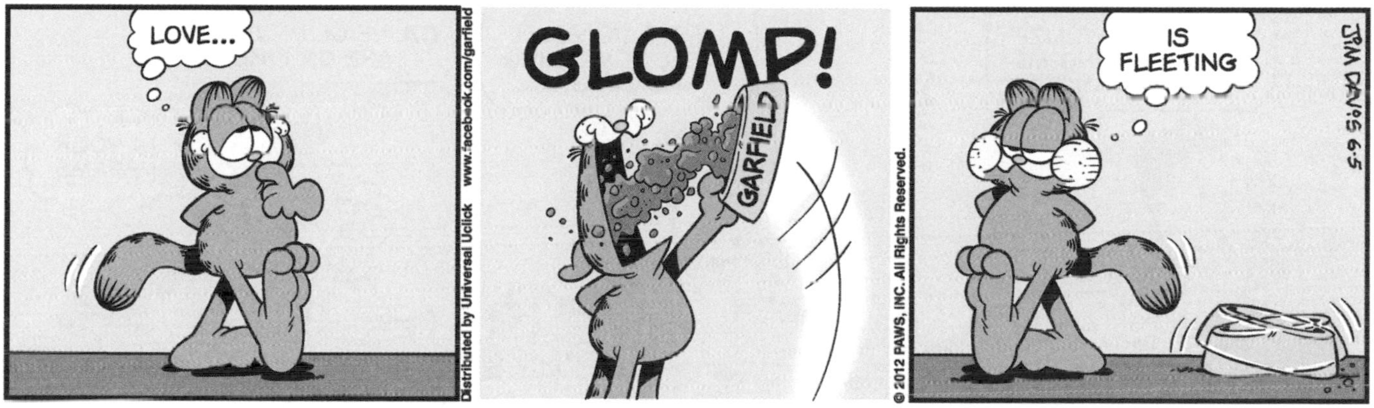
LOVE...
Distributed by Universal Uclick www.facebook.com/garfield
GLOMP!
GARFIELD
© 2012 PAWS, INC. All Rights Reserved.
IS FLEETING
JIM DAVIS 6-5

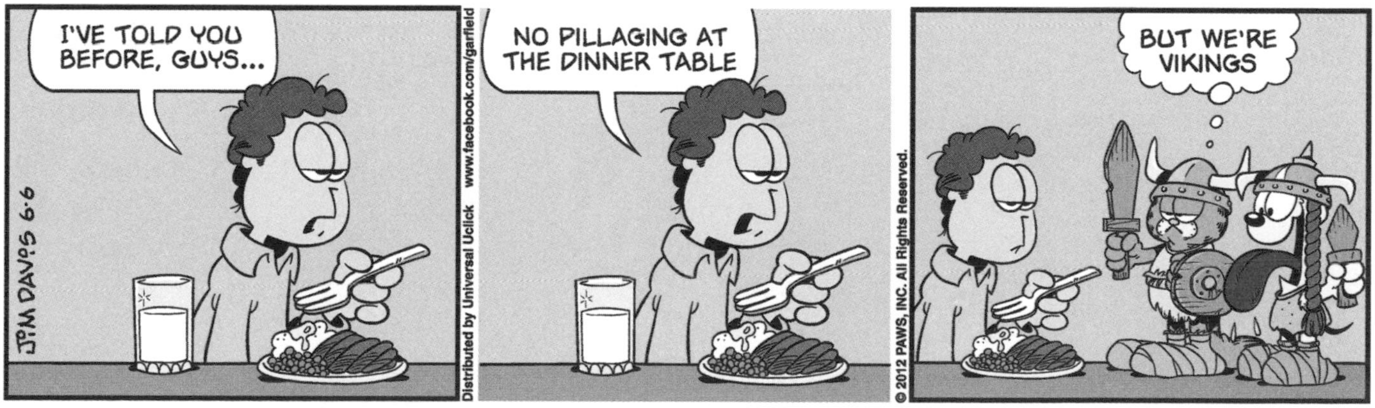
I'VE TOLD YOU BEFORE, GUYS...
JIM DAVIS 6-6
Distributed by Universal Uclick www.facebook.com/garfield
NO PILLAGING AT THE DINNER TABLE
© 2012 PAWS, INC. All Rights Reserved.
BUT WE'RE VIKINGS

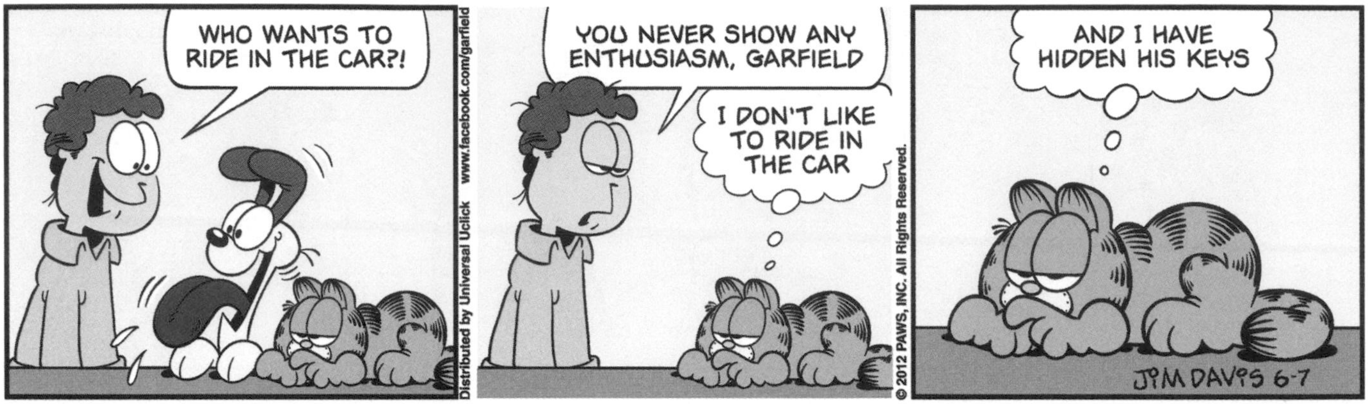
WHO WANTS TO RIDE IN THE CAR?!
Distributed by Universal Uclick www.facebook.com/garfield
YOU NEVER SHOW ANY ENTHUSIASM, GARFIELD
I DON'T LIKE TO RIDE IN THE CAR
© 2012 PAWS, INC. All Rights Reserved.
AND I HAVE HIDDEN HIS KEYS
JIM DAVIS 6-7

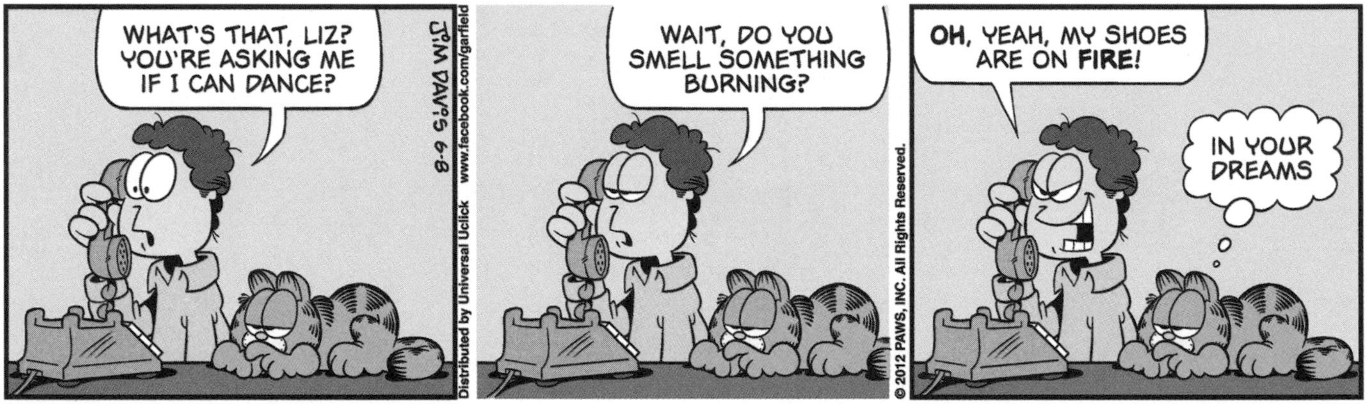
WHAT'S THAT, LIZ? YOU'RE ASKING ME IF I CAN DANCE?
JIM DAVIS 6-8
Distributed by Universal Uclick www.facebook.com/garfield
WAIT, DO YOU SMELL SOMETHING BURNING?
© 2012 PAWS, INC. All Rights Reserved.
OH, YEAH, MY SHOES ARE ON FIRE!
IN YOUR DREAMS

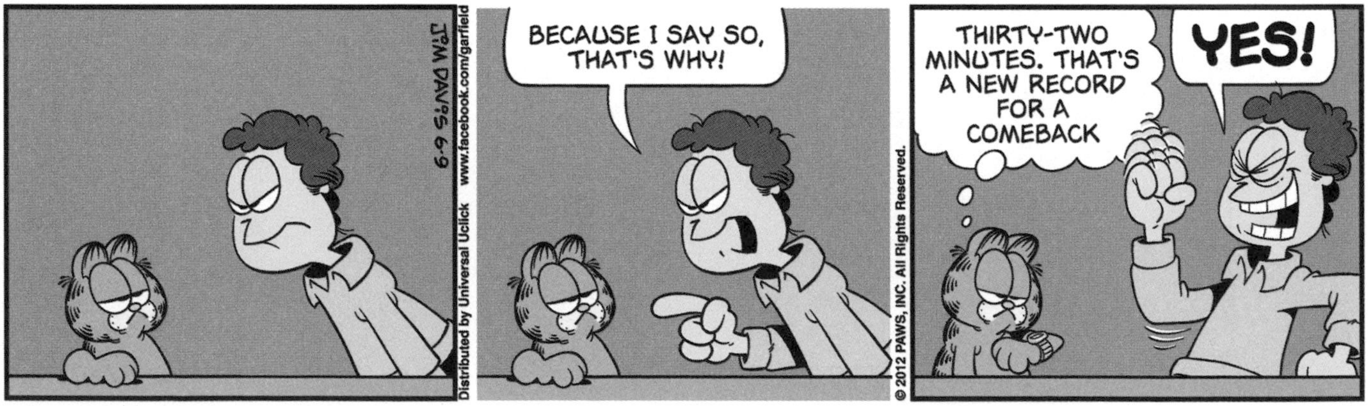
JIM DAVIS 6-9
Distributed by Universal Uclick www.facebook.com/garfield
BECAUSE I SAY SO, THAT'S WHY!
© 2012 PAWS, INC. All Rights Reserved.
THIRTY-TWO MINUTES. THAT'S A NEW RECORD FOR A COMEBACK
YES!

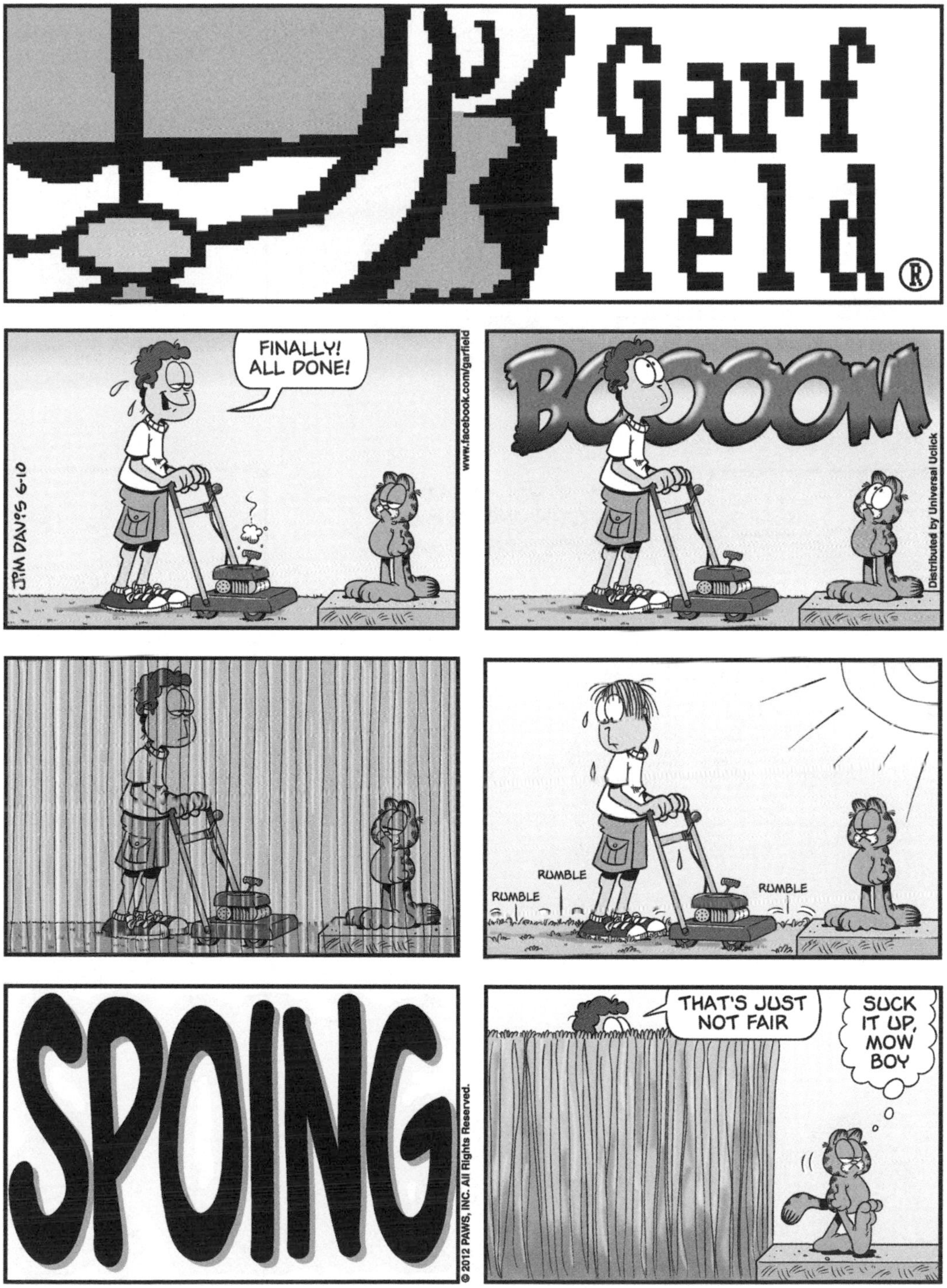

Garfield ®
FINALLY! ALL DONE!
JIM DAVIS 6-10
www.facebook.com/garfield
BOOOOM
Distributed by Universal Uclick
RUMBLE
RUMBLE
RUMBLE
SPOING
© 2012 PAWS, INC. All Rights Reserved.
THAT'S JUST NOT FAIR
SUCK IT UP, MOW BOY

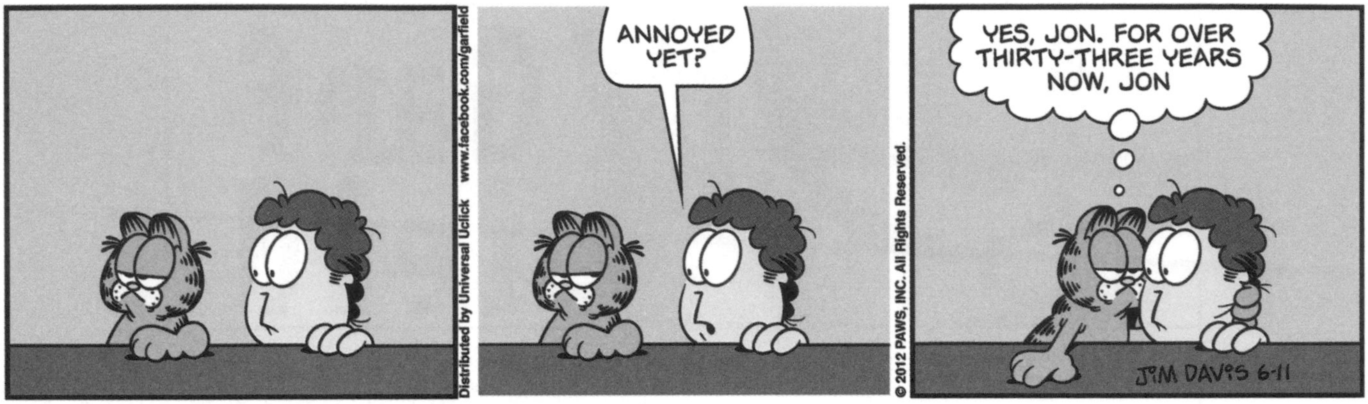
ANNOYED YET?
YES, JON. FOR OVER THIRTY-THREE YEARS NOW, JON
Distributed by Universal Uclick www.facebook.com/garfield
© 2012 PAWS, INC. All Rights Reserved.
JIM DAVIS 6-11

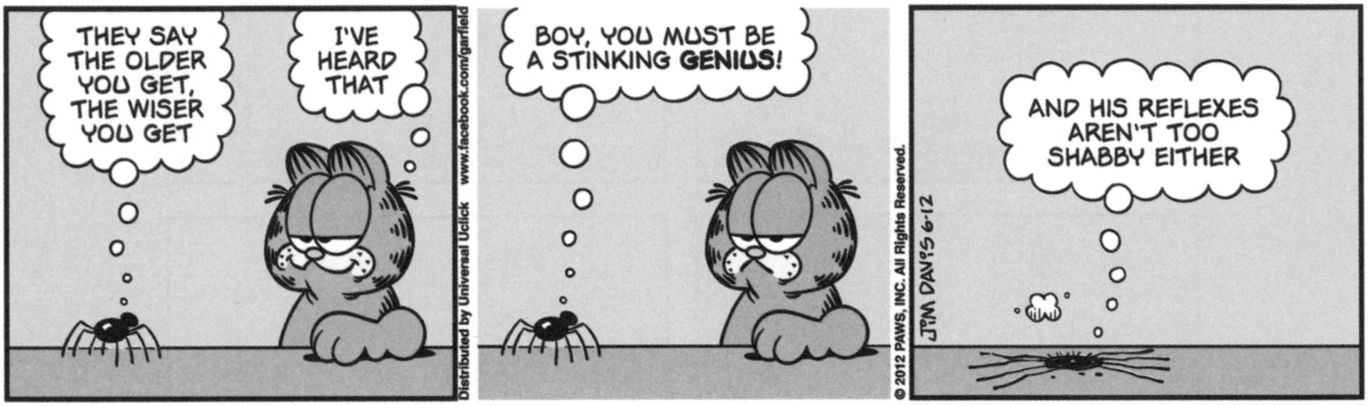
THEY SAY THE OLDER YOU GET, THE WISER YOU GET
I'VE HEARD THAT
BOY, YOU MUST BE A STINKING **GENIUS**!
AND HIS REFLEXES AREN'T TOO SHABBY EITHER
Distributed by Universal Uclick www.facebook.com/garfield
© 2012 PAWS, INC. All Rights Reserved.
JIM DAVIS 6-12

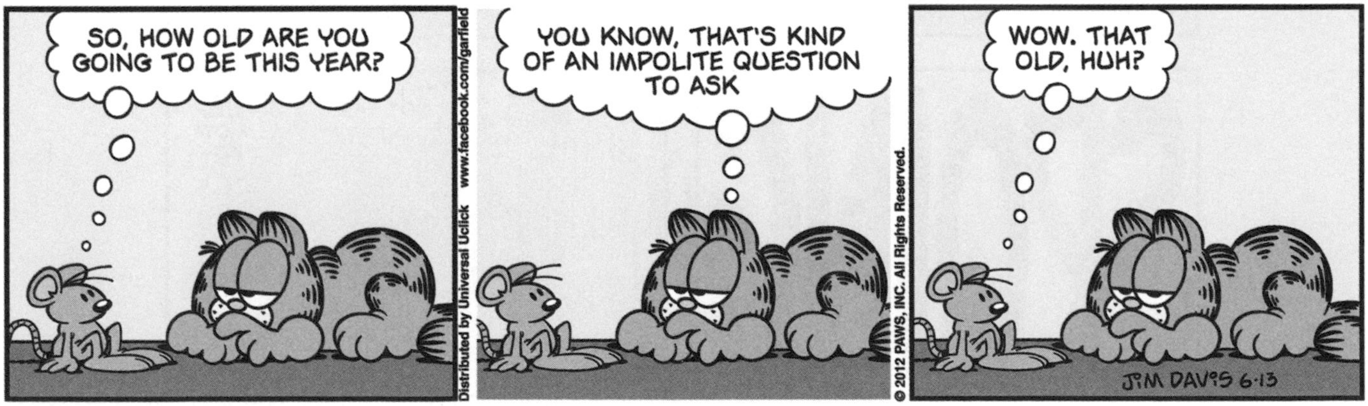
SO, HOW OLD ARE YOU GOING TO BE THIS YEAR?
YOU KNOW, THAT'S KIND OF AN IMPOLITE QUESTION TO ASK
WOW. THAT OLD, HUH?
Distributed by Universal Uclick www.facebook.com/garfield
© 2012 PAWS, INC. All Rights Reserved.
JIM DAVIS 6-13

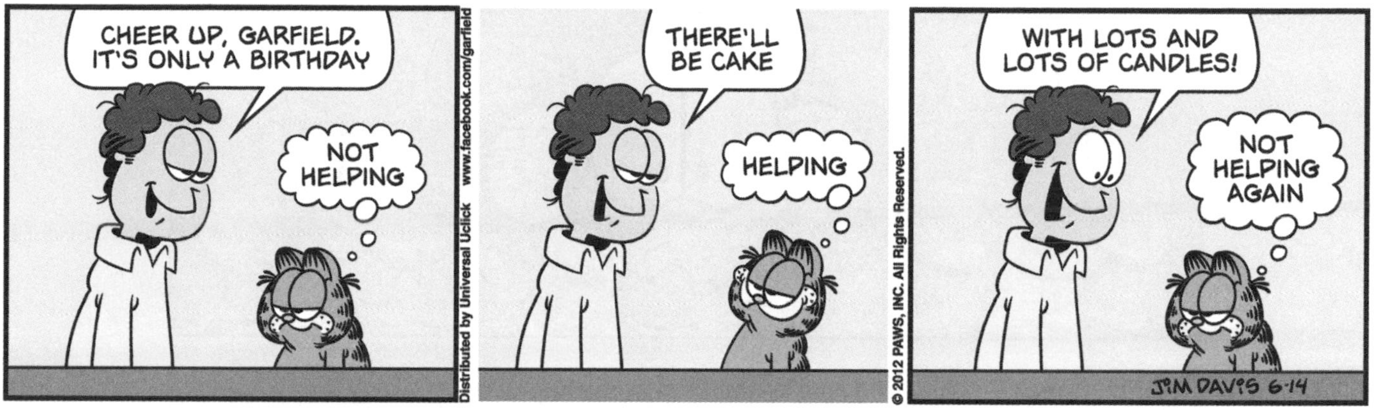
CHEER UP, GARFIELD. IT'S ONLY A BIRTHDAY
NOT HELPING
Distributed by Universal Uclick www.facebook.com/garfield
THERE'LL BE CAKE
HELPING
© 2012 PAWS, INC. All Rights Reserved.
WITH LOTS AND LOTS OF CANDLES!
NOT HELPING AGAIN
JIM DAVIS 6-14

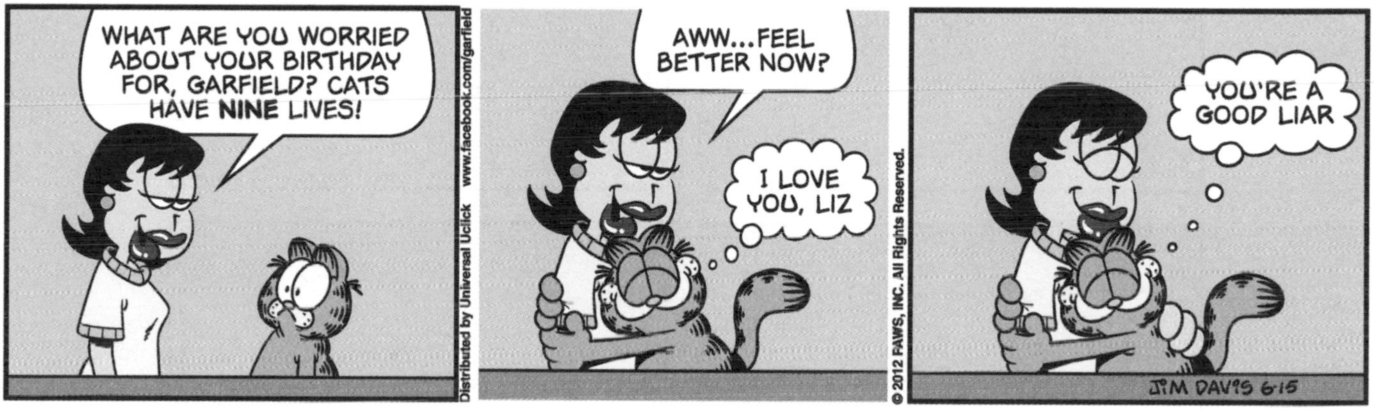
WHAT ARE YOU WORRIED ABOUT YOUR BIRTHDAY FOR, GARFIELD? CATS HAVE **NINE** LIVES!
Distributed by Universal Uclick www.facebook.com/garfield
AWW...FEEL BETTER NOW?
I LOVE YOU, LIZ
© 2012 PAWS, INC. All Rights Reserved.
YOU'RE A GOOD LIAR
JIM DAVIS 6-15

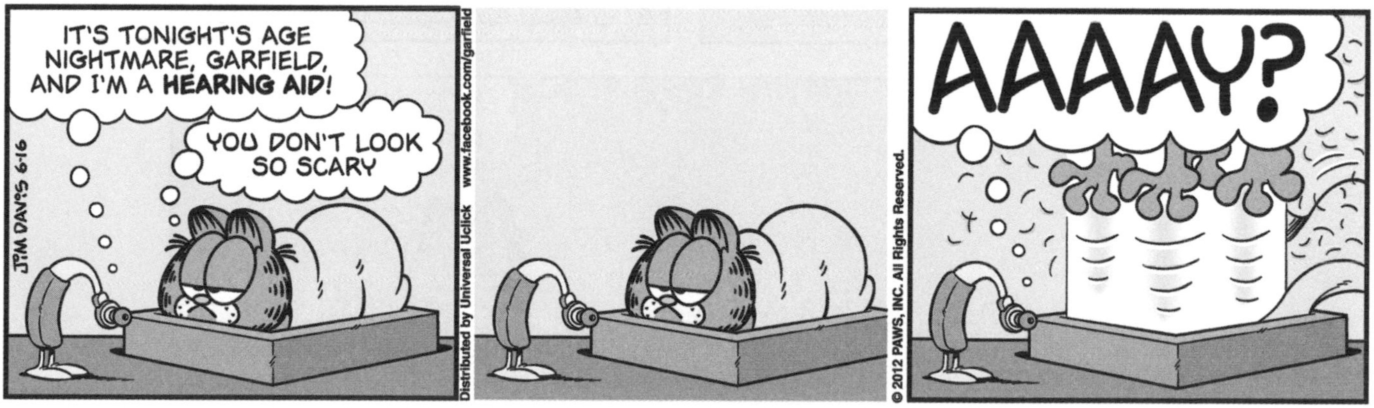
IT'S TONIGHT'S AGE NIGHTMARE, GARFIELD, AND I'M A **HEARING AID**!
YOU DON'T LOOK SO SCARY
JIM DAVIS 6-16
Distributed by Universal Uclick www.facebook.com/garfield
© 2012 PAWS, INC. All Rights Reserved.
AAAAY?

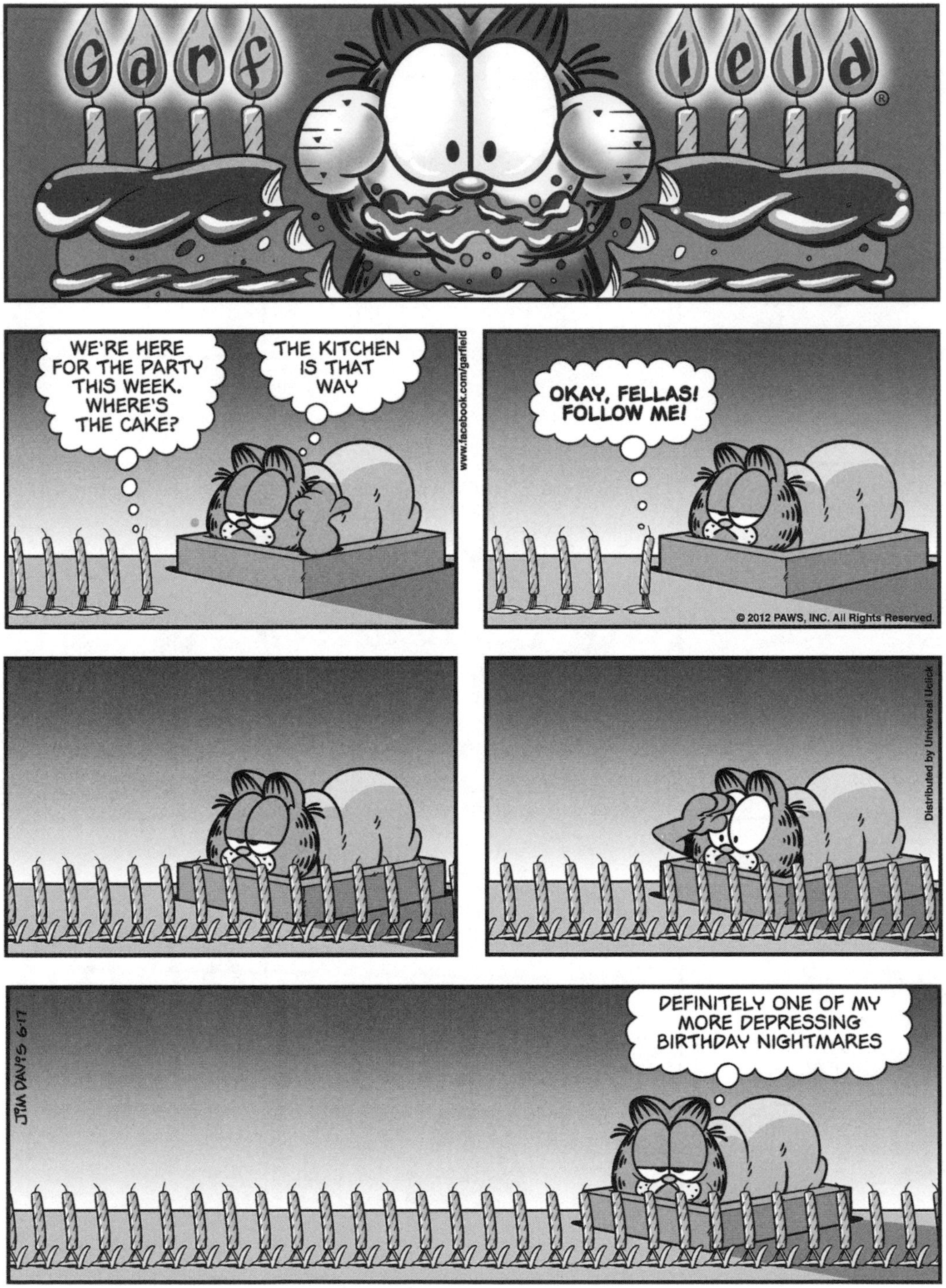
Garfield
WE'RE HERE FOR THE PARTY THIS WEEK. WHERE'S THE CAKE?
THE KITCHEN IS THAT WAY
www.facebook.com/garfield
OKAY, FELLAS! FOLLOW ME!
© 2012 PAWS, INC. All Rights Reserved.
Distributed by Universal Uclick
JIM DAVIS 6-17
DEFINITELY ONE OF MY MORE DEPRESSING BIRTHDAY NIGHTMARES

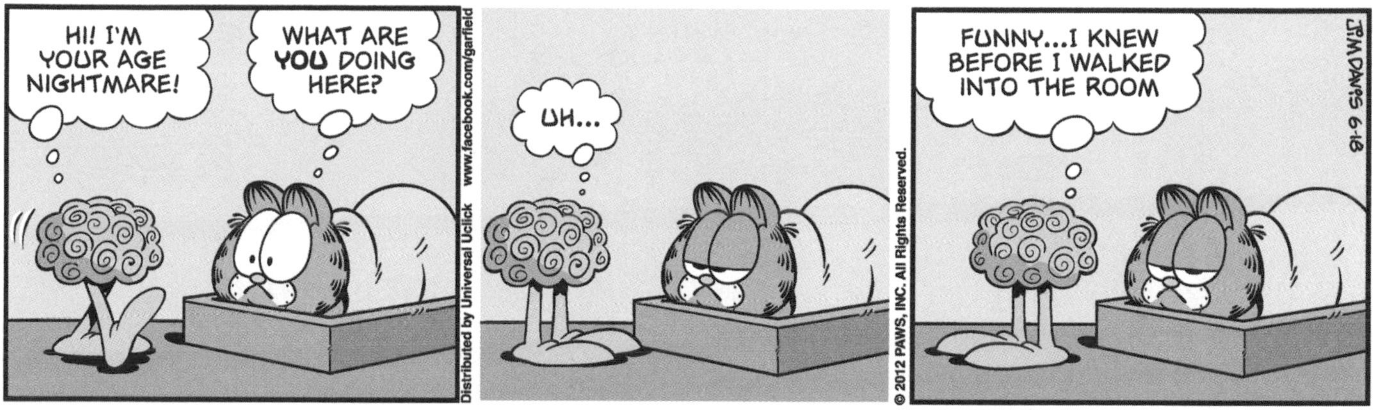
HI! I'M YOUR AGE NIGHTMARE!
WHAT ARE YOU DOING HERE?
Distributed by Universal Uclick www.facebook.com/garfield
UH...
© 2012 PAWS, INC. All Rights Reserved.
FUNNY...I KNEW BEFORE I WALKED INTO THE ROOM
JIM DAVIS 6-18

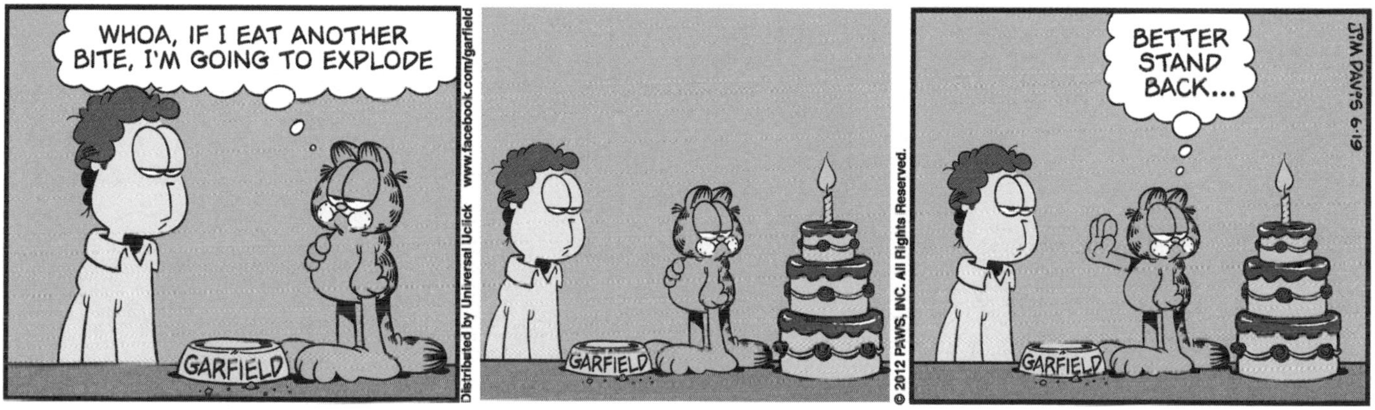
WHOA, IF I EAT ANOTHER BITE, I'M GOING TO EXPLODE
GARFIELD
Distributed by Universal Uclick www.facebook.com/garfield
GARFIELD
© 2012 PAWS, INC. All Rights Reserved.
BETTER STAND BACK...
GARFIELD
JIM DAVIS 6-19

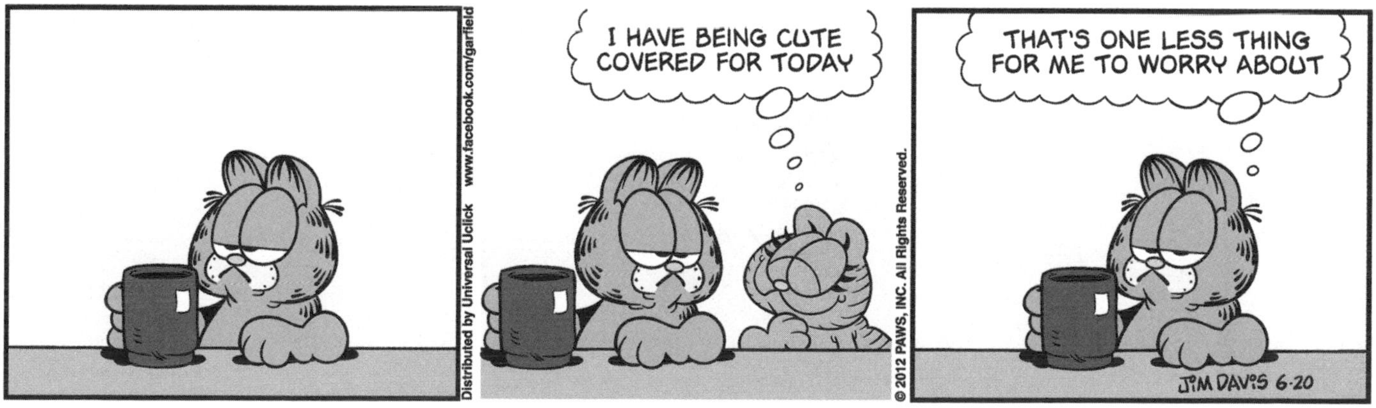
Distributed by Universal Uclick www.facebook.com/garfield
I HAVE BEING CUTE COVERED FOR TODAY
© 2012 PAWS, INC. All Rights Reserved.
THAT'S ONE LESS THING FOR ME TO WORRY ABOUT
JIM DAVIS 6-20

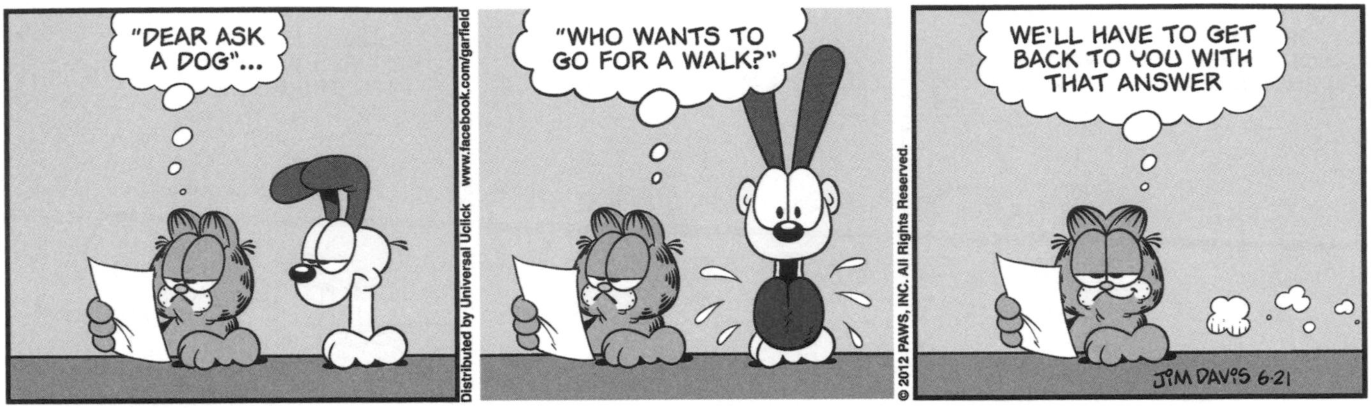
"DEAR ASK A DOG"...
Distributed by Universal Uclick www.facebook.com/garfield
"WHO WANTS TO GO FOR A WALK?"
© 2012 PAWS, INC. All Rights Reserved.
WE'LL HAVE TO GET BACK TO YOU WITH THAT ANSWER
JIM DAVIS 6-21

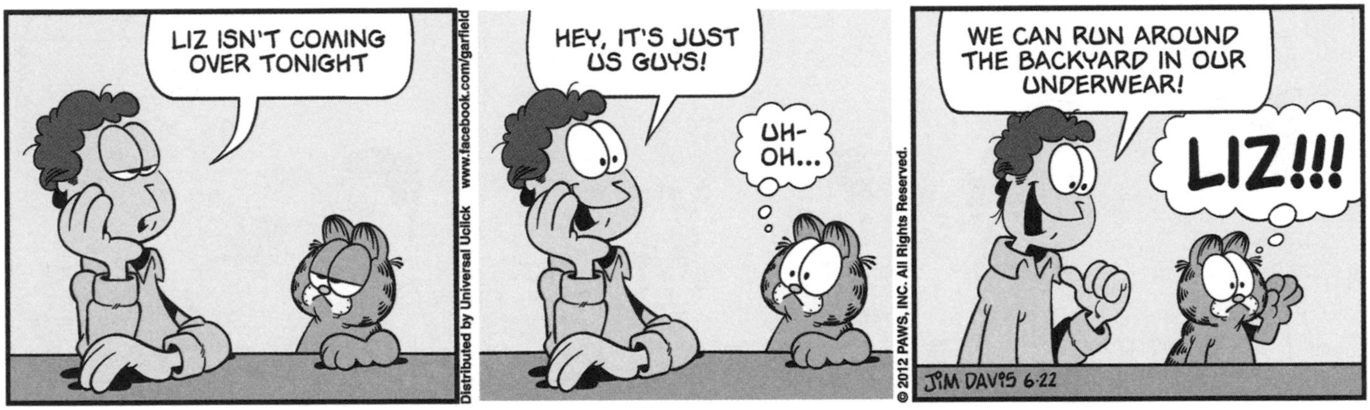
LIZ ISN'T COMING OVER TONIGHT
Distributed by Universal Uclick www.facebook.com/garfield
HEY, IT'S JUST US GUYS!
UH-OH...
© 2012 PAWS, INC. All Rights Reserved.
WE CAN RUN AROUND THE BACKYARD IN OUR UNDERWEAR!
LIZ!!!
JIM DAVIS 6-22

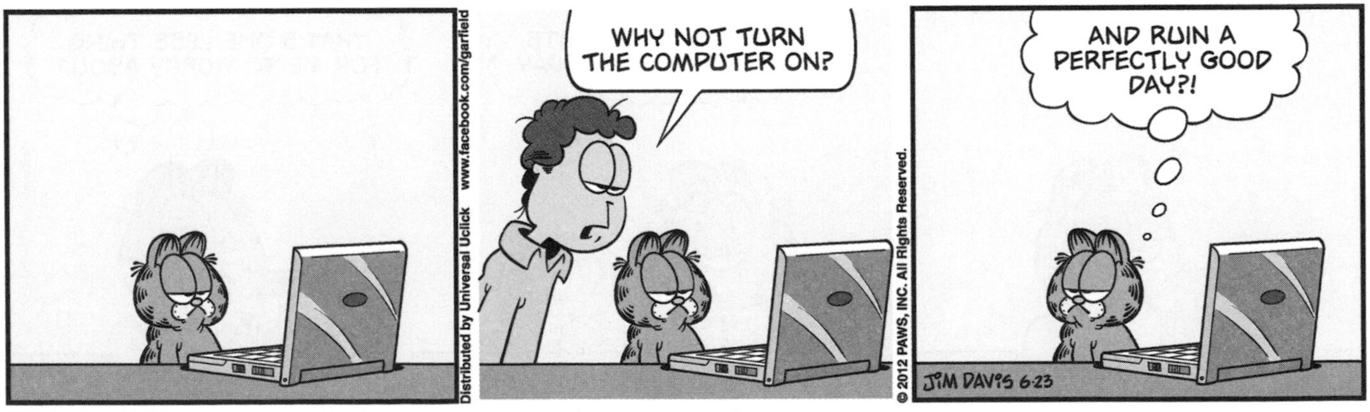
Distributed by Universal Uclick www.facebook.com/garfield
WHY NOT TURN THE COMPUTER ON?
© 2012 PAWS, INC. All Rights Reserved.
AND RUIN A PERFECTLY GOOD DAY?!
JIM DAVIS 6-23

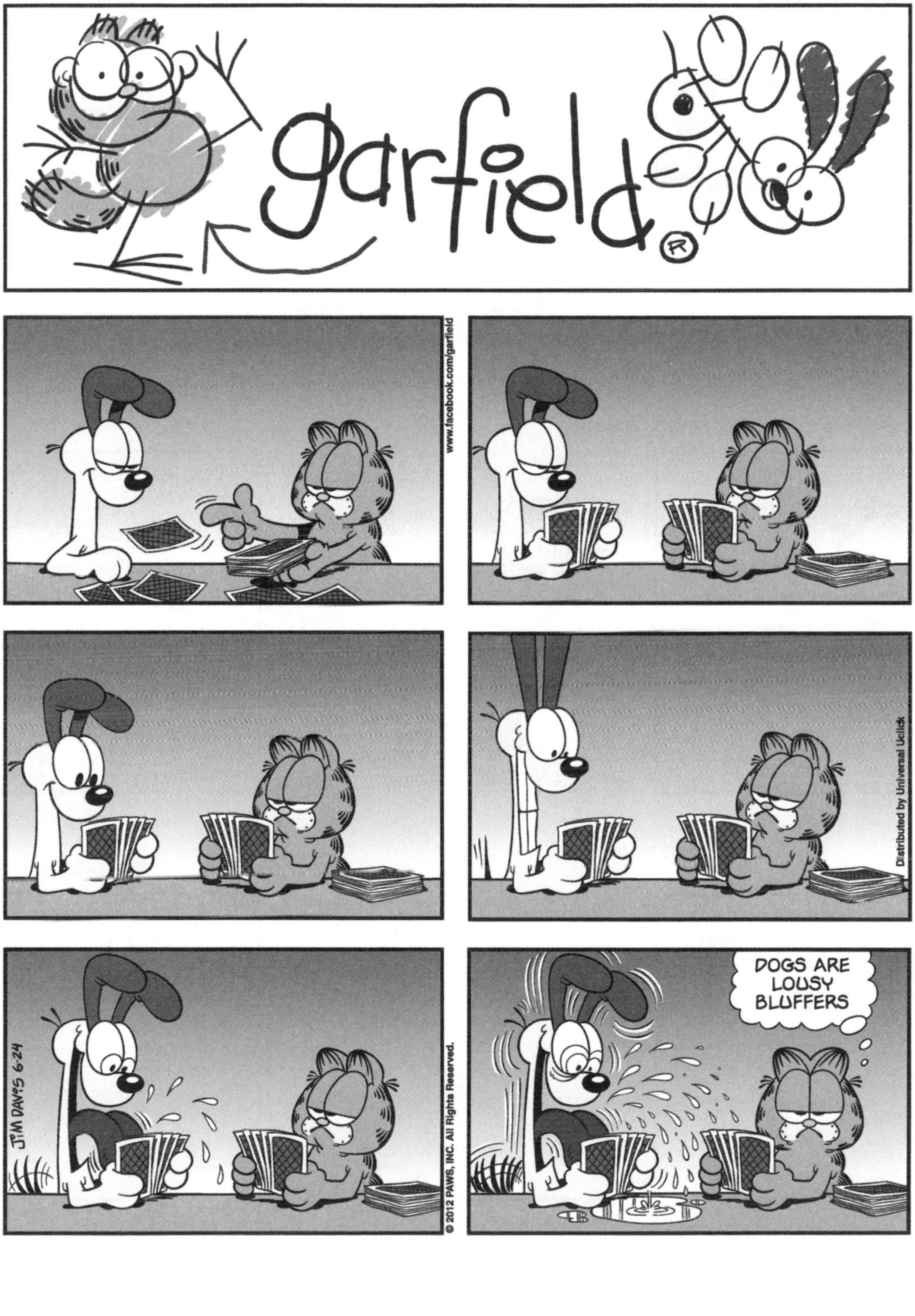
garfield®
www.facebook.com/garfield
Distributed by Universal Uclick
JIM DAVIS 6-24
© 2012 PAWS, INC. All Rights Reserved.
DOGS ARE LOUSY BLUFFERS

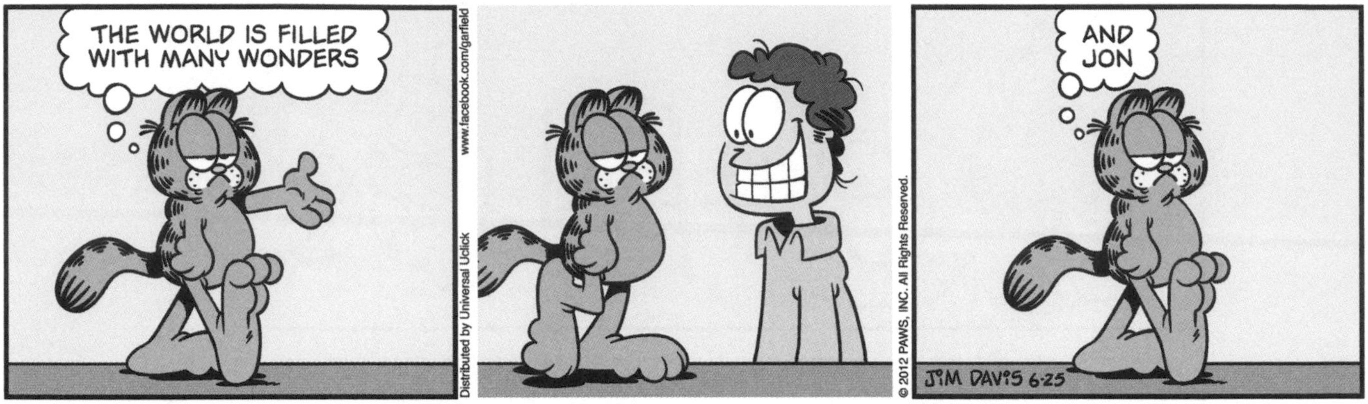
THE WORLD IS FILLED WITH MANY WONDERS
Distributed by Universal Uclick www.facebook.com/garfield
AND JON
© 2012 PAWS, INC. All Rights Reserved.
JIM DAVIS 6-25

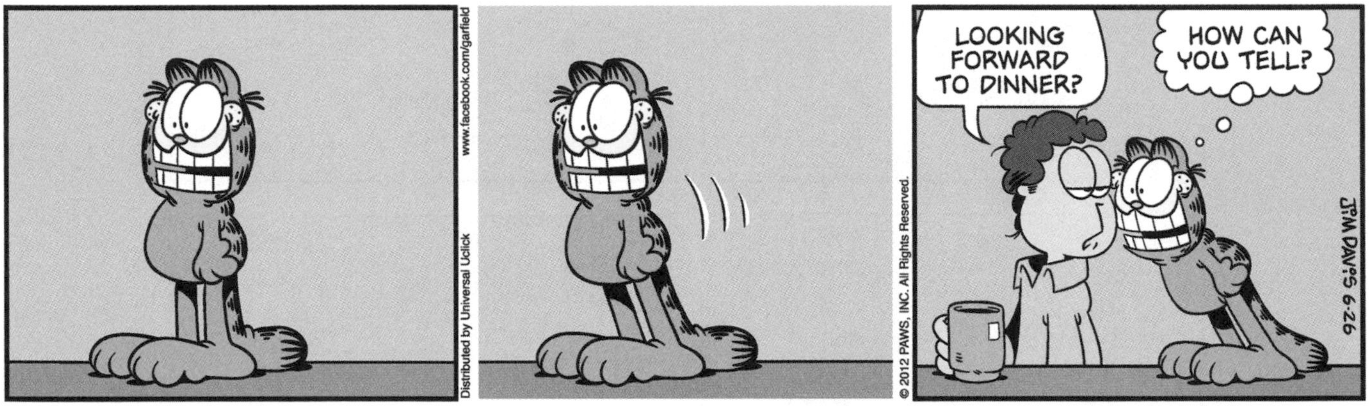
Distributed by Universal Uclick www.facebook.com/garfield
© 2012 PAWS, INC. All Rights Reserved.
LOOKING FORWARD TO DINNER?
HOW CAN YOU TELL?
JIM DAVIS 6-26

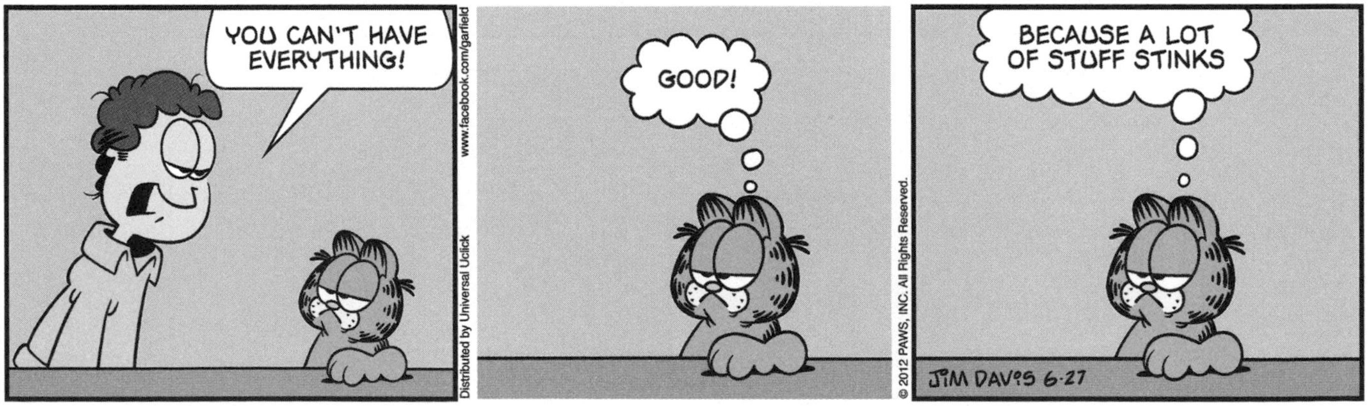
YOU CAN'T HAVE EVERYTHING!
Distributed by Universal Uclick www.facebook.com/garfield
GOOD!
© 2012 PAWS, INC. All Rights Reserved.
BECAUSE A LOT OF STUFF STINKS
JIM DAVIS 6-27

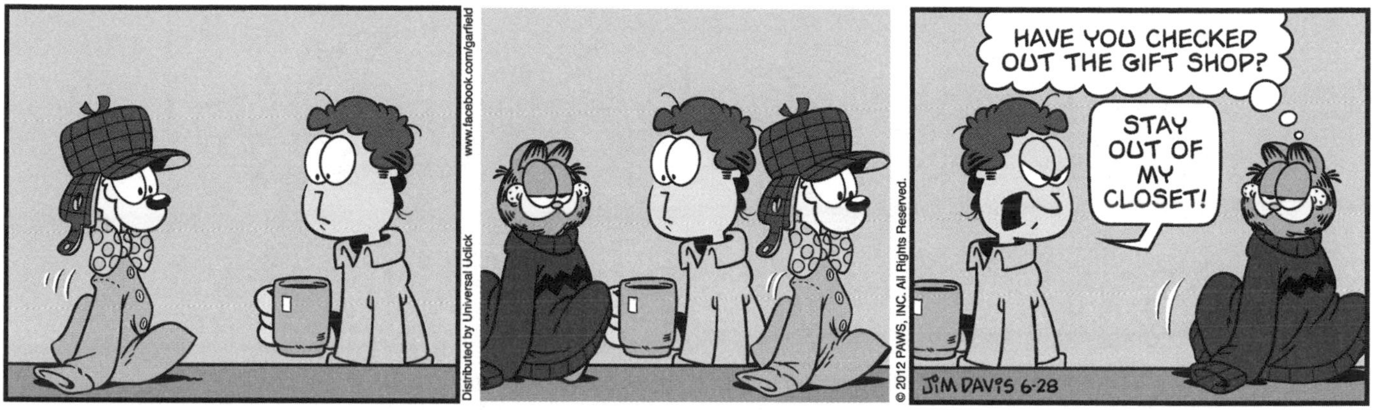
HAVE YOU CHECKED OUT THE GIFT SHOP?
STAY OUT OF MY CLOSET!
JIM DAVIS 6-28
Distributed by Universal Uclick
www.facebook.com/garfield
© 2012 PAWS, INC. All Rights Reserved.

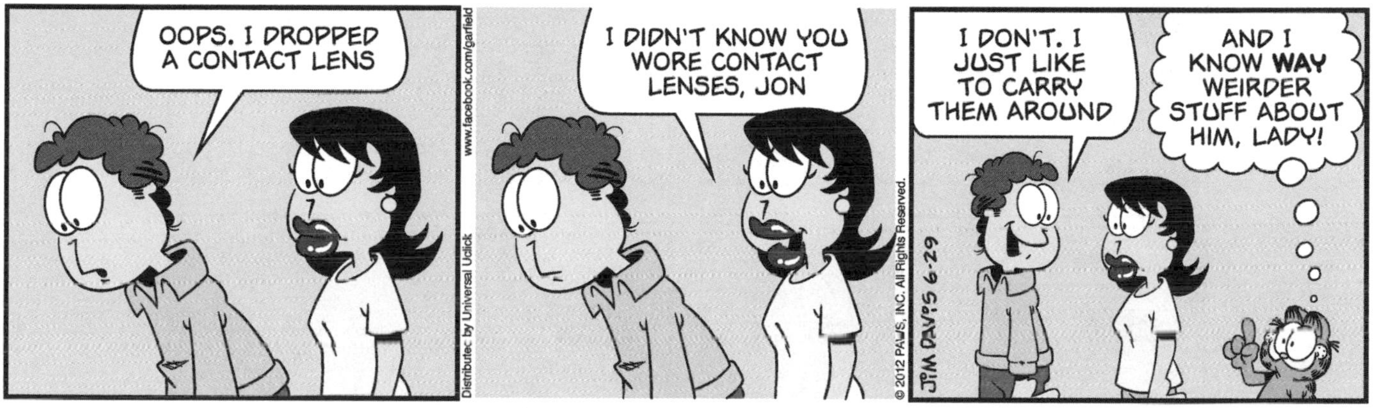
OOPS. I DROPPED A CONTACT LENS
I DIDN'T KNOW YOU WORE CONTACT LENSES, JON
I DON'T. I JUST LIKE TO CARRY THEM AROUND
AND I KNOW **WAY** WEIRDER STUFF ABOUT HIM, LADY!
JIM DAVIS 6-29
Distributed by Universal Uclick
www.facebook.com/garfield
© 2012 PAWS, INC. All Rights Reserved.

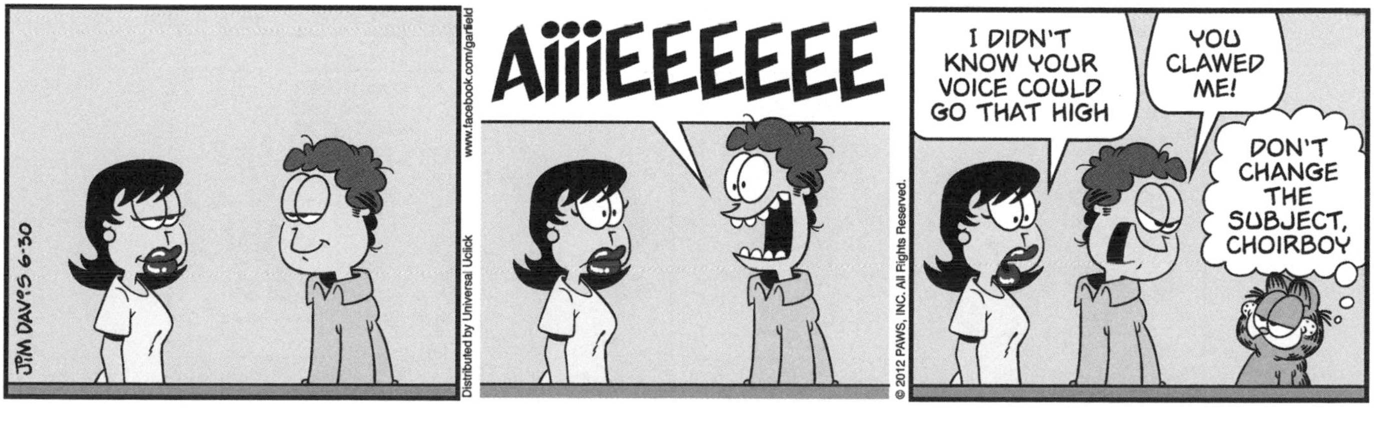
JIM DAVIS 6-30
AiiiEEEEEEE
I DIDN'T KNOW YOUR VOICE COULD GO THAT HIGH
YOU CLAWED ME!
DON'T CHANGE THE SUBJECT, CHOIRBOY
Distributed by Universal Uclick
www.facebook.com/garfield
© 2012 PAWS, INC. All Rights Reserved.

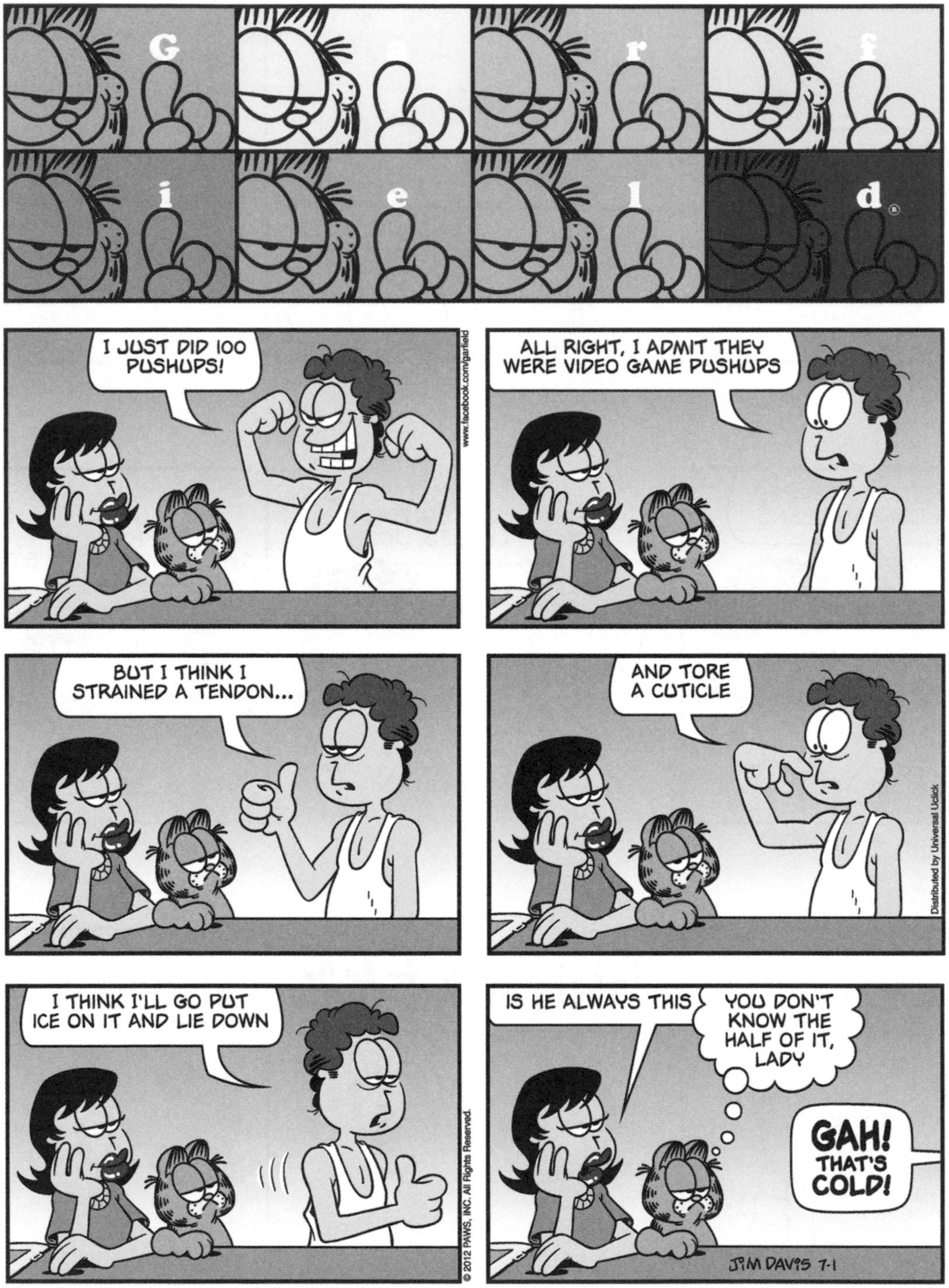
Garfield®
I JUST DID 100 PUSHUPS!
www.facebook.com/garfield
ALL RIGHT, I ADMIT THEY WERE VIDEO GAME PUSHUPS
BUT I THINK I STRAINED A TENDON...
AND TORE A CUTICLE
Distributed by Universal Uclick
I THINK I'LL GO PUT ICE ON IT AND LIE DOWN
© 2012 PAWS, INC. All Rights Reserved.
IS HE ALWAYS THIS
YOU DON'T KNOW THE HALF OF IT, LADY
GAH! THAT'S COLD!
JIM DAVIS 7-1

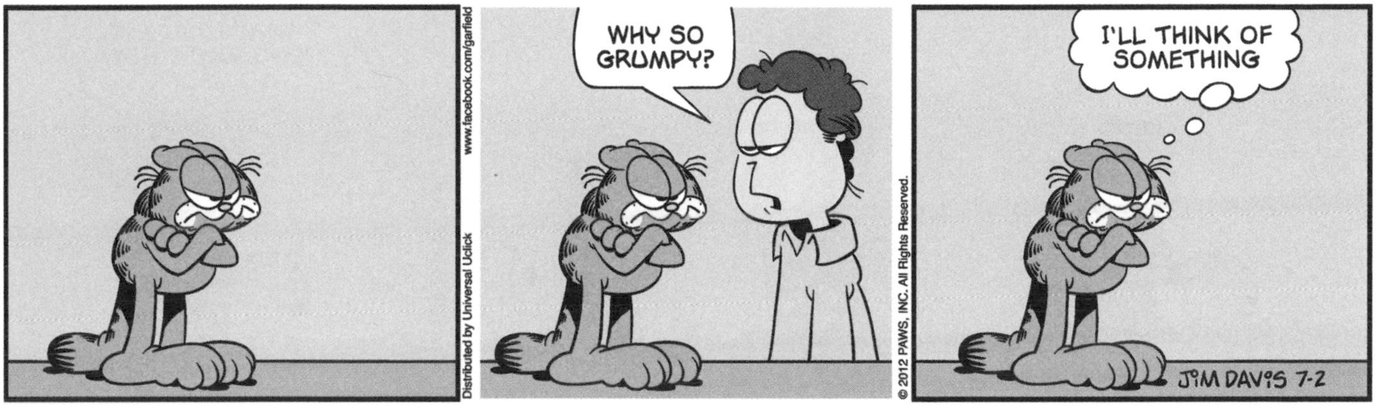
Distributed by Universal Uclick
www.facebook.com/garfield
WHY SO GRUMPY?
© 2012 PAWS, INC. All Rights Reserved.
I'LL THINK OF SOMETHING
JIM DAVIS 7-2

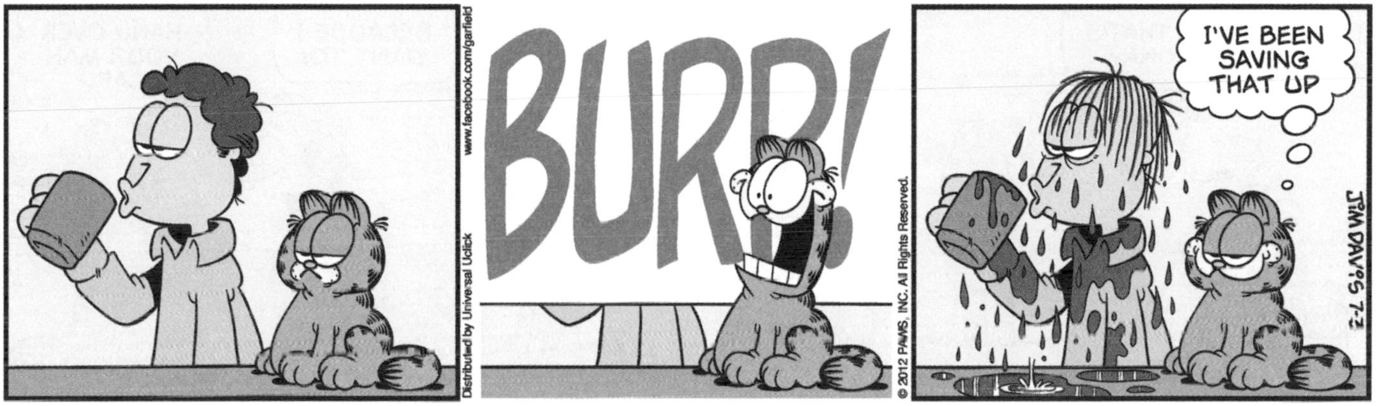
Distributed by Universal Uclick
www.facebook.com/garfield
BURP!
© 2012 PAWS, INC. All Rights Reserved.
I'VE BEEN SAVING THAT UP
JIM DAVIS 7-3

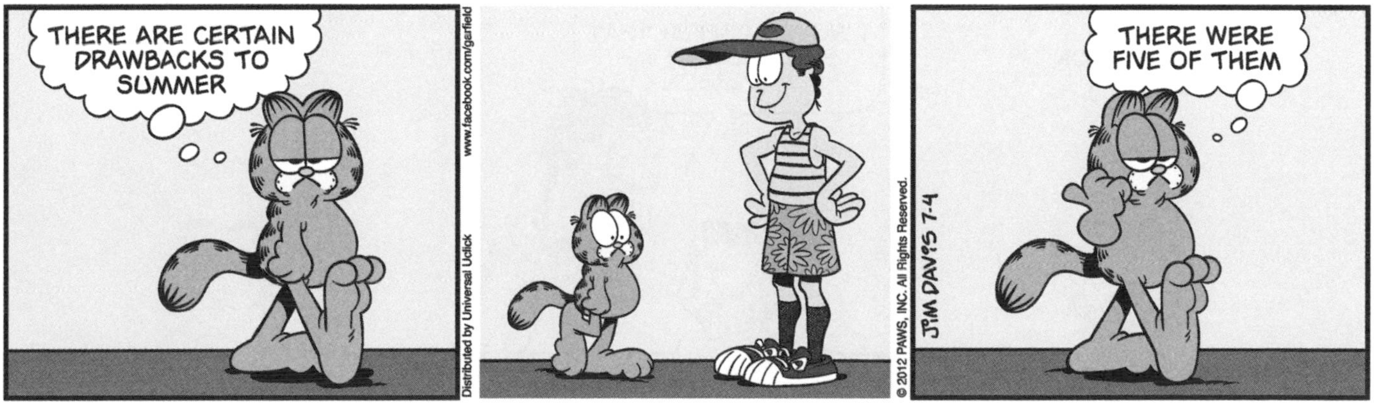
THERE ARE CERTAIN DRAWBACKS TO SUMMER
Distributed by Universal Uclick
www.facebook.com/garfield
© 2012 PAWS, INC. All Rights Reserved.
JIM DAVIS 7-4
THERE WERE FIVE OF THEM

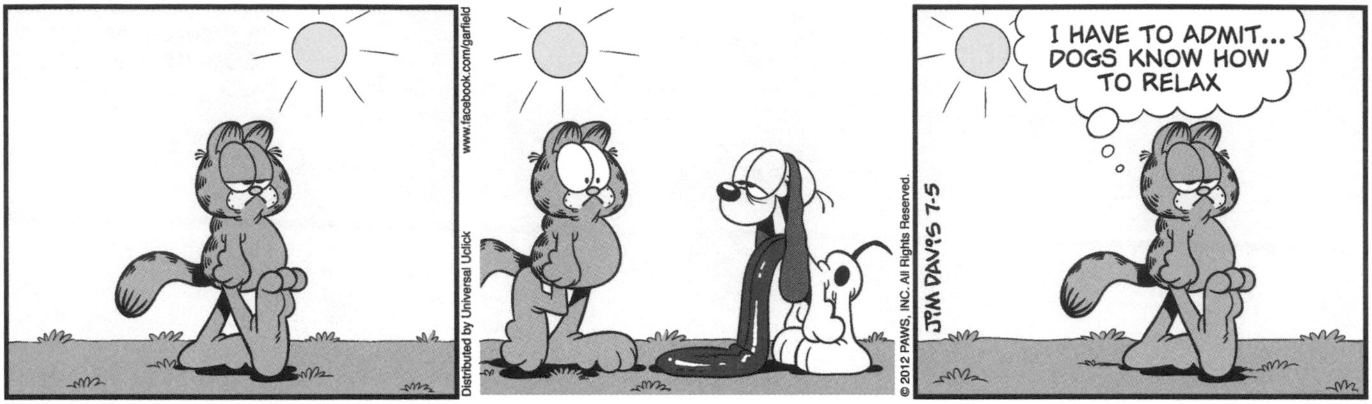
Distributed by Universal Uclick
www.facebook.com/garfield
© 2012 PAWS, INC. All Rights Reserved.
JIM DAVIS 7-5
I HAVE TO ADMIT... DOGS KNOW HOW TO RELAX

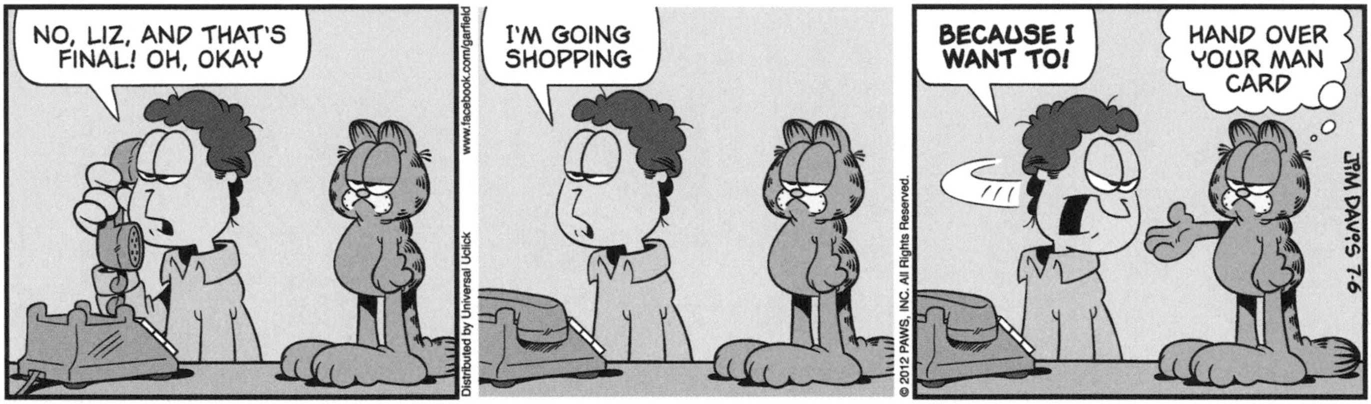
NO, LIZ, AND THAT'S FINAL! OH, OKAY
Distributed by Universal Uclick
www.facebook.com/garfield
I'M GOING SHOPPING
© 2012 PAWS, INC. All Rights Reserved.
BECAUSE I WANT TO!
HAND OVER YOUR MAN CARD
JIM DAVIS 7-6

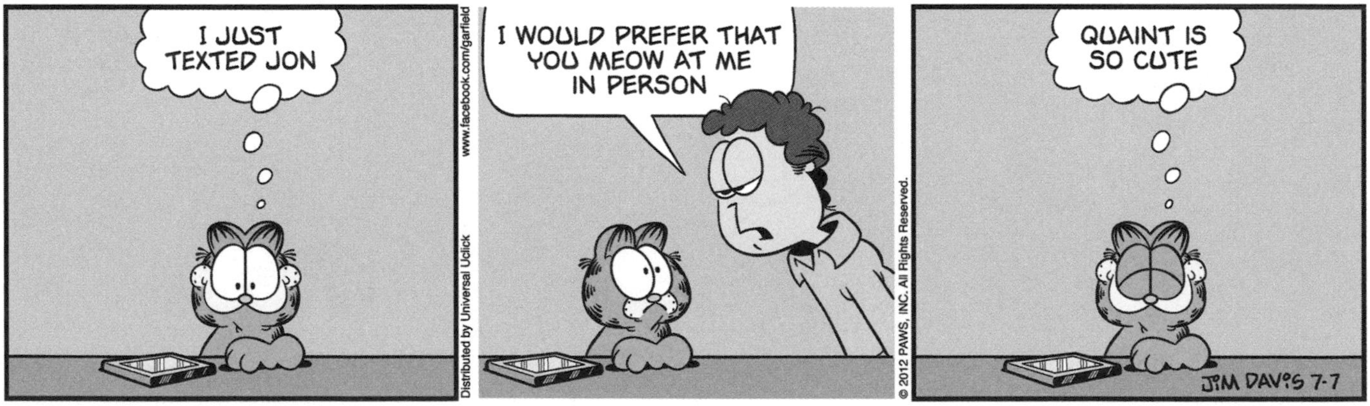
I JUST TEXTED JON
Distributed by Universal Uclick
www.facebook.com/garfield
I WOULD PREFER THAT YOU MEOW AT ME IN PERSON
© 2012 PAWS, INC. All Rights Reserved.
QUAINT IS SO CUTE
JIM DAVIS 7-7

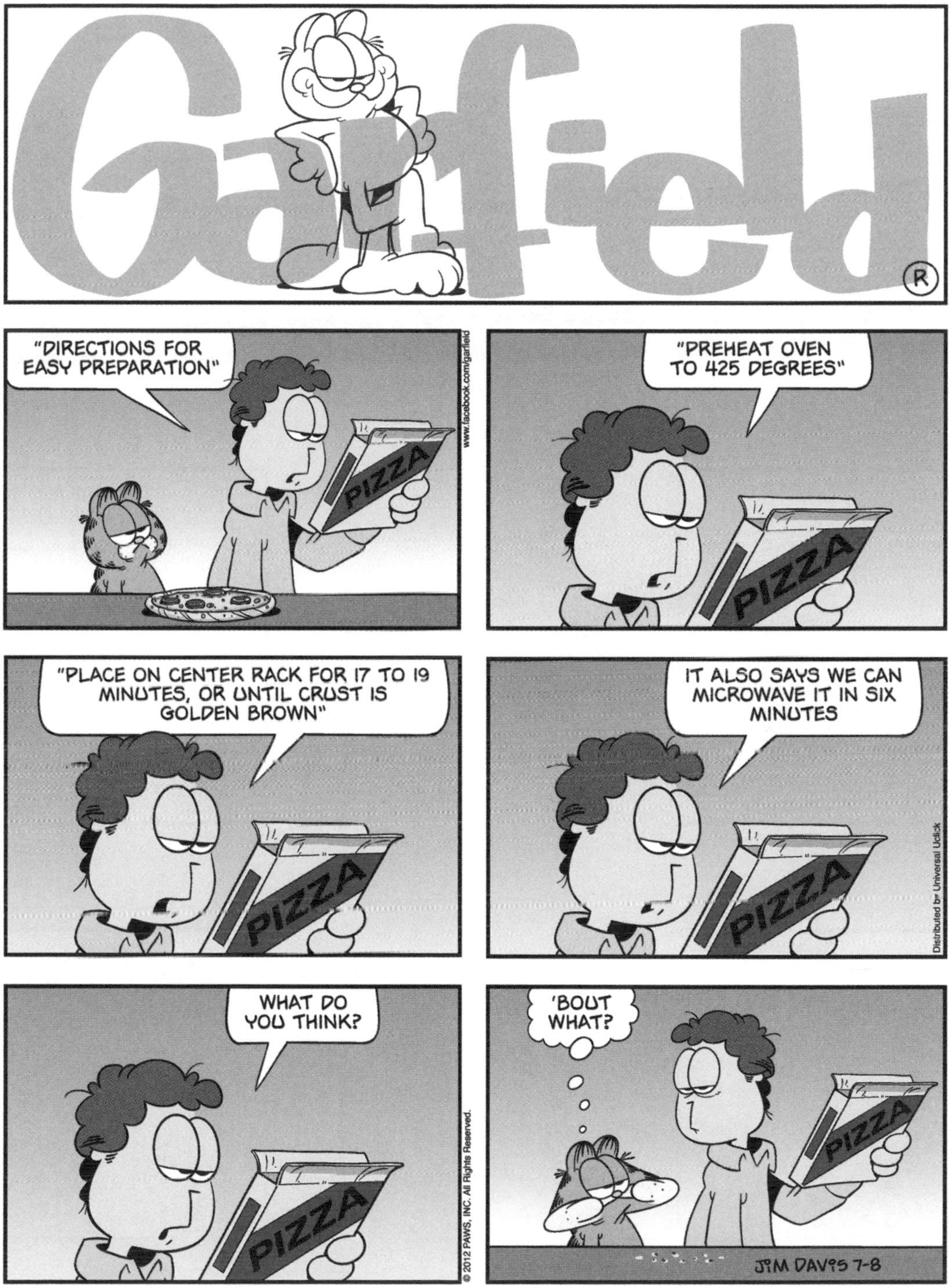
Garfield ®
"DIRECTIONS FOR EASY PREPARATION"
www.facebook.com/garfield
"PREHEAT OVEN TO 425 DEGREES"
"PLACE ON CENTER RACK FOR 17 TO 19 MINUTES, OR UNTIL CRUST IS GOLDEN BROWN"
IT ALSO SAYS WE CAN MICROWAVE IT IN SIX MINUTES
Distributed by Universal Uclick
WHAT DO YOU THINK?
© 2012 PAWS, INC. All Rights Reserved.
'BOUT WHAT?
JIM DAVIS 7-8
PIZZA

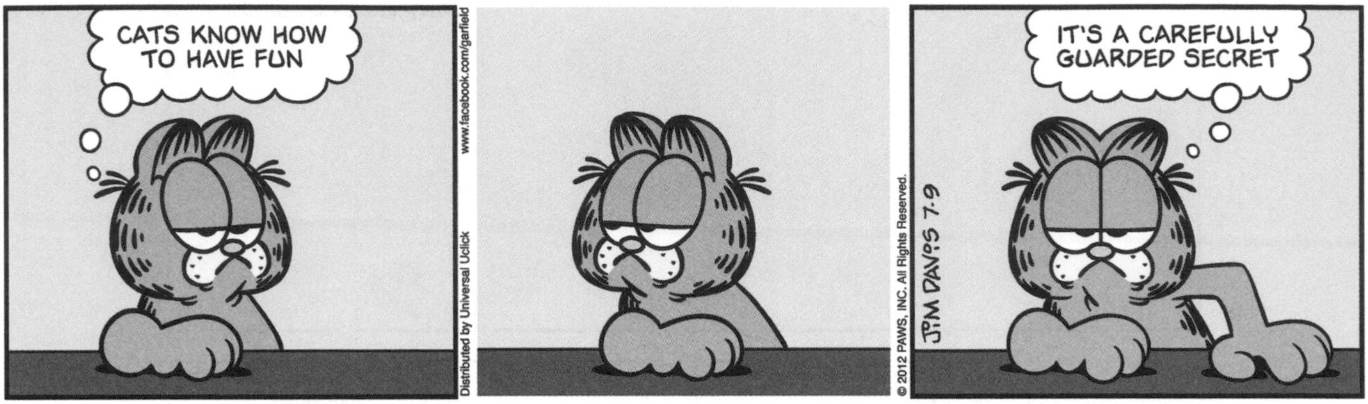
CATS KNOW HOW TO HAVE FUN
IT'S A CAREFULLY GUARDED SECRET
JIM DAVIS 7·9
Distributed by Universal Uclick www.facebook.com/garfield
© 2012 PAWS, INC. All Rights Reserved.

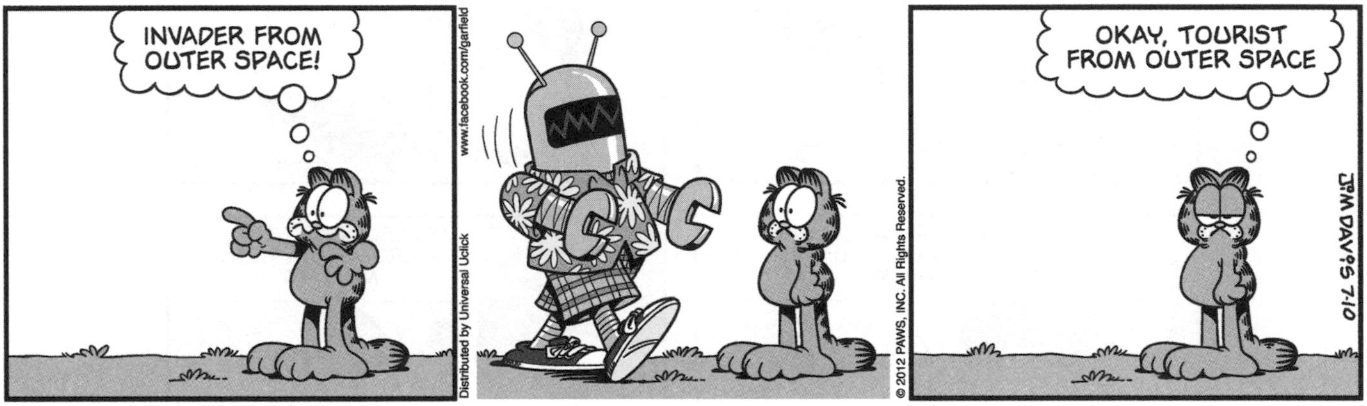
INVADER FROM OUTER SPACE!
OKAY, TOURIST FROM OUTER SPACE
JIM DAVIS 7·10
Distributed by Universal Uclick www.facebook.com/garfield
© 2012 PAWS, INC. All Rights Reserved.

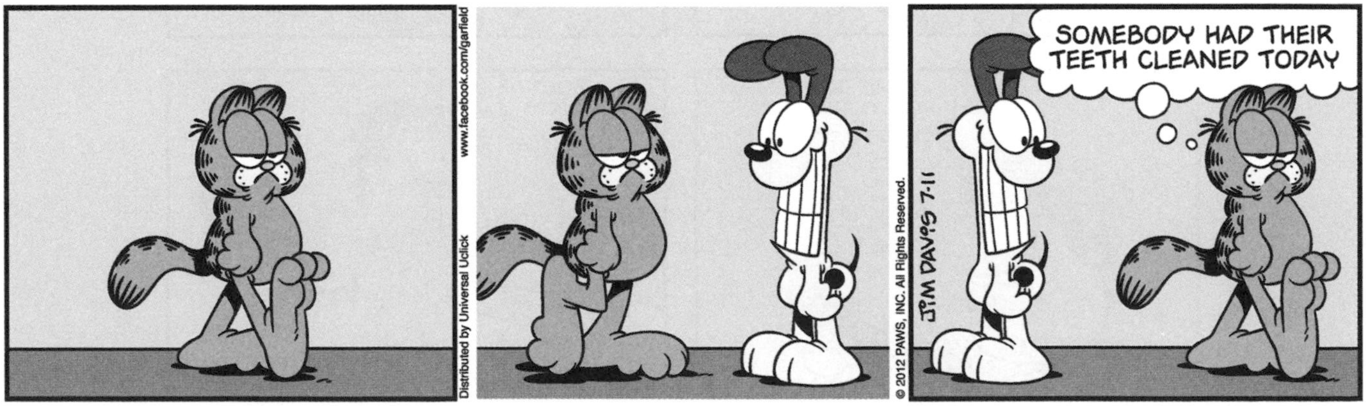
SOMEBODY HAD THEIR TEETH CLEANED TODAY
JIM DAVIS 7·11
Distributed by Universal Uclick www.facebook.com/garfield
© 2012 PAWS, INC. All Rights Reserved.

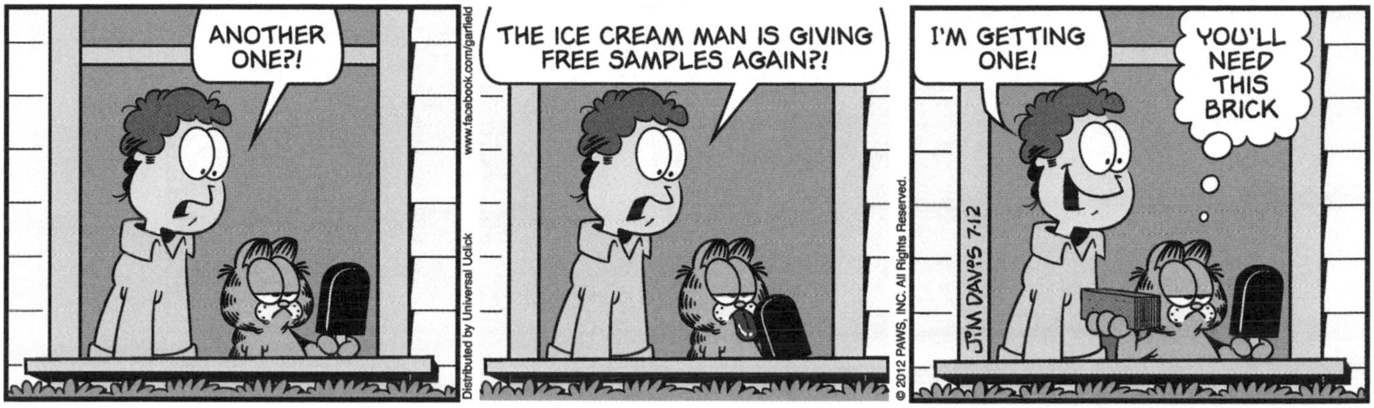
ANOTHER ONE?!
THE ICE CREAM MAN IS GIVING FREE SAMPLES AGAIN?!
I'M GETTING ONE!
YOU'LL NEED THIS BRICK
JIM DAVIS 7-12
Distributed by Universal Uclick www.facebook.com/garfield
© 2012 PAWS, INC. All Rights Reserved.

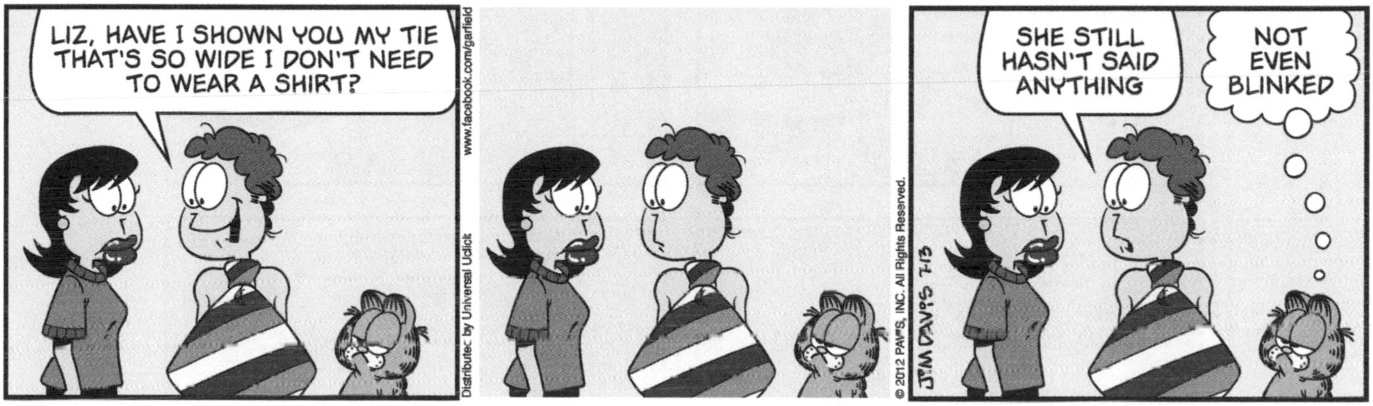
LIZ, HAVE I SHOWN YOU MY TIE THAT'S SO WIDE I DON'T NEED TO WEAR A SHIRT?
SHE STILL HASN'T SAID ANYTHING
NOT EVEN BLINKED
JIM DAVIS 7-13
Distributed by Universal Uclick www.facebook.com/garfield
© 2012 PAWS, INC. All Rights Reserved.

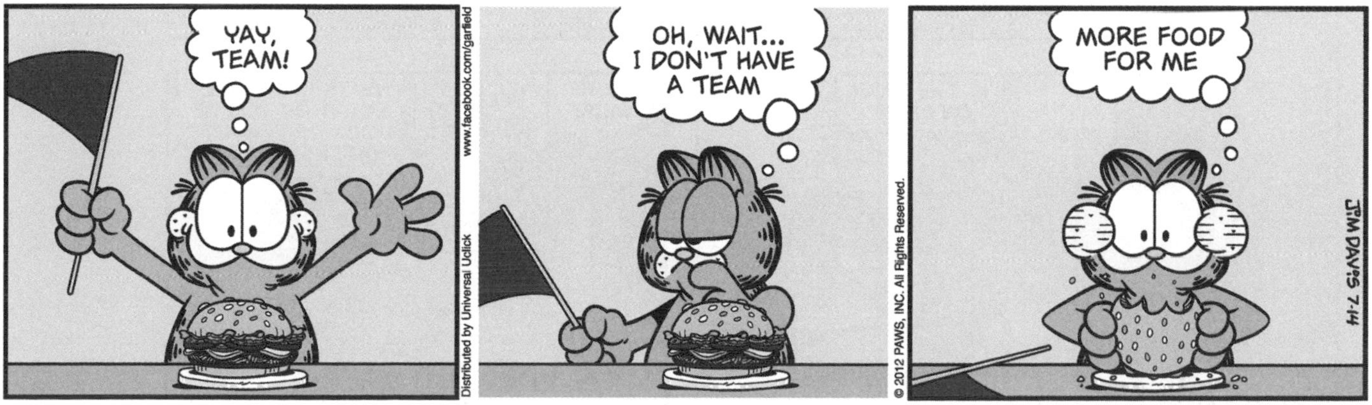
YAY, TEAM!
OH, WAIT... I DON'T HAVE A TEAM
MORE FOOD FOR ME
JIM DAVIS 7-14
Distributed by Universal Uclick www.facebook.com/garfield
© 2012 PAWS, INC. All Rights Reserved.

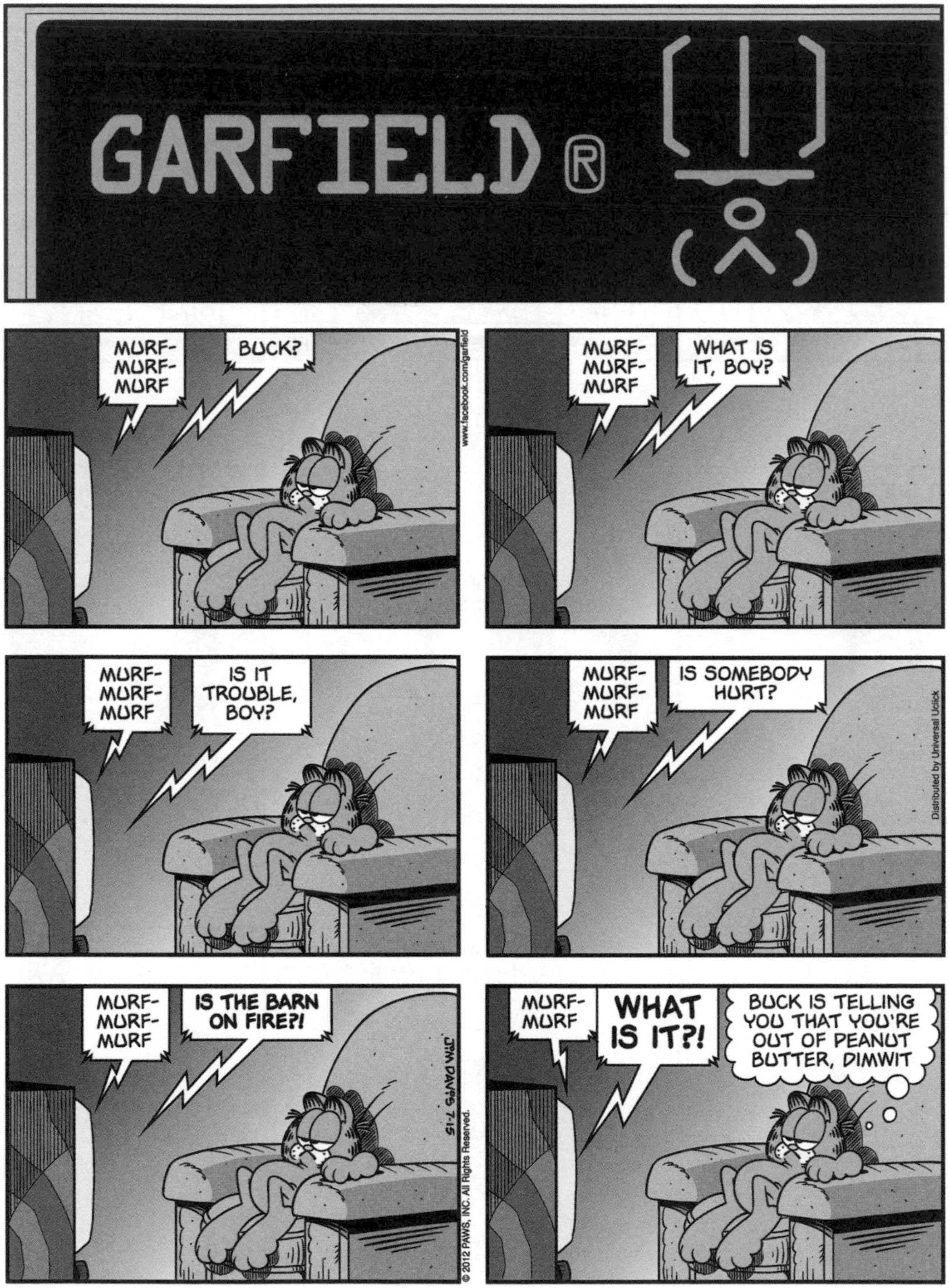
GARFIELD®
MURF-MURF-MURF
BUCK?
www.facebook.com/garfield
MURF-MURF-MURF
WHAT IS IT, BOY?
MURF-MURF-MURF
IS IT TROUBLE, BOY?
MURF-MURF-MURF
IS SOMEBODY HURT?
Distributed by Universal Uclick
MURF-MURF-MURF
IS THE BARN ON FIRE?!
JIM DAVIS 7-15
© 2012 PAWS, INC. All Rights Reserved.
MURF-MURF
WHAT IS IT?!
BUCK IS TELLING YOU THAT YOU'RE OUT OF PEANUT BUTTER, DIMWIT

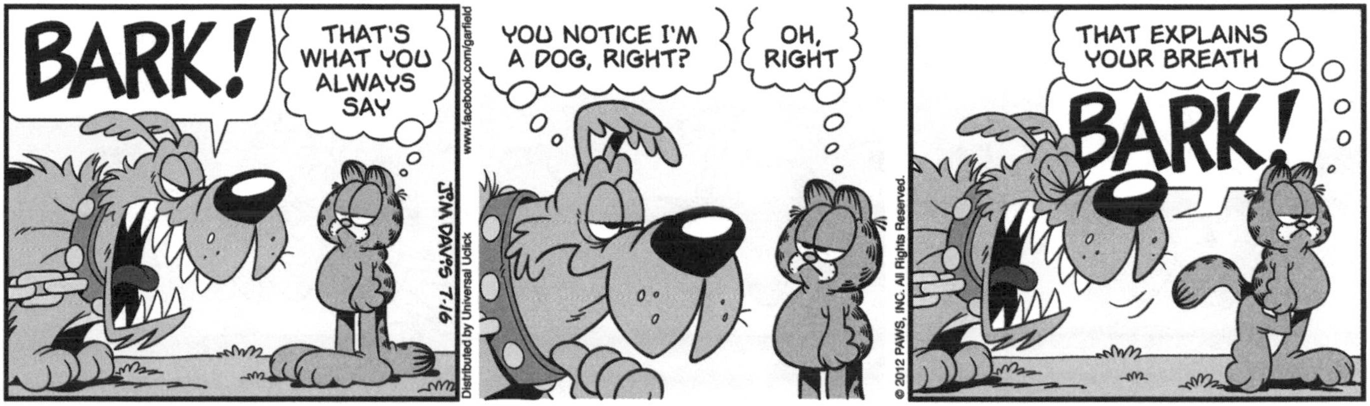
BARK!
THAT'S WHAT YOU ALWAYS SAY
JIM DAVIS 7-16
www.facebook.com/garfield
Distributed by Universal Uclick
YOU NOTICE I'M A DOG, RIGHT?
OH, RIGHT
© 2012 PAWS, INC. All Rights Reserved.
THAT EXPLAINS YOUR BREATH
BARK!

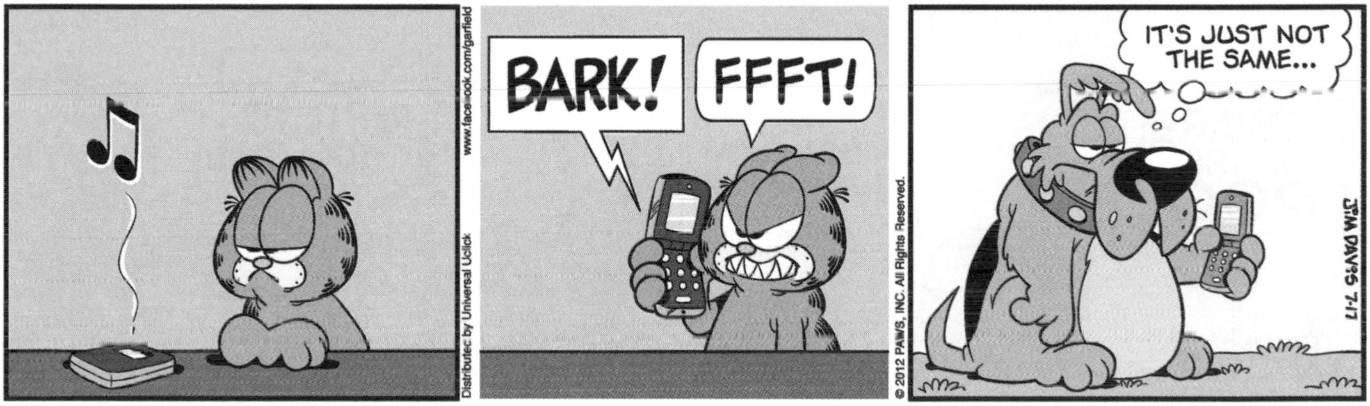
www.facebook.com/garfield
Distributed by Universal Uclick
BARK!
FFFT!
© 2012 PAWS, INC. All Rights Reserved.
IT'S JUST NOT THE SAME...
JIM DAVIS 7-17

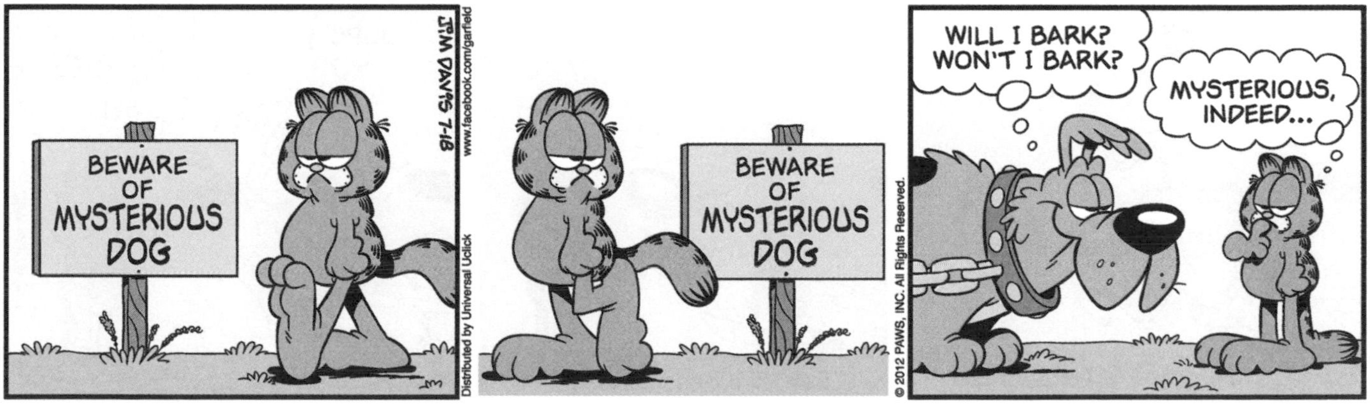
BEWARE OF MYSTERIOUS DOG
JIM DAVIS 7-18
www.facebook.com/garfield
Distributed by Universal Uclick
BEWARE OF MYSTERIOUS DOG
© 2012 PAWS, INC. All Rights Reserved.
WILL I BARK? WON'T I BARK?
MYSTERIOUS, INDEED...

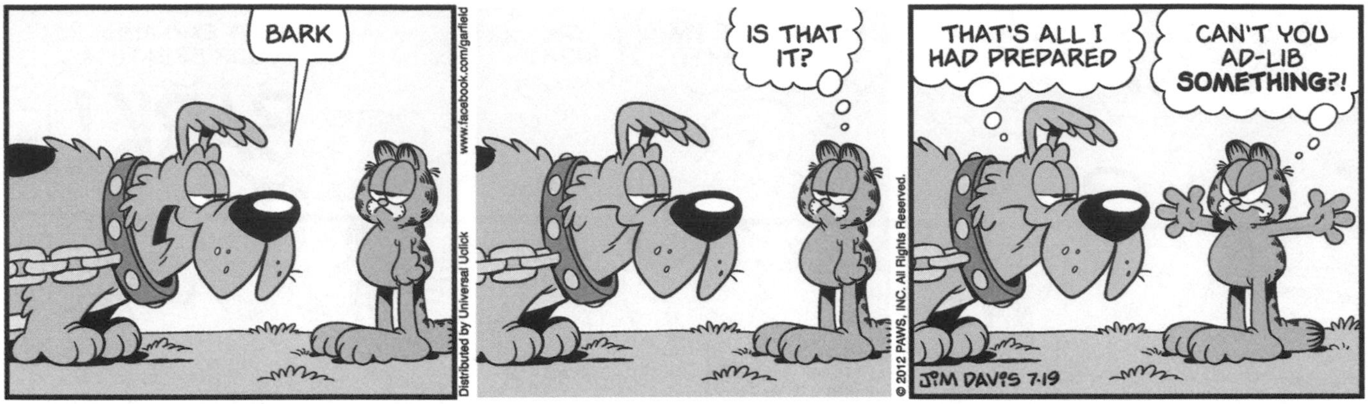
BARK
IS THAT IT?
THAT'S ALL I HAD PREPARED
CAN'T YOU AD-LIB **SOMETHING**?!
JIM DAVIS 7-19
Distributed by Universal Uclick
www.facebook.com/garfield
© 2012 PAWS, INC. All Rights Reserved.

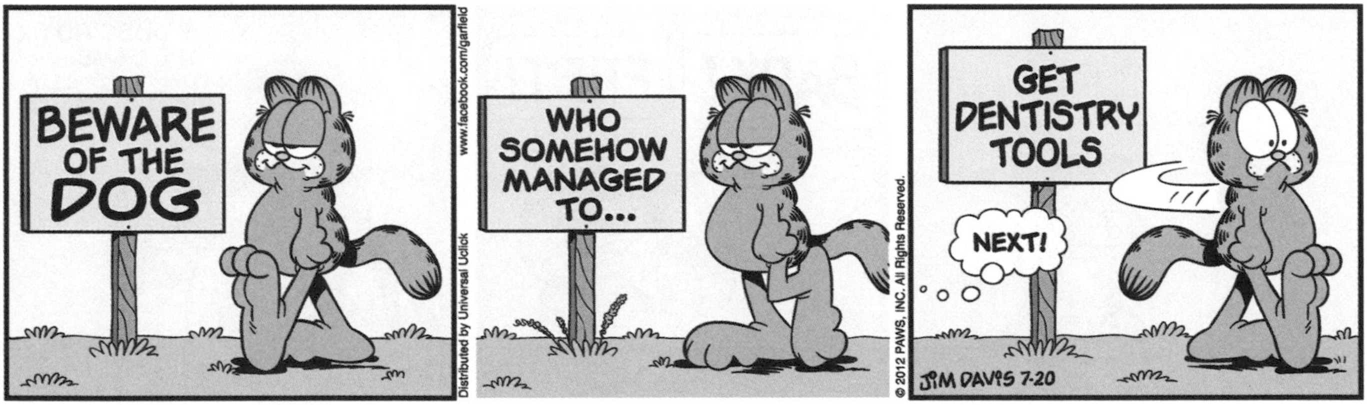
BEWARE OF THE DOG
WHO SOMEHOW MANAGED TO...
GET DENTISTRY TOOLS
NEXT!
JIM DAVIS 7-20
Distributed by Universal Uclick
www.facebook.com/garfield
© 2012 PAWS, INC. All Rights Reserved.

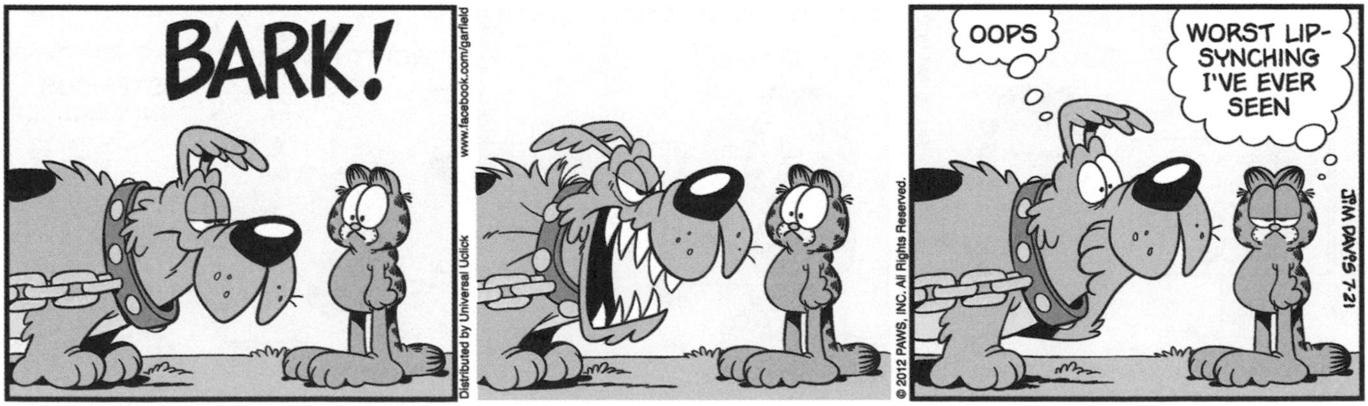
BARK!
OOPS
WORST LIP-SYNCHING I'VE EVER SEEN
JIM DAVIS 7-21
Distributed by Universal Uclick
www.facebook.com/garfield
© 2012 PAWS, INC. All Rights Reserved.

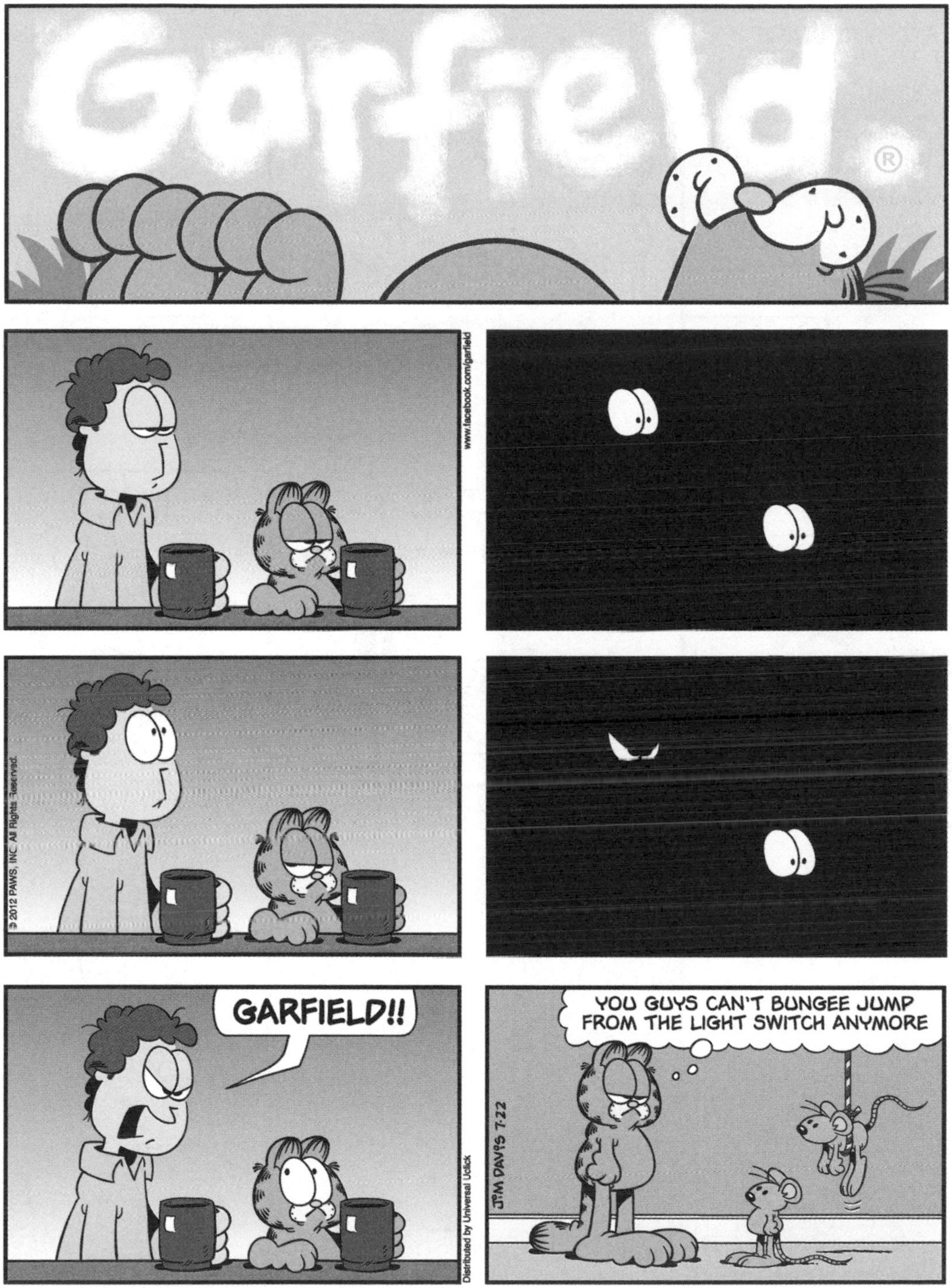
Garfield®
www.facebook.com/garfield
© 2012 PAWS, INC. All Rights Reserved.
GARFIELD!!
Distributed by Universal Uclick
YOU GUYS CAN'T BUNGEE JUMP FROM THE LIGHT SWITCH ANYMORE
JIM DAVIS 7-22

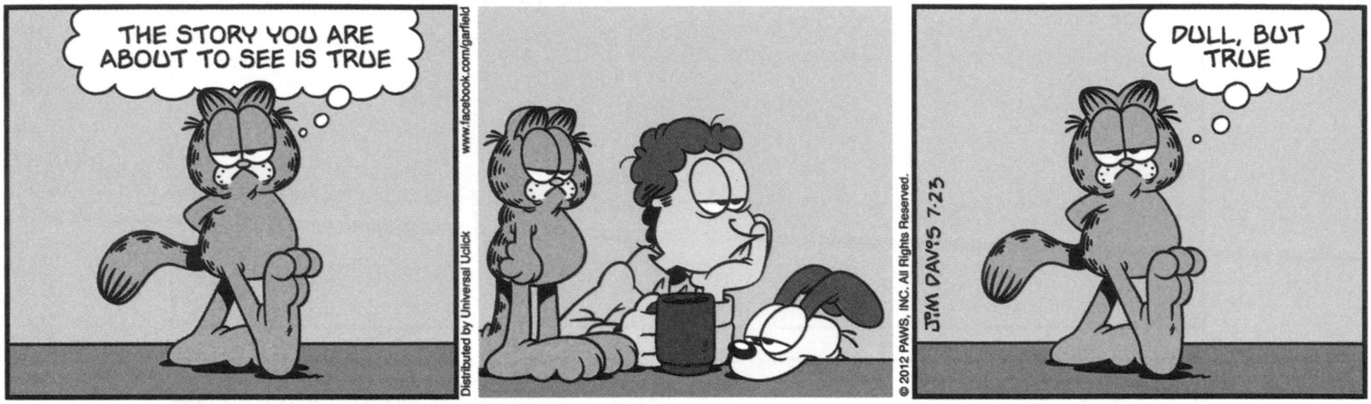
THE STORY YOU ARE ABOUT TO SEE IS TRUE
DULL, BUT TRUE
JIM DAVIS 7-23
Distributed by Universal Uclick
www.facebook.com/garfield
© 2012 PAWS, INC. All Rights Reserved.

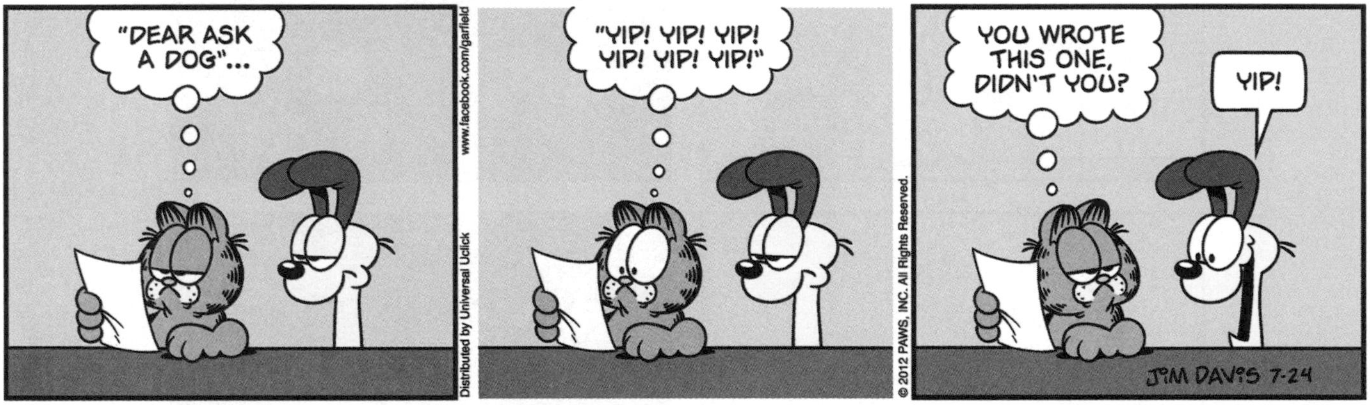
"DEAR ASK A DOG"...
"YIP! YIP! YIP! YIP! YIP! YIP!"
YOU WROTE THIS ONE, DIDN'T YOU?
YIP!
JIM DAVIS 7-24
Distributed by Universal Uclick
www.facebook.com/garfield
© 2012 PAWS, INC. All Rights Reserved.

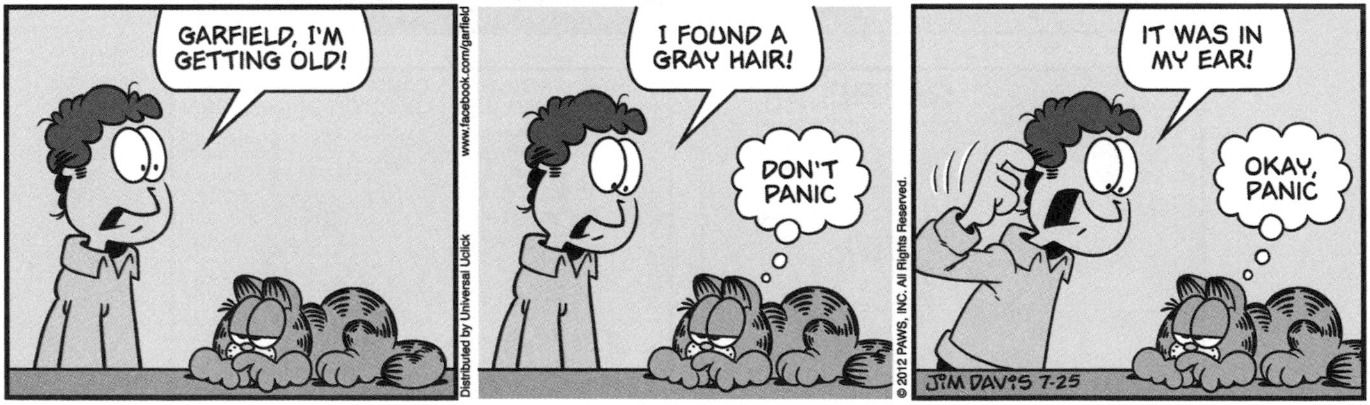
GARFIELD, I'M GETTING OLD!
I FOUND A GRAY HAIR!
DON'T PANIC
IT WAS IN MY EAR!
OKAY, PANIC
JIM DAVIS 7-25
Distributed by Universal Uclick
www.facebook.com/garfield
© 2012 PAWS, INC. All Rights Reserved.

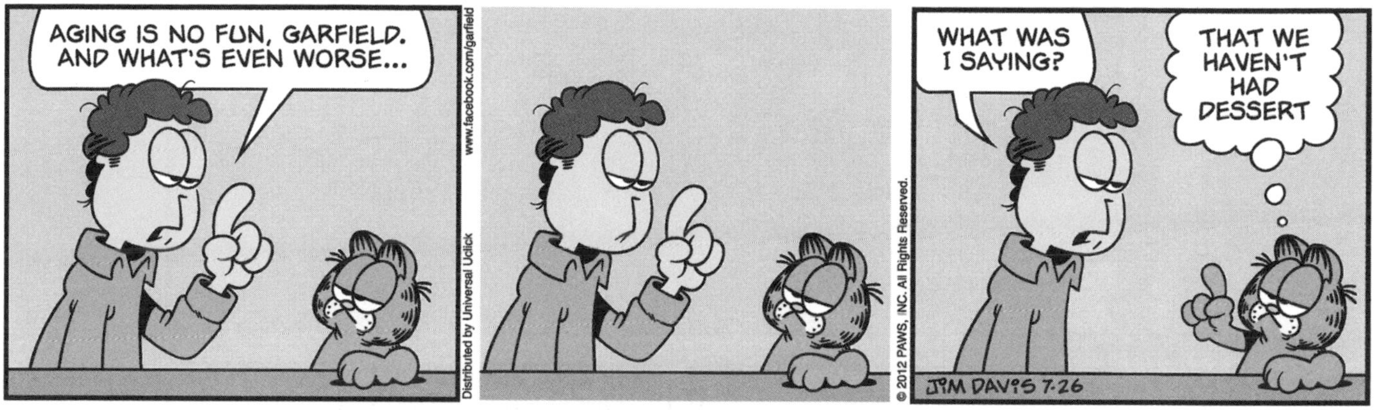
AGING IS NO FUN, GARFIELD. AND WHAT'S EVEN WORSE...
WHAT WAS I SAYING?
THAT WE HAVEN'T HAD DESSERT
JIM DAVIS 7-26
Distributed by Universal Uclick www.facebook.com/garfield
© 2012 PAWS, INC. All Rights Reserved.

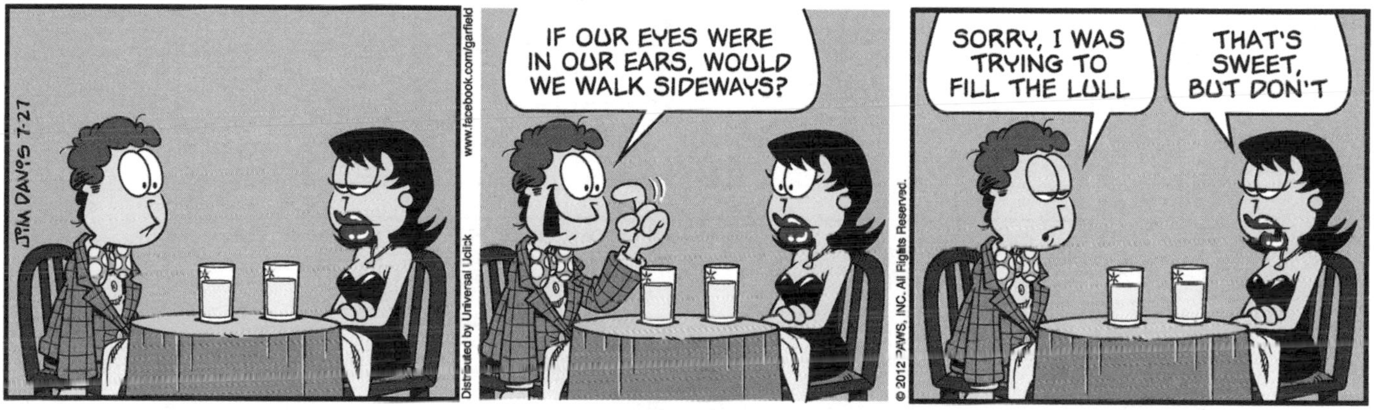
JIM DAVIS 7-27
IF OUR EYES WERE IN OUR EARS, WOULD WE WALK SIDEWAYS?
SORRY, I WAS TRYING TO FILL THE LULL
THAT'S SWEET, BUT DON'T
Distributed by Universal Uclick www.facebook.com/garfield
© 2012 PAWS, INC. All Rights Reserved.

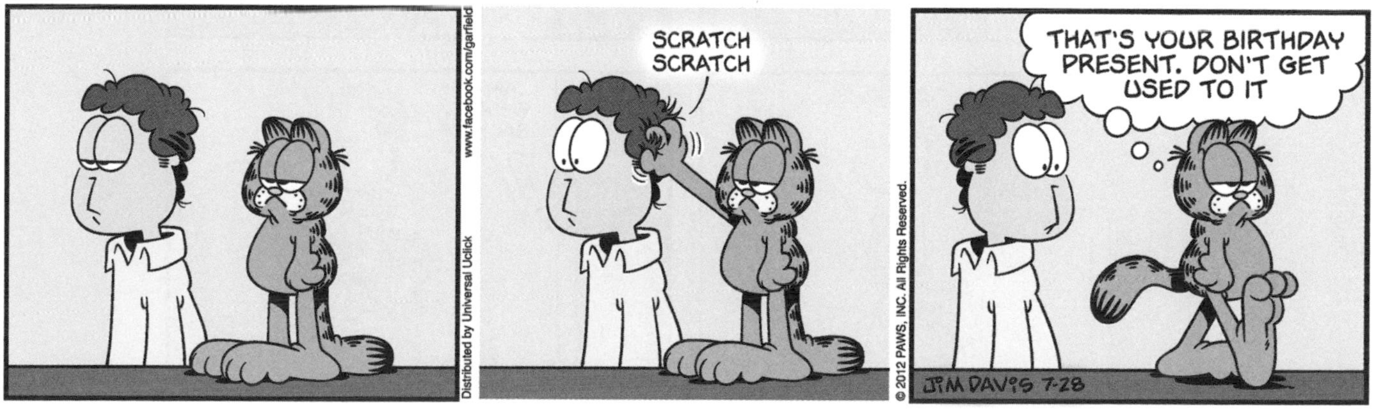
SCRATCH SCRATCH
THAT'S YOUR BIRTHDAY PRESENT. DON'T GET USED TO IT
JIM DAVIS 7-28
Distributed by Universal Uclick www.facebook.com/garfield
© 2012 PAWS, INC. All Rights Reserved.

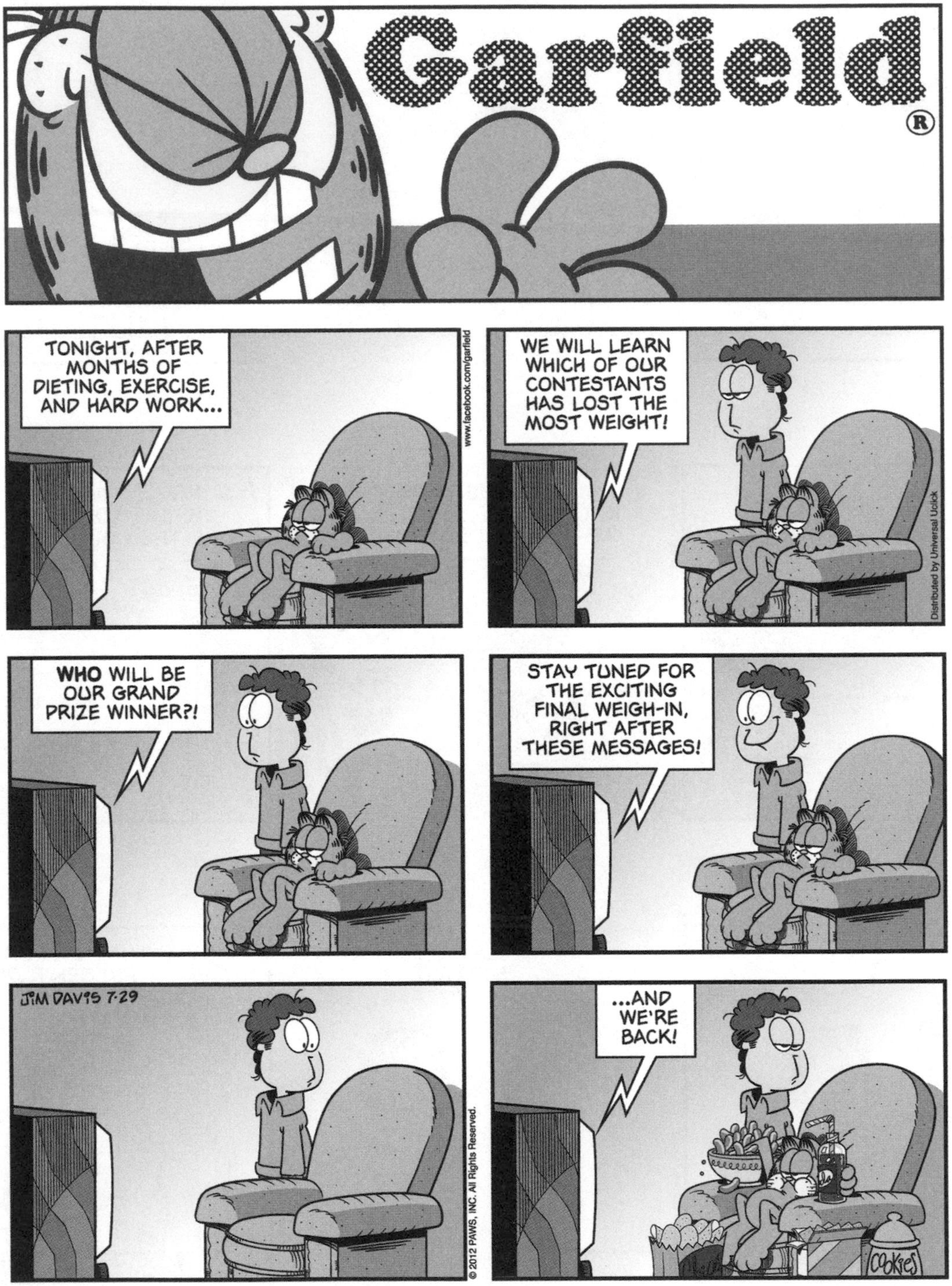
Garfield®
TONIGHT, AFTER MONTHS OF DIETING, EXERCISE, AND HARD WORK...
www.facebook.com/garfield
WE WILL LEARN WHICH OF OUR CONTESTANTS HAS LOST THE MOST WEIGHT!
Distributed by Universal Uclick
WHO WILL BE OUR GRAND PRIZE WINNER?!
STAY TUNED FOR THE EXCITING FINAL WEIGH-IN, RIGHT AFTER THESE MESSAGES!
JIM DAVIS 7-29
© 2012 PAWS, INC. All Rights Reserved.
...AND WE'RE BACK!
COOKIES

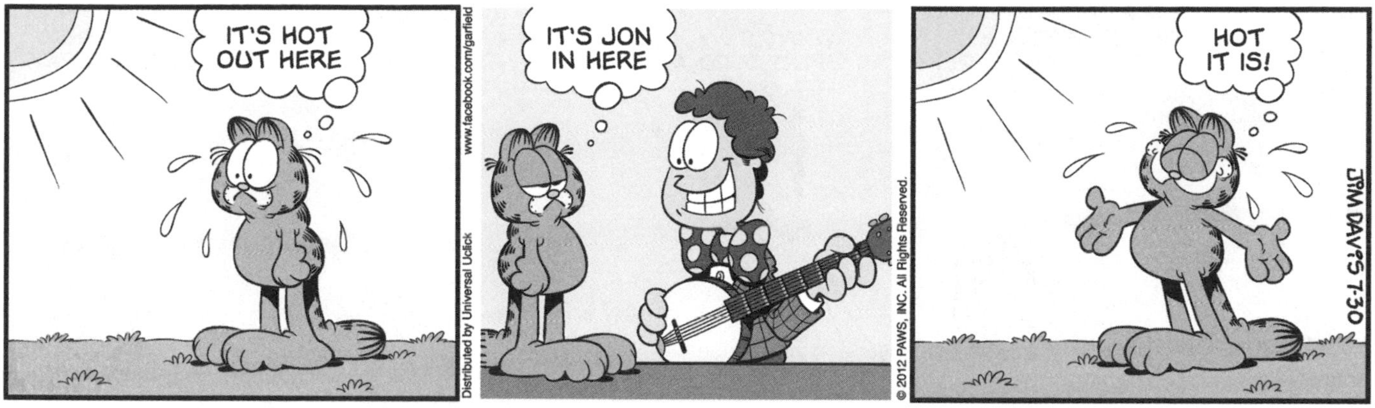
IT'S HOT OUT HERE
IT'S JON IN HERE
HOT IT IS!
JIM DAVIS 7-30
Distributed by Universal Uclick www.facebook.com/garfield
© 2012 PAWS, INC. All Rights Reserved.

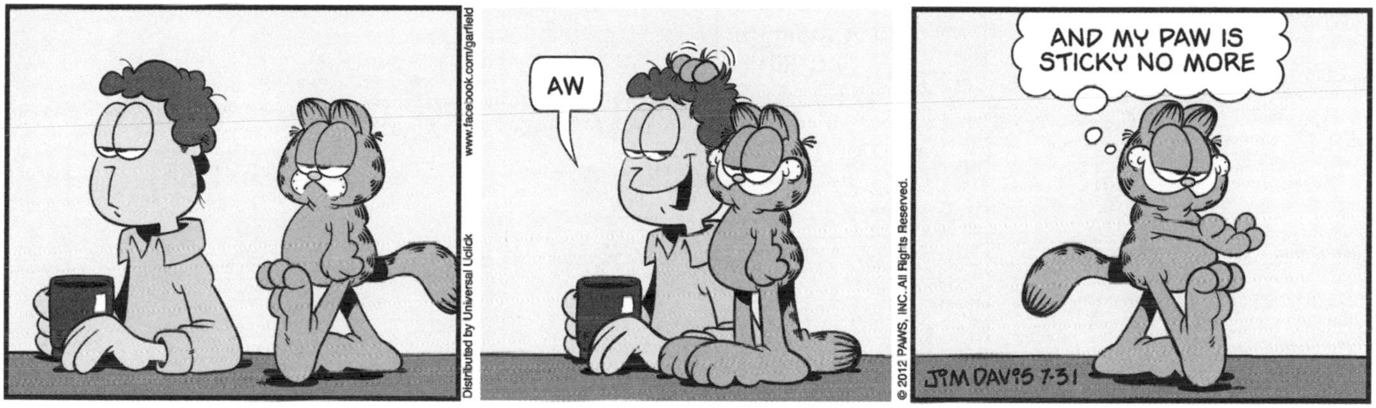
AW
AND MY PAW IS STICKY NO MORE
JIM DAVIS 7-31
Distributed by Universal Uclick www.facebook.com/garfield
© 2012 PAWS, INC. All Rights Reserved.

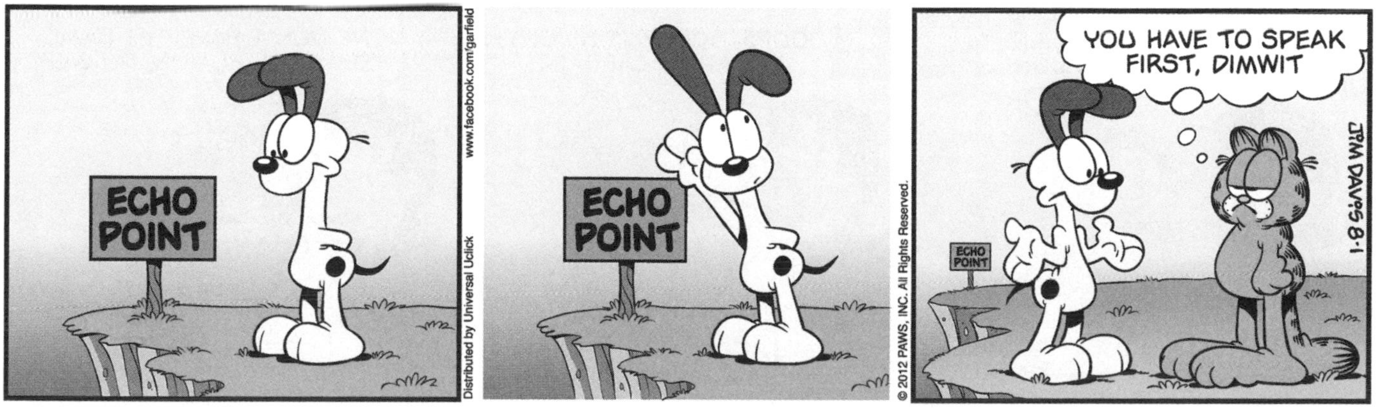
ECHO POINT
ECHO POINT
ECHO POINT
YOU HAVE TO SPEAK FIRST, DIMWIT
JIM DAVIS 8-1
Distributed by Universal Uclick www.facebook.com/garfield
© 2012 PAWS, INC. All Rights Reserved.

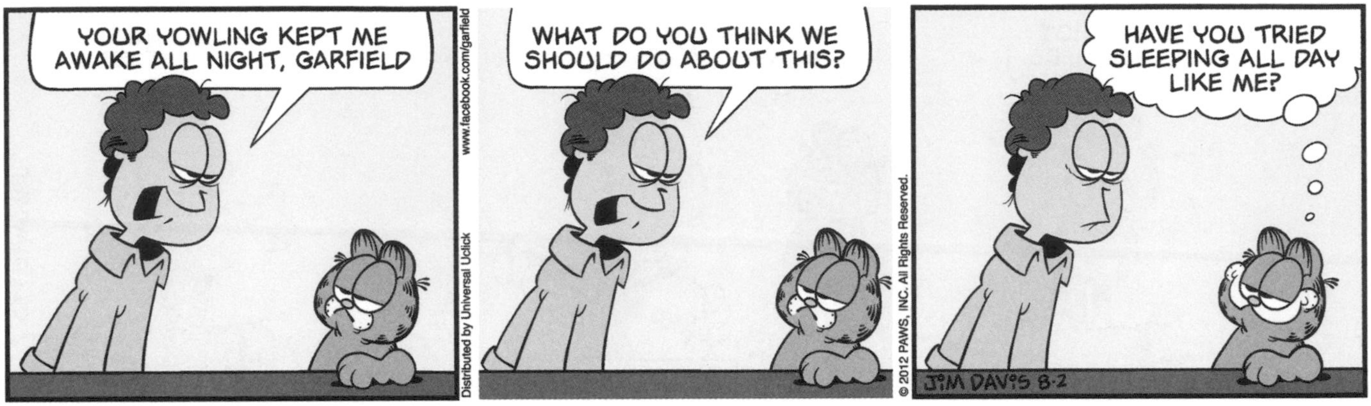
YOUR YOWLING KEPT ME AWAKE ALL NIGHT, GARFIELD
Distributed by Universal Uclick www.facebook.com/garfield
WHAT DO YOU THINK WE SHOULD DO ABOUT THIS?
© 2012 PAWS, INC. All Rights Reserved.
HAVE YOU TRIED SLEEPING ALL DAY LIKE ME?
JIM DAVIS 8-2

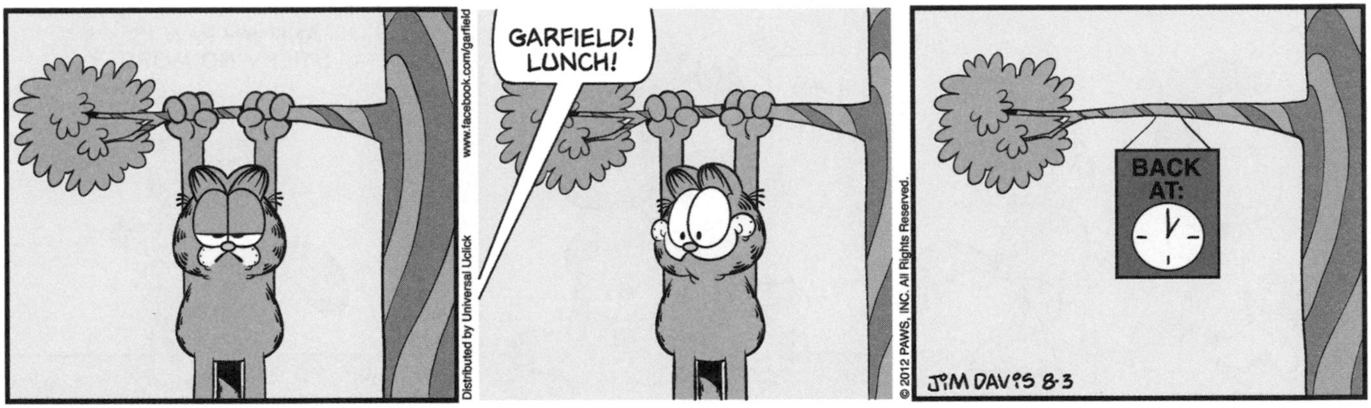
Distributed by Universal Uclick www.facebook.com/garfield
GARFIELD! LUNCH!
© 2012 PAWS, INC. All Rights Reserved.
BACK AT:
JIM DAVIS 8-3

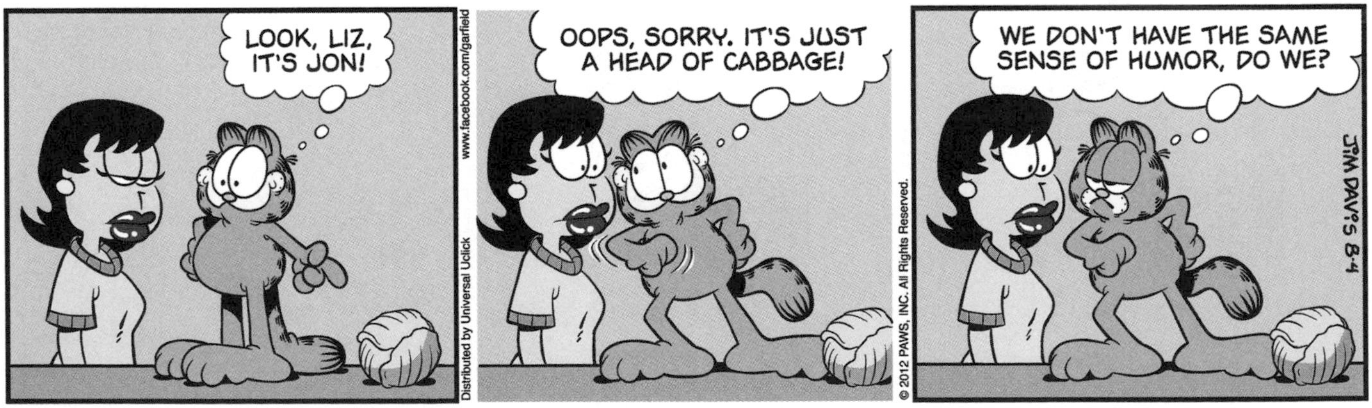
LOOK, LIZ, IT'S JON!
Distributed by Universal Uclick www.facebook.com/garfield
OOPS, SORRY. IT'S JUST A HEAD OF CABBAGE!
© 2012 PAWS, INC. All Rights Reserved.
WE DON'T HAVE THE SAME SENSE OF HUMOR, DO WE?
JIM DAVIS 8-4

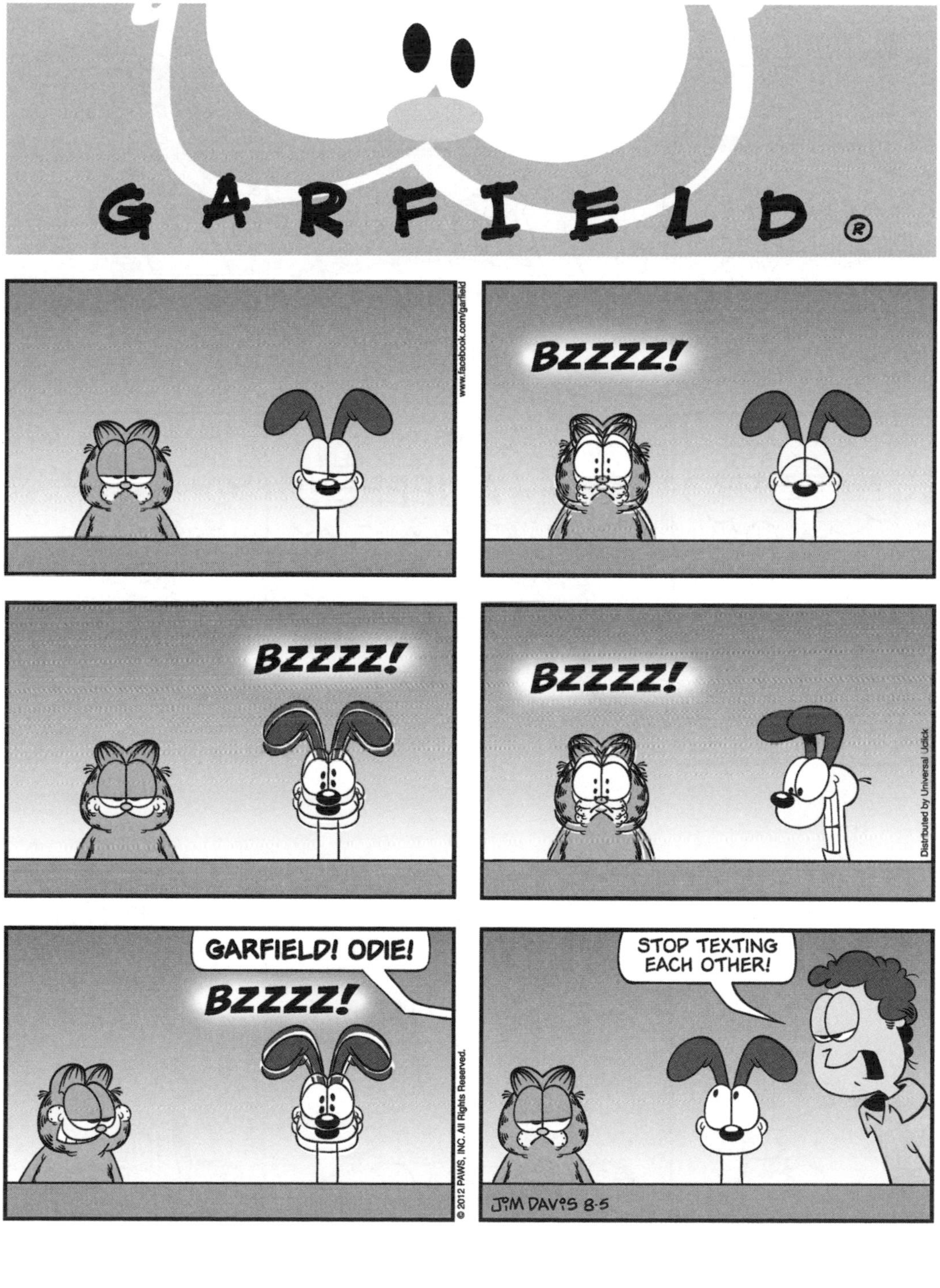
GARFIELD®
www.facebook.com/garfield
BZZZZ!
BZZZZ!
BZZZZ!
Distributed by Universal Uclick
GARFIELD! ODIE!
BZZZZ!
© 2012 PAWS, INC. All Rights Reserved.
STOP TEXTING EACH OTHER!
JIM DAVIS 8-5

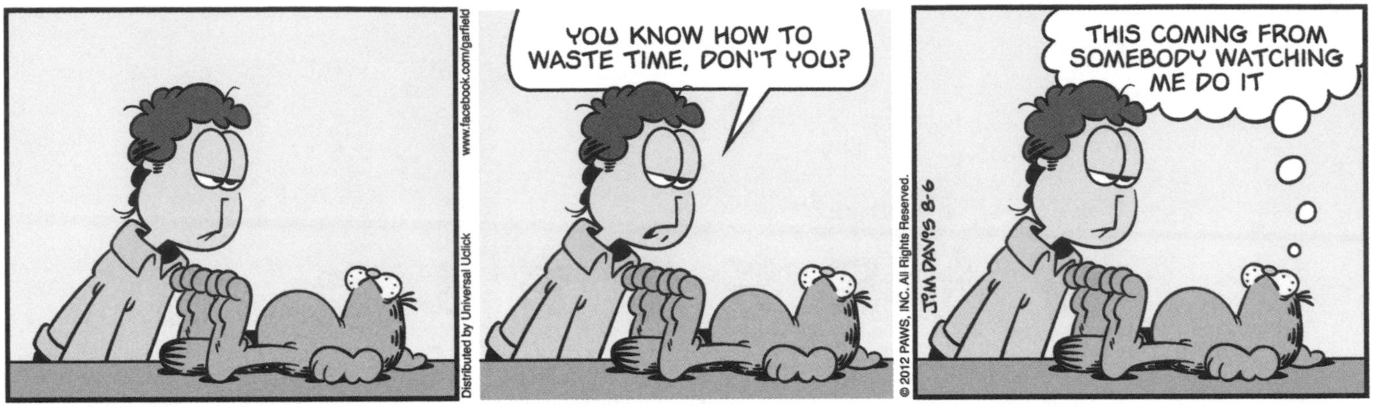
YOU KNOW HOW TO WASTE TIME, DON'T YOU?
THIS COMING FROM SOMEBODY WATCHING ME DO IT
www.facebook.com/garfield
Distributed by Universal Uclick
© 2012 PAWS, INC. All Rights Reserved.
JIM DAVIS 8-6

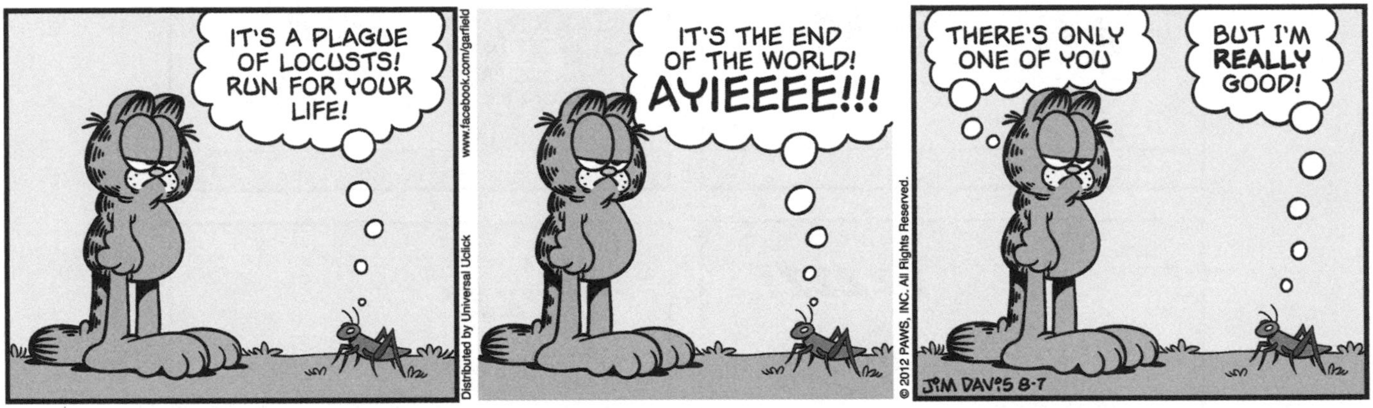
IT'S A PLAGUE OF LOCUSTS! RUN FOR YOUR LIFE!
IT'S THE END OF THE WORLD! AYIEEEEE!!!
THERE'S ONLY ONE OF YOU
BUT I'M REALLY GOOD!
www.facebook.com/garfield
Distributed by Universal Uclick
© 2012 PAWS, INC. All Rights Reserved.
JIM DAVIS 8-7

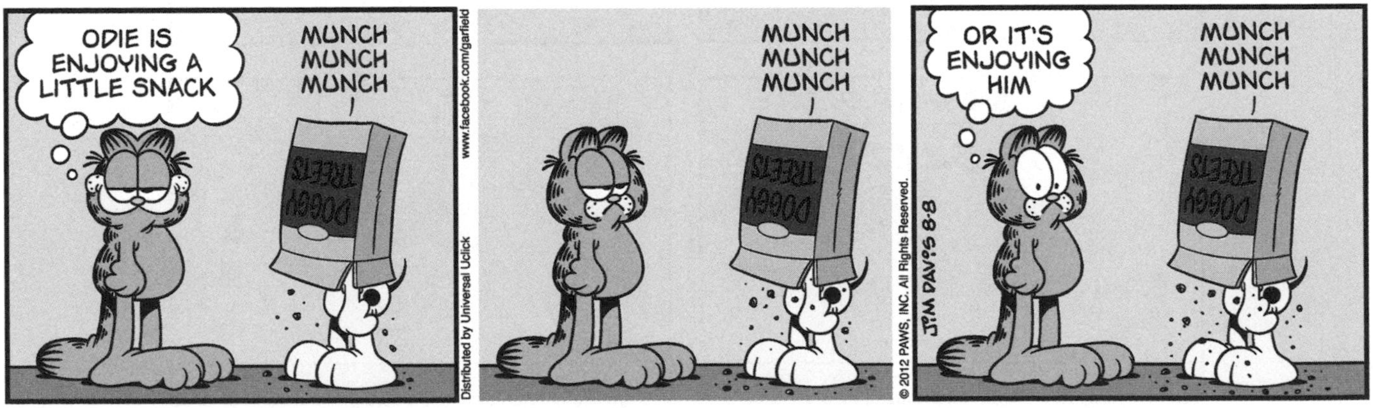
ODIE IS ENJOYING A LITTLE SNACK
MUNCH MUNCH MUNCH
DOGGY TREETS
MUNCH MUNCH MUNCH
OR IT'S ENJOYING HIM
MUNCH MUNCH MUNCH
www.facebook.com/garfield
Distributed by Universal Uclick
© 2012 PAWS, INC. All Rights Reserved.
JIM DAVIS 8-8

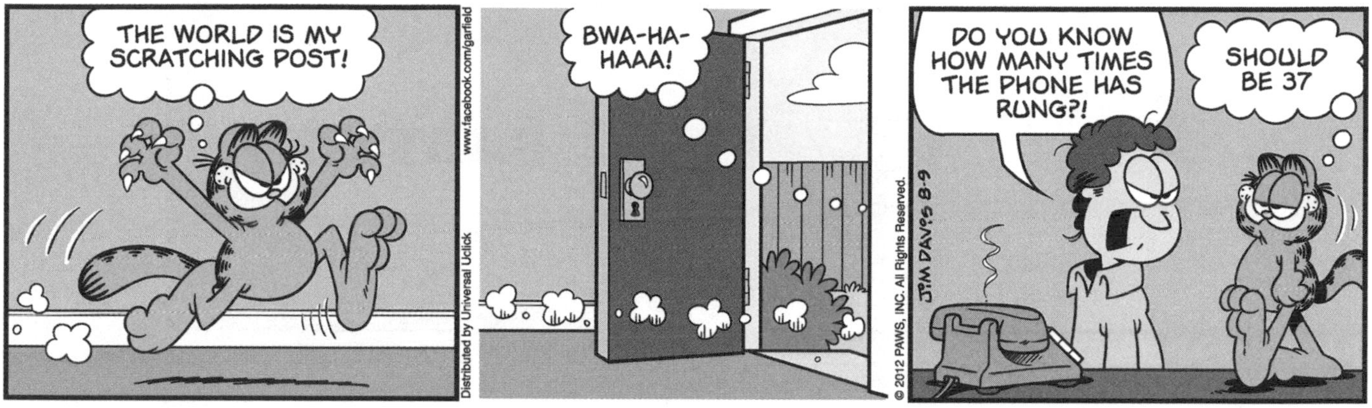
THE WORLD IS MY SCRATCHING POST!
Distributed by Universal Uclick
www.facebook.com/garfield
BWA-HA-HAAA!
© 2012 PAWS, INC. All Rights Reserved.
JIM DAVIS 8-9
DO YOU KNOW HOW MANY TIMES THE PHONE HAS RUNG?!
SHOULD BE 37

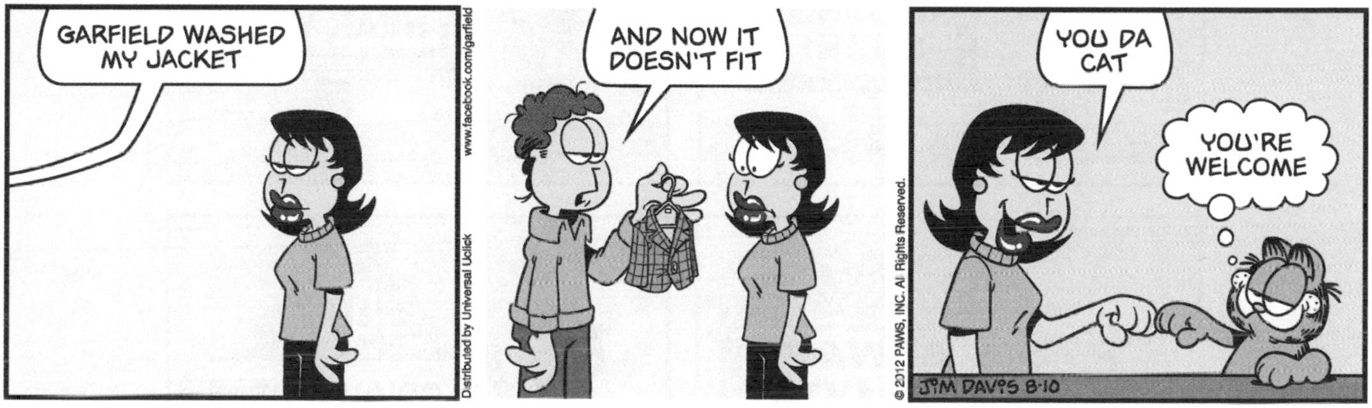
GARFIELD WASHED MY JACKET
Distributed by Universal Uclick
www.facebook.com/garfield
AND NOW IT DOESN'T FIT
© 2012 PAWS, INC. All Rights Reserved.
YOU DA CAT
YOU'RE WELCOME
JIM DAVIS 8-10

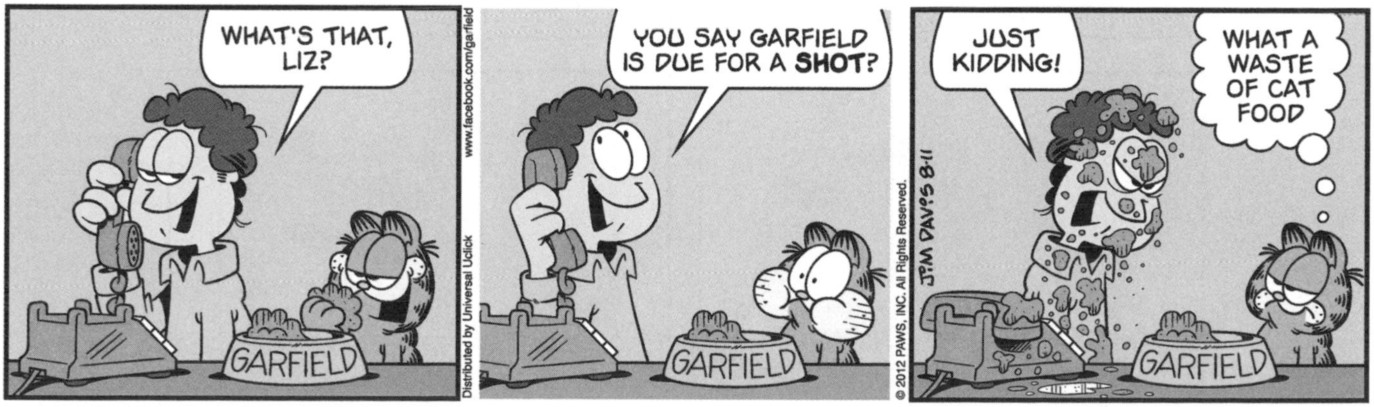
WHAT'S THAT, LIZ?
GARFIELD
Distributed by Universal Uclick
www.facebook.com/garfield
YOU SAY GARFIELD IS DUE FOR A SHOT?
GARFIELD
© 2012 PAWS, INC. All Rights Reserved.
JIM DAVIS 8-11
JUST KIDDING!
WHAT A WASTE OF CAT FOOD
GARFIELD

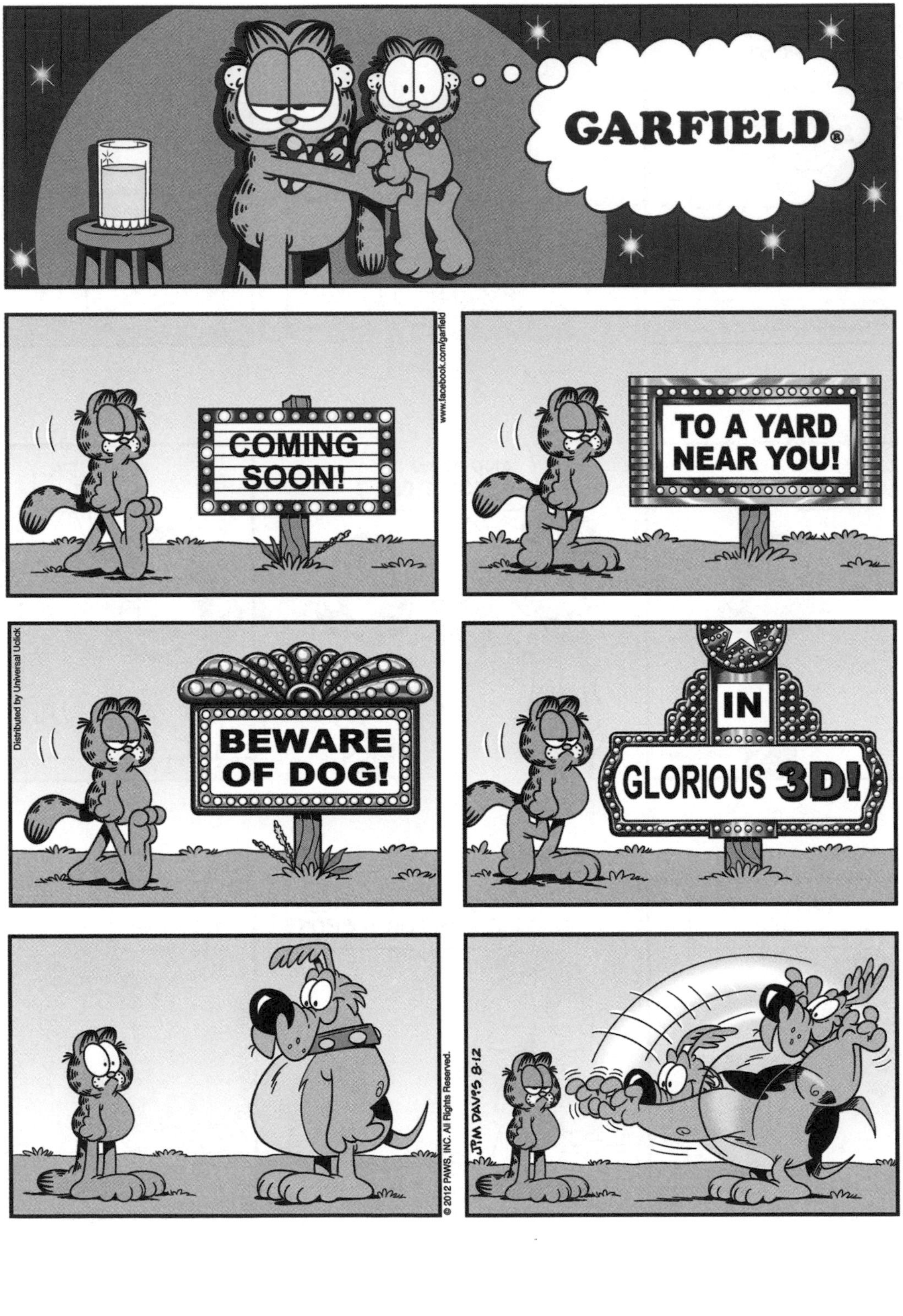

GARFIELD®
COMING SOON!
TO A YARD NEAR YOU!
BEWARE OF DOG!
IN
GLORIOUS 3D!
www.facebook.com/garfield
Distributed by Universal Uclick
© 2012 PAWS, INC. All Rights Reserved.
JPM DAVIS 8-12

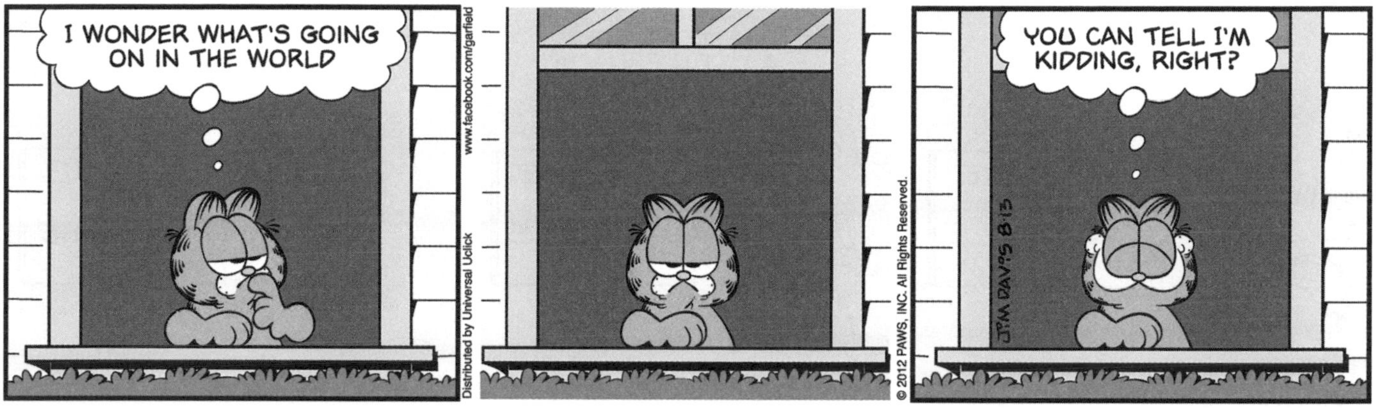
I WONDER WHAT'S GOING ON IN THE WORLD
www.facebook.com/garfield
Distributed by Universal Uclick
© 2012 PAWS, INC. All Rights Reserved.
YOU CAN TELL I'M KIDDING, RIGHT?
JIM DAVIS 8-13

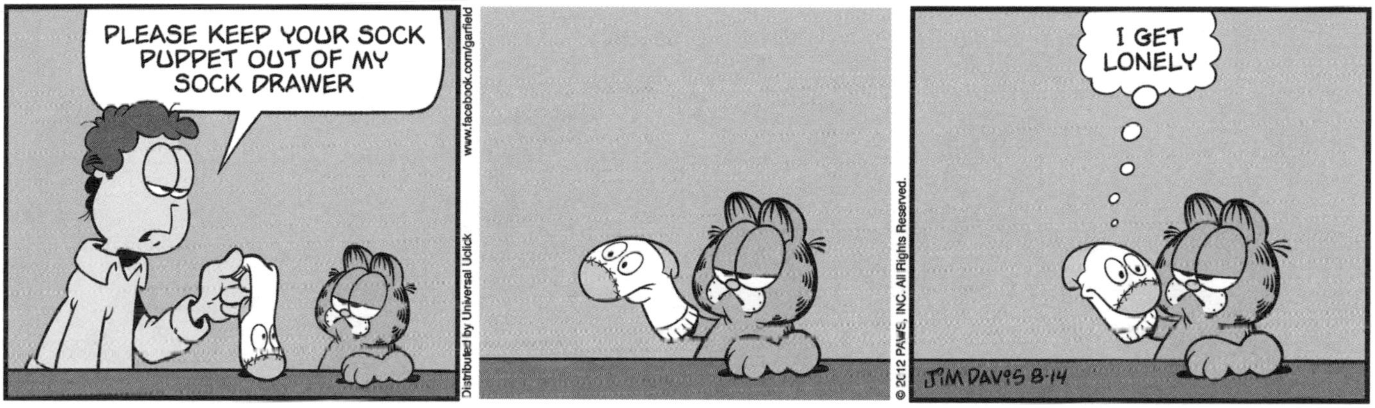
PLEASE KEEP YOUR SOCK PUPPET OUT OF MY SOCK DRAWER
www.facebook.com/garfield
Distributed by Universal Uclick
© 2012 PAWS, INC. All Rights Reserved.
I GET LONELY
JIM DAVIS 8-14

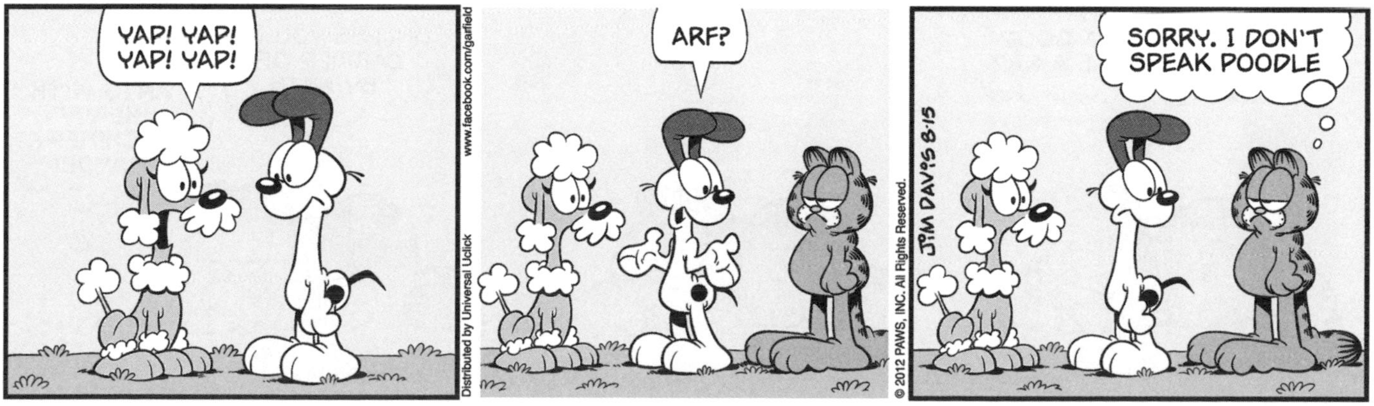
YAP! YAP! YAP! YAP!
www.facebook.com/garfield
Distributed by Universal Uclick
ARF?
© 2012 PAWS, INC. All Rights Reserved.
JIM DAVIS 8-15
SORRY. I DON'T SPEAK POODLE

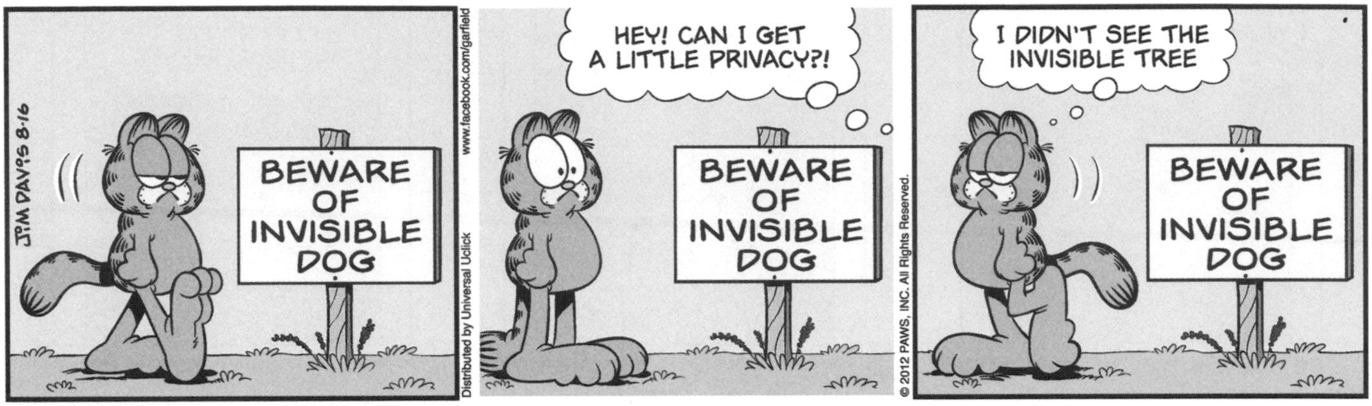
JIM DAVIS 8-16
BEWARE OF INVISIBLE DOG
HEY! CAN I GET A LITTLE PRIVACY?!
BEWARE OF INVISIBLE DOG
I DIDN'T SEE THE INVISIBLE TREE
BEWARE OF INVISIBLE DOG
Distributed by Universal Uclick www.facebook.com/garfield
© 2012 PAWS, INC. All Rights Reserved.

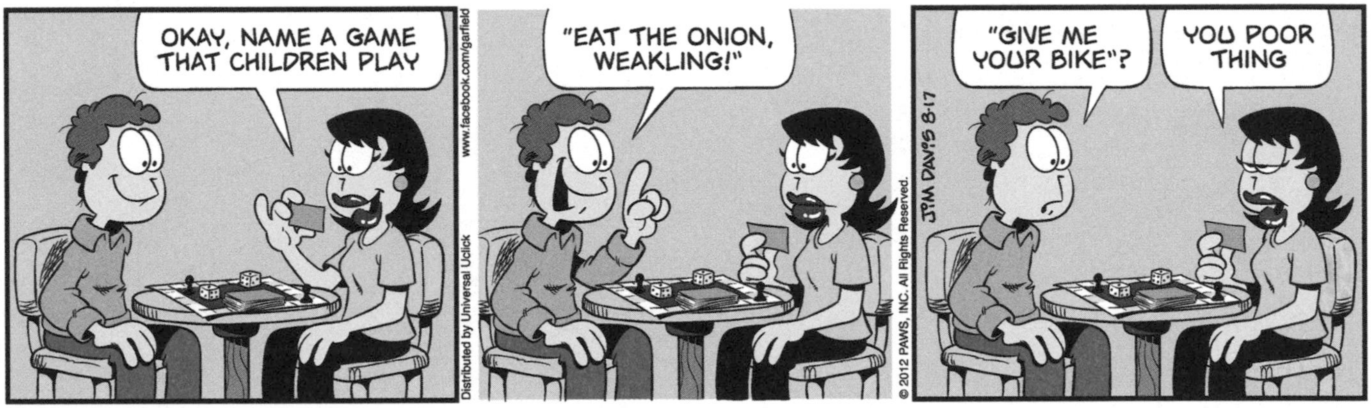
OKAY, NAME A GAME THAT CHILDREN PLAY
"EAT THE ONION, WEAKLING!"
"GIVE ME YOUR BIKE"?
YOU POOR THING
JIM DAVIS 8-17
Distributed by Universal Uclick www.facebook.com/garfield
© 2012 PAWS, INC. All Rights Reserved.

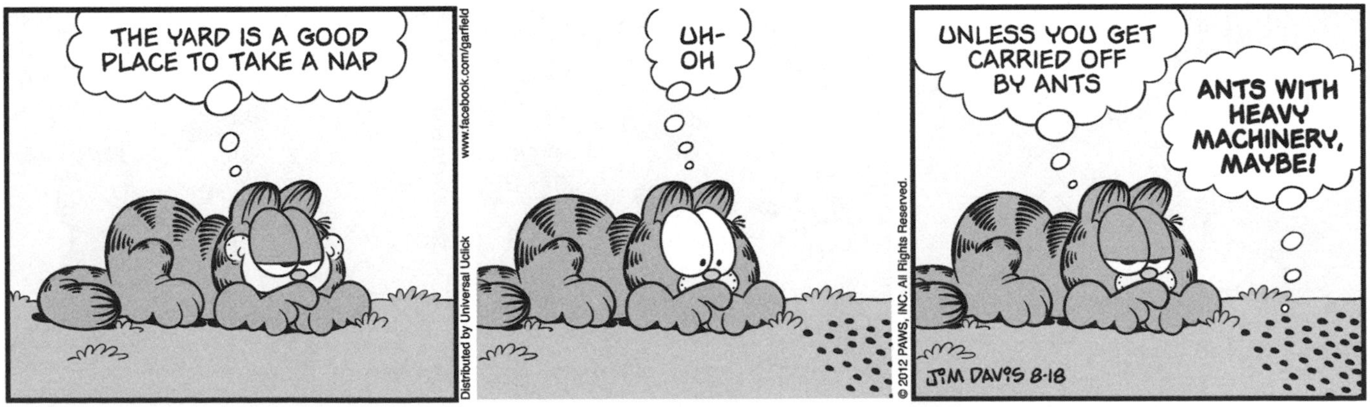
THE YARD IS A GOOD PLACE TO TAKE A NAP
UH-OH
UNLESS YOU GET CARRIED OFF BY ANTS
ANTS WITH HEAVY MACHINERY, MAYBE!
JIM DAVIS 8-18
Distributed by Universal Uclick www.facebook.com/garfield
© 2012 PAWS, INC. All Rights Reserved.

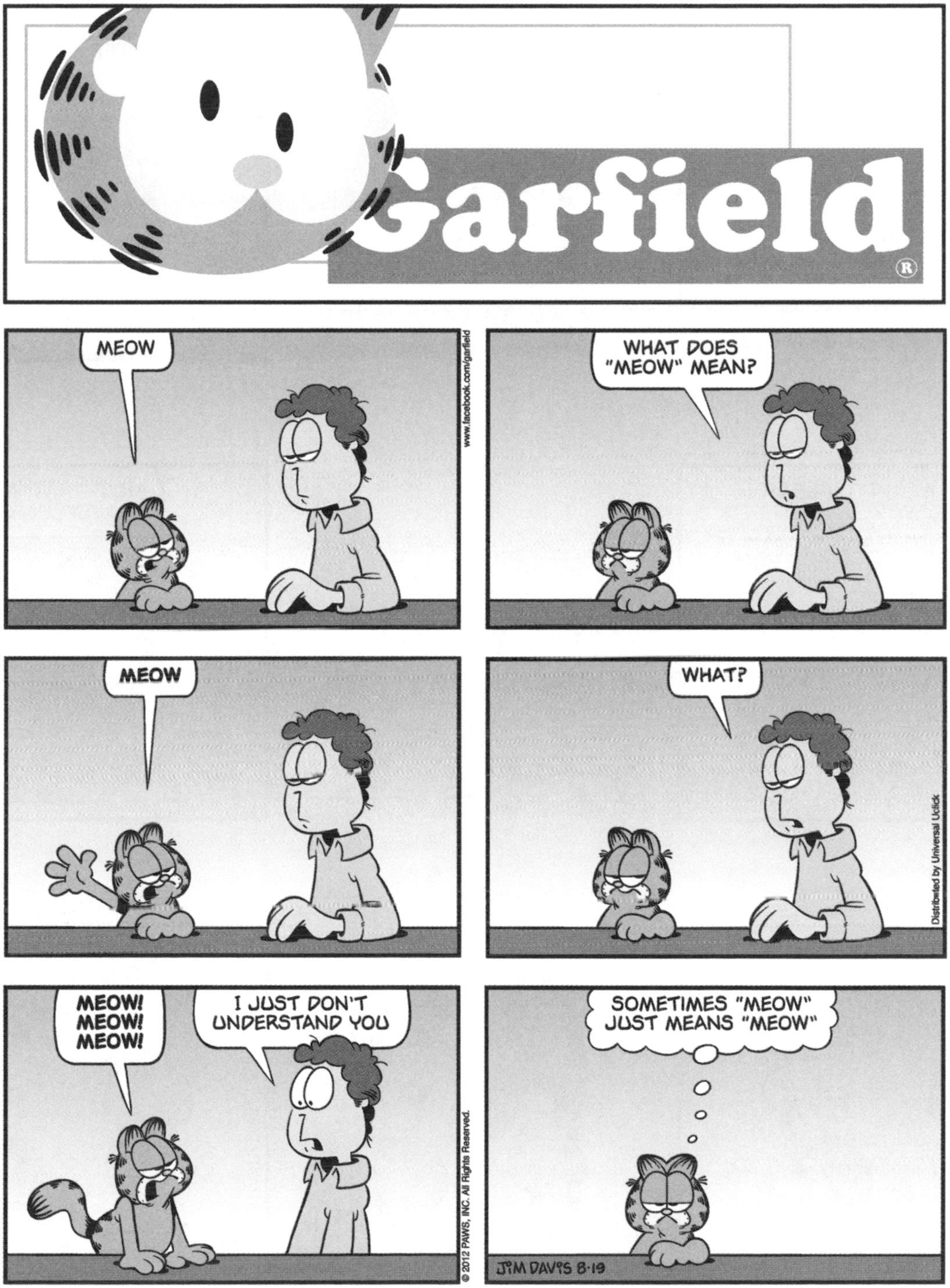
Garfield®
MEOW
www.facebook.com/garfield
WHAT DOES "MEOW" MEAN?
MEOW
WHAT?
Distributed by Universal Uclick
MEOW! MEOW! MEOW!
I JUST DON'T UNDERSTAND YOU
© 2012 PAWS, INC. All Rights Reserved.
SOMETIMES "MEOW" JUST MEANS "MEOW"
JIM DAVIS 8-19

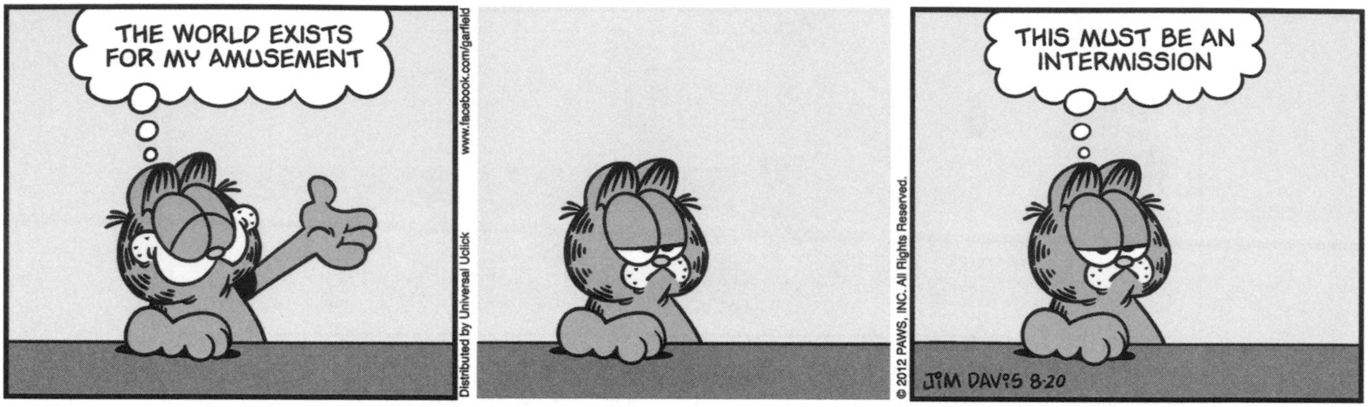
THE WORLD EXISTS FOR MY AMUSEMENT
THIS MUST BE AN INTERMISSION
JIM DAVIS 8-20
www.facebook.com/garfield
Distributed by Universal Uclick
© 2012 PAWS, INC. All Rights Reserved.

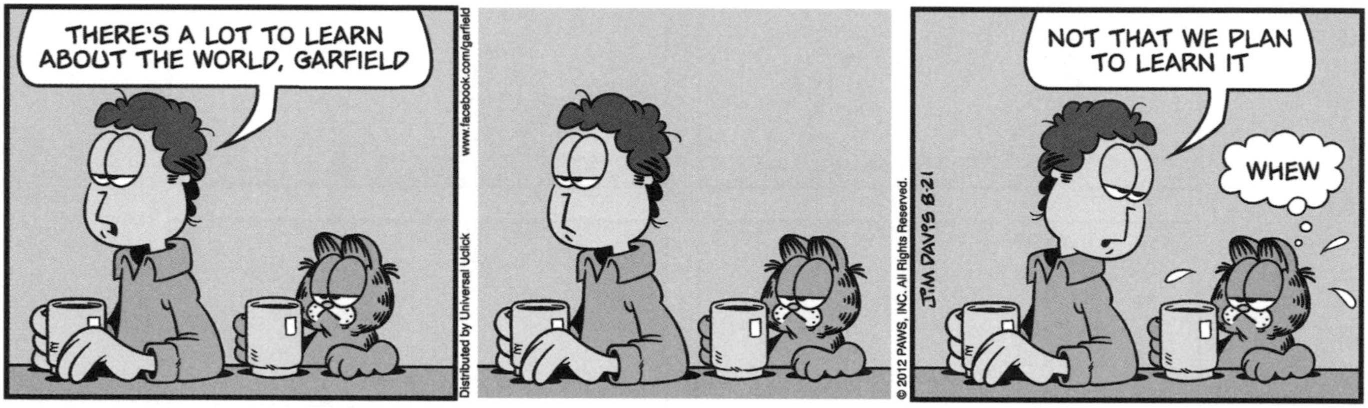
THERE'S A LOT TO LEARN ABOUT THE WORLD, GARFIELD
NOT THAT WE PLAN TO LEARN IT
WHEW
JIM DAVIS 8-21
www.facebook.com/garfield
Distributed by Universal Uclick
© 2012 PAWS, INC. All Rights Reserved.

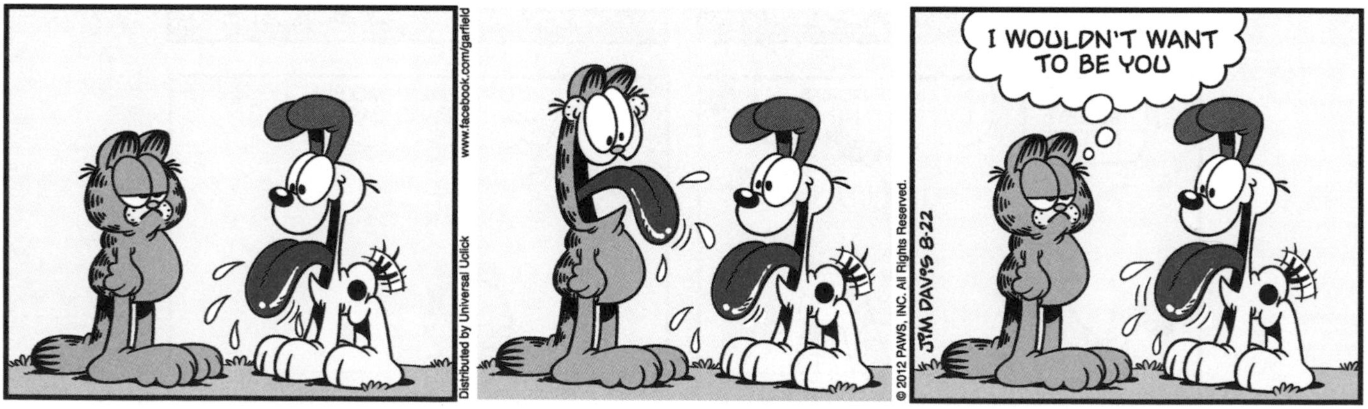
I WOULDN'T WANT TO BE YOU
JIM DAVIS 8-22
www.facebook.com/garfield
Distributed by Universal Uclick
© 2012 PAWS, INC. All Rights Reserved.

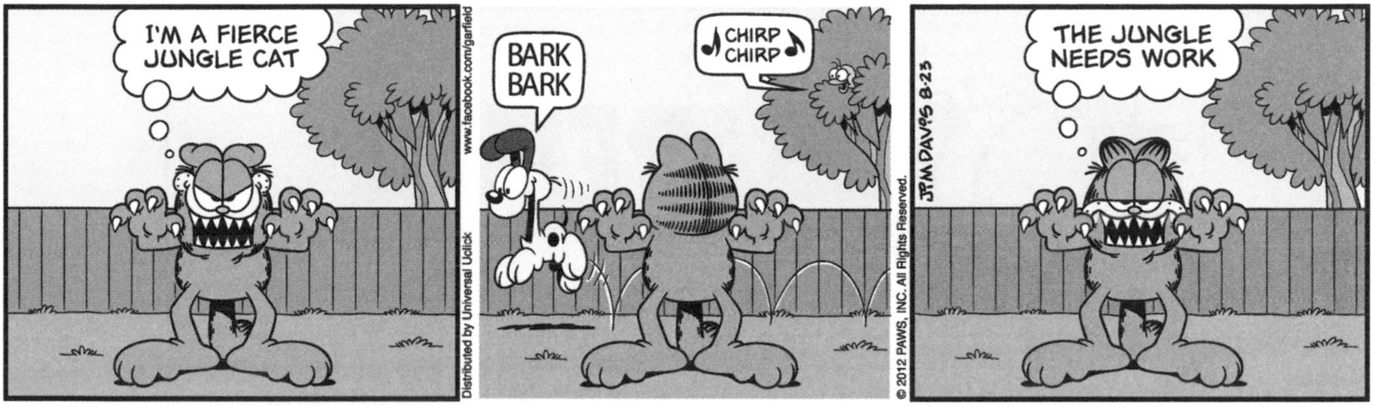
I'M A FIERCE JUNGLE CAT
BARK BARK
CHIRP CHIRP
THE JUNGLE NEEDS WORK
Distributed by Universal Uclick
www.facebook.com/garfield
© 2012 PAWS, INC. All Rights Reserved.
JIM DAVIS 8-23

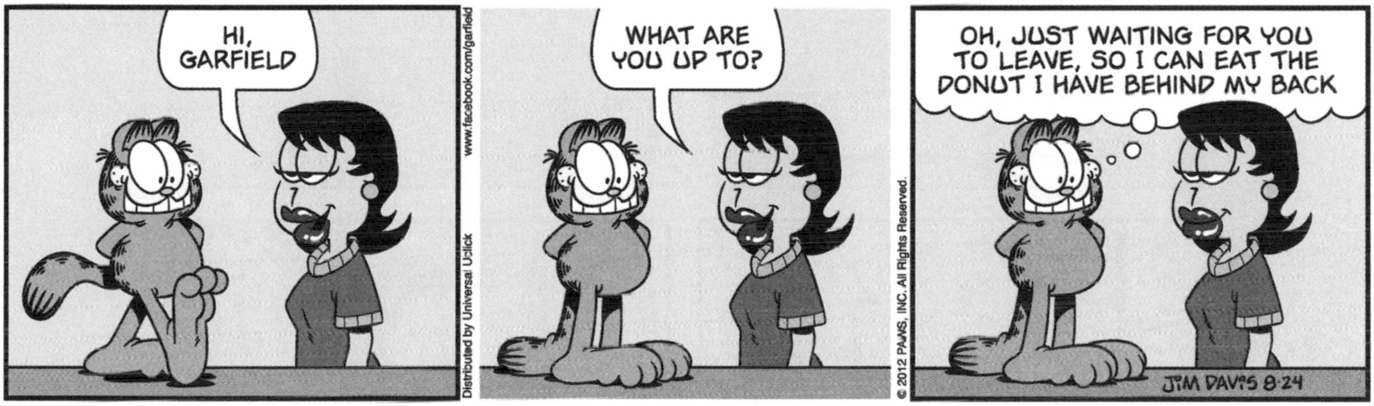
HI, GARFIELD
WHAT ARE YOU UP TO?
OH, JUST WAITING FOR YOU TO LEAVE, SO I CAN EAT THE DONUT I HAVE BEHIND MY BACK
Distributed by Universal Uclick
www.facebook.com/garfield
© 2012 PAWS, INC. All Rights Reserved.
JIM DAVIS 8-24

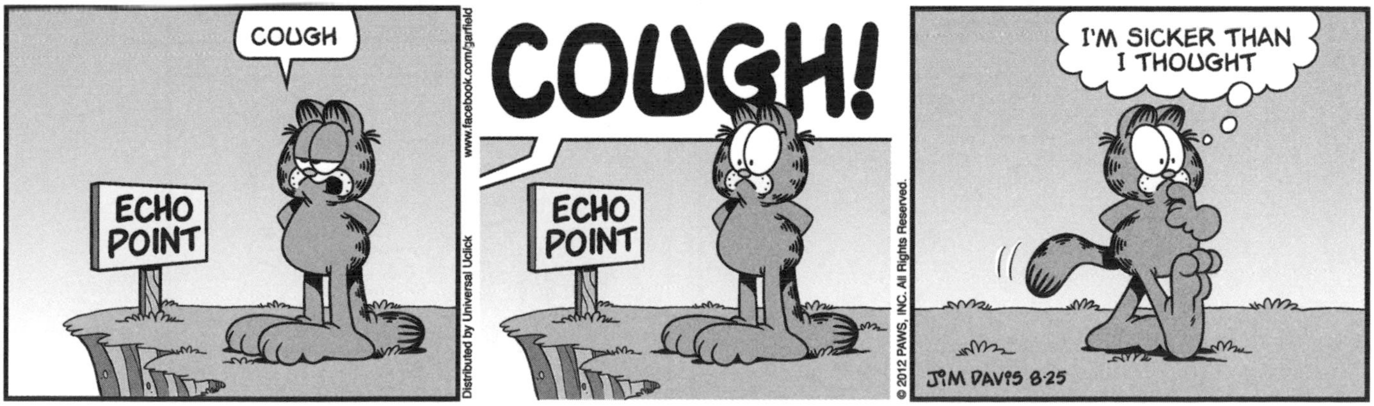
ECHO POINT
COUGH
COUGH!
ECHO POINT
I'M SICKER THAN I THOUGHT
Distributed by Universal Uclick
www.facebook.com/garfield
© 2012 PAWS, INC. All Rights Reserved.
JIM DAVIS 8-25

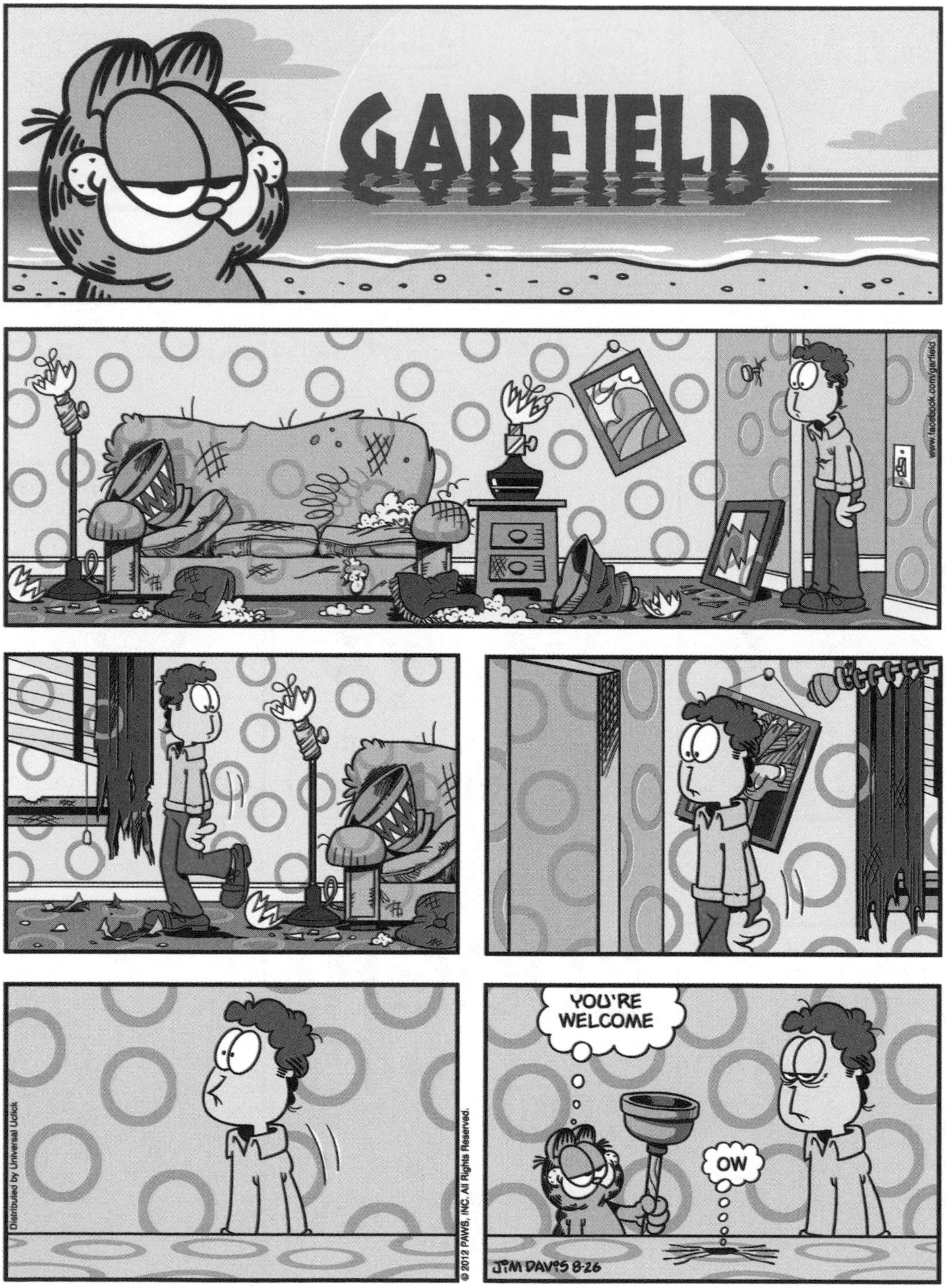
GARFIELD
www.facebook.com/garfield
Distributed by Universal Uclick
© 2012 PAWS, INC. All Rights Reserved.
YOU'RE WELCOME
OW
JIM DAVIS 8-26

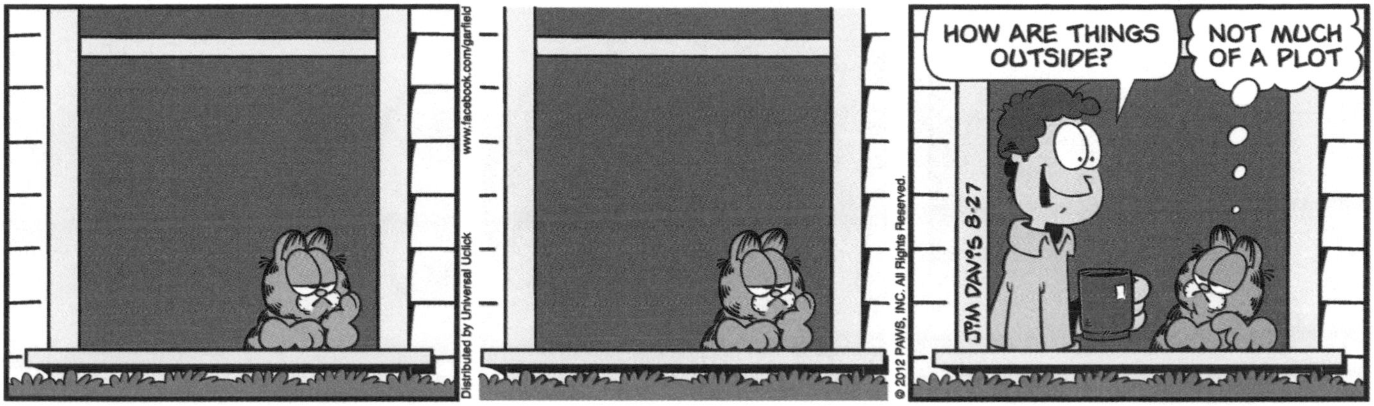
HOW ARE THINGS OUTSIDE?
NOT MUCH OF A PLOT
JIM DAVIS 8-27
Distributed by Universal Uclick www.facebook.com/garfield
© 2012 PAWS, INC. All Rights Reserved.

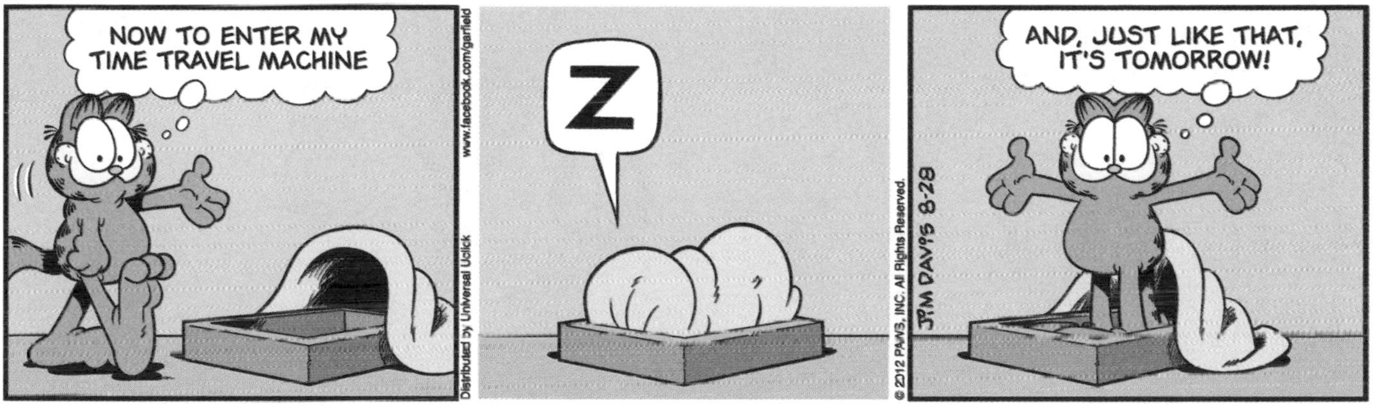
NOW TO ENTER MY TIME TRAVEL MACHINE
Z
AND, JUST LIKE THAT, IT'S TOMORROW!
JIM DAVIS 8-28
Distributed by Universal Uclick www.facebook.com/garfield
© 2012 PAWS, INC. All Rights Reserved.

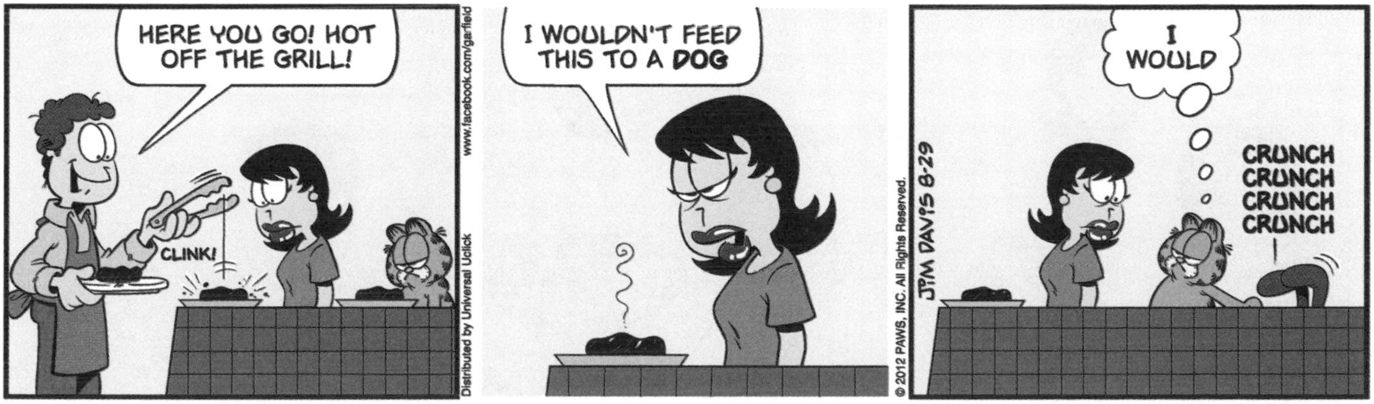
HERE YOU GO! HOT OFF THE GRILL!
CLINK!
I WOULDN'T FEED THIS TO A **DOG**
I WOULD
CRUNCH
CRUNCH
CRUNCH
CRUNCH
JIM DAVIS 8-29
Distributed by Universal Uclick www.facebook.com/garfield
© 2012 PAWS, INC. All Rights Reserved.

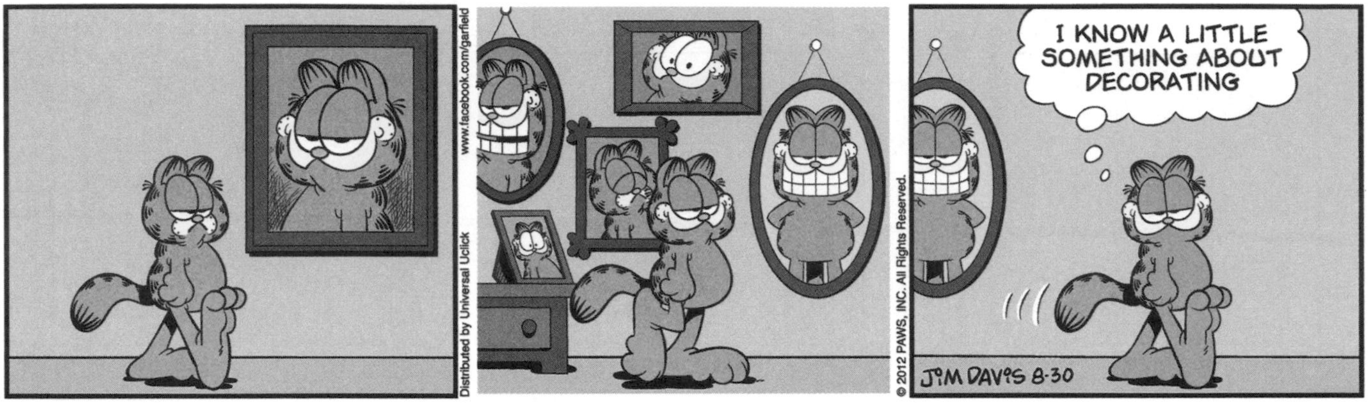
www.facebook.com/garfield
Distributed by Universal Uclick
I KNOW A LITTLE SOMETHING ABOUT DECORATING
© 2012 PAWS, INC. All Rights Reserved.
JIM DAVIS 8-30

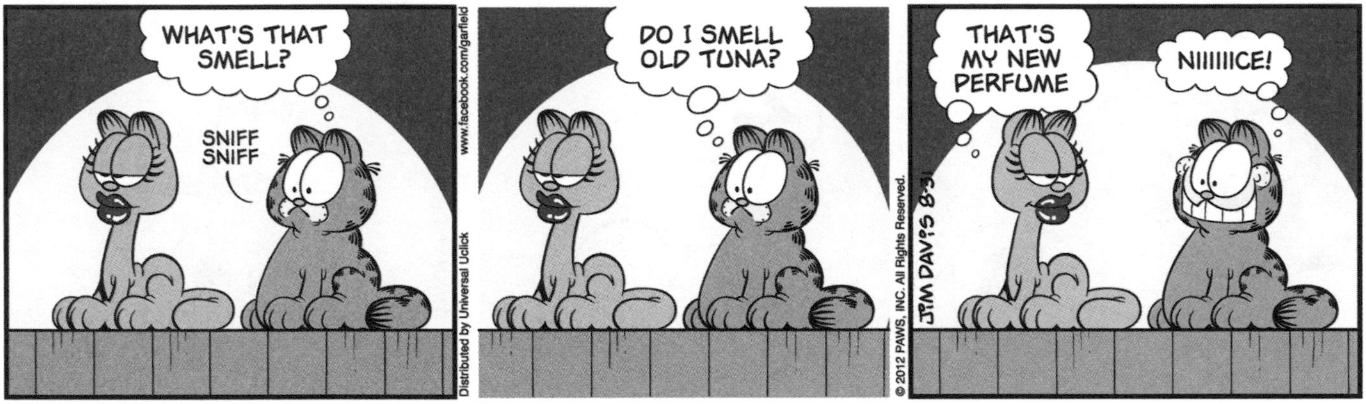
WHAT'S THAT SMELL?
SNIFF SNIFF
www.facebook.com/garfield
Distributed by Universal Uclick
DO I SMELL OLD TUNA?
© 2012 PAWS, INC. All Rights Reserved.
JIM DAVIS 8-31
THAT'S MY NEW PERFUME
NIIIIIICE!

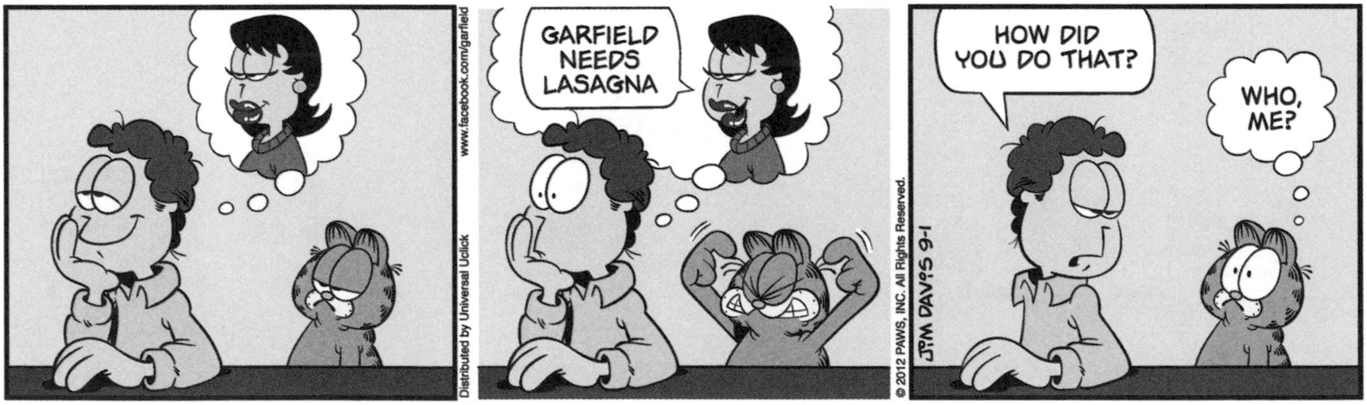
www.facebook.com/garfield
Distributed by Universal Uclick
GARFIELD NEEDS LASAGNA
© 2012 PAWS, INC. All Rights Reserved.
JIM DAVIS 9-1
HOW DID YOU DO THAT?
WHO, ME?

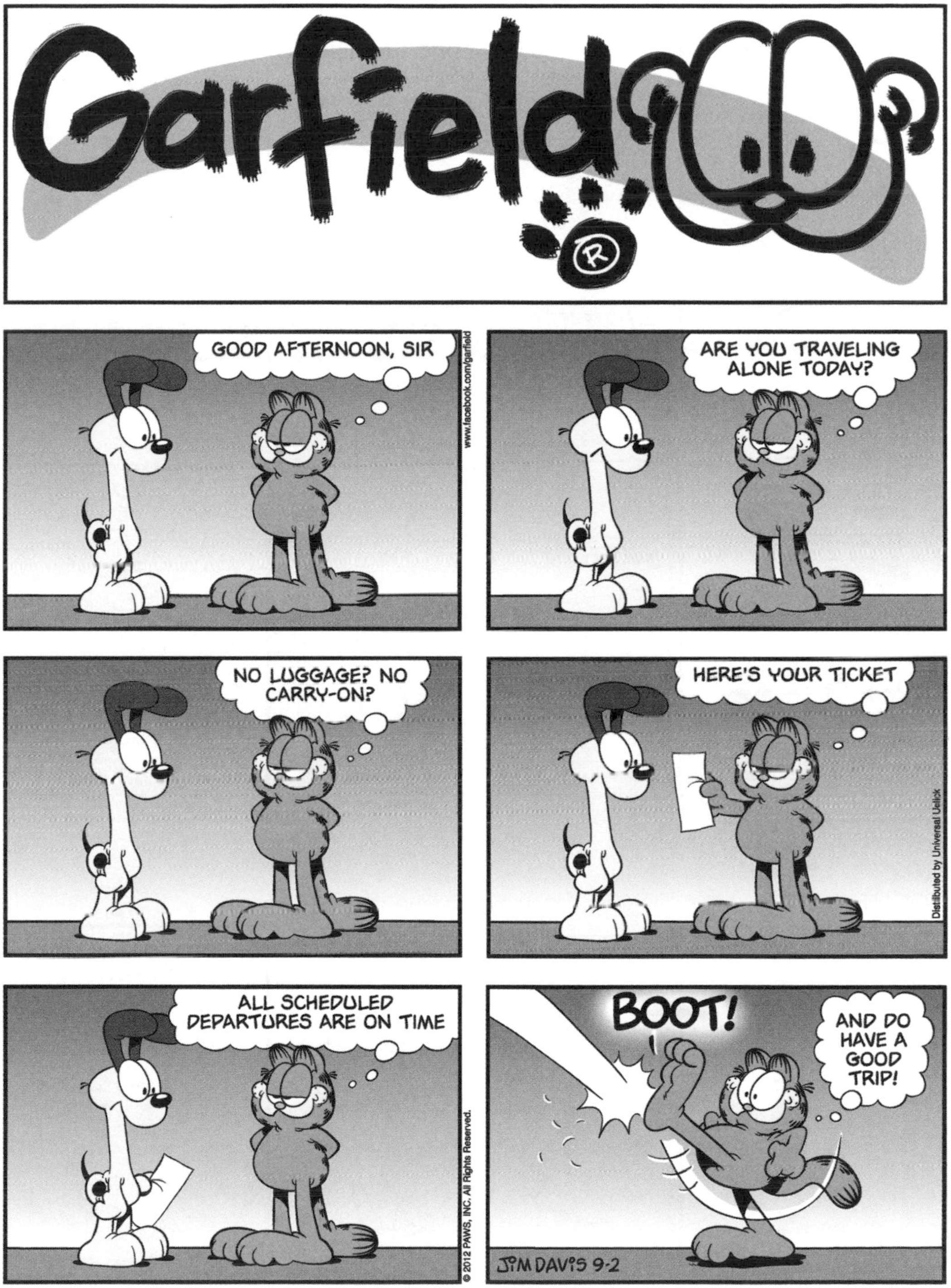
Garfield®
GOOD AFTERNOON, SIR
www.facebook.com/garfield
ARE YOU TRAVELING ALONE TODAY?
NO LUGGAGE? NO CARRY-ON?
HERE'S YOUR TICKET
Distributed by Universal Uclick
ALL SCHEDULED DEPARTURES ARE ON TIME
© 2012 PAWS, INC. All Rights Reserved.
BOOT!
AND DO HAVE A GOOD TRIP!
JIM DAVIS 9-2

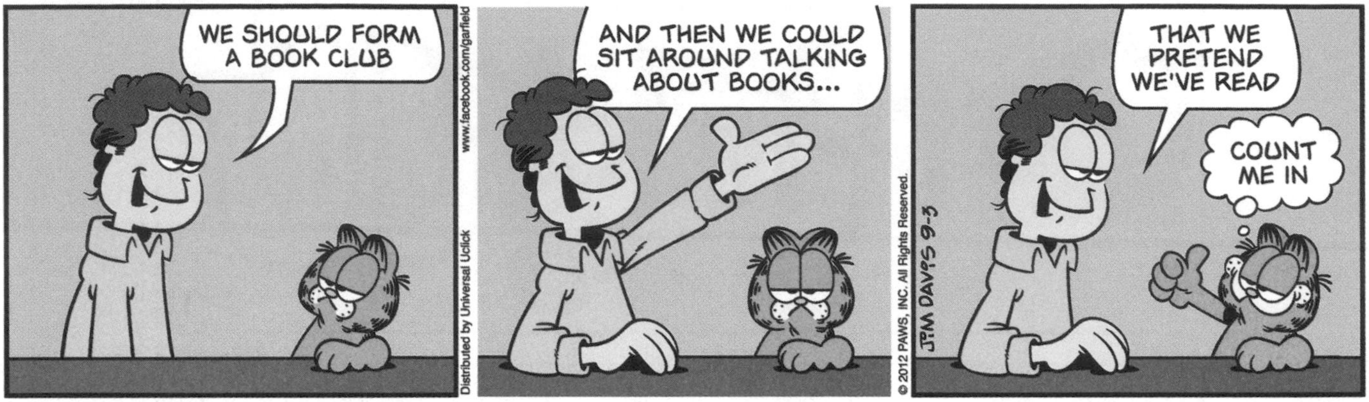
WE SHOULD FORM A BOOK CLUB
www.facebook.com/garfield
Distributed by Universal Uclick
AND THEN WE COULD SIT AROUND TALKING ABOUT BOOKS...
© 2012 PAWS, INC. All Rights Reserved.
JIM DAVIS 9-3
THAT WE PRETEND WE'VE READ
COUNT ME IN

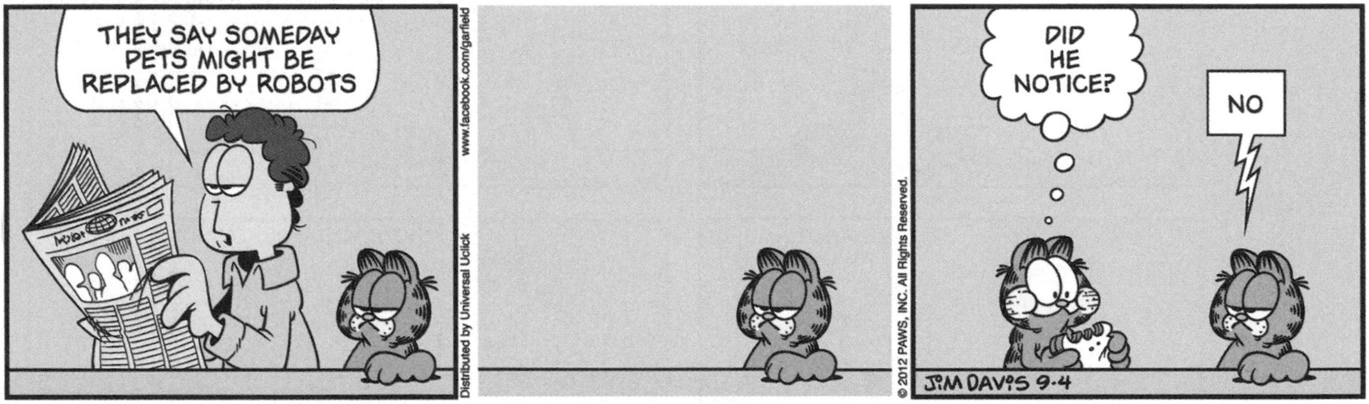
THEY SAY SOMEDAY PETS MIGHT BE REPLACED BY ROBOTS
www.facebook.com/garfield
Distributed by Universal Uclick
© 2012 PAWS, INC. All Rights Reserved.
DID HE NOTICE?
NO
JIM DAVIS 9-4

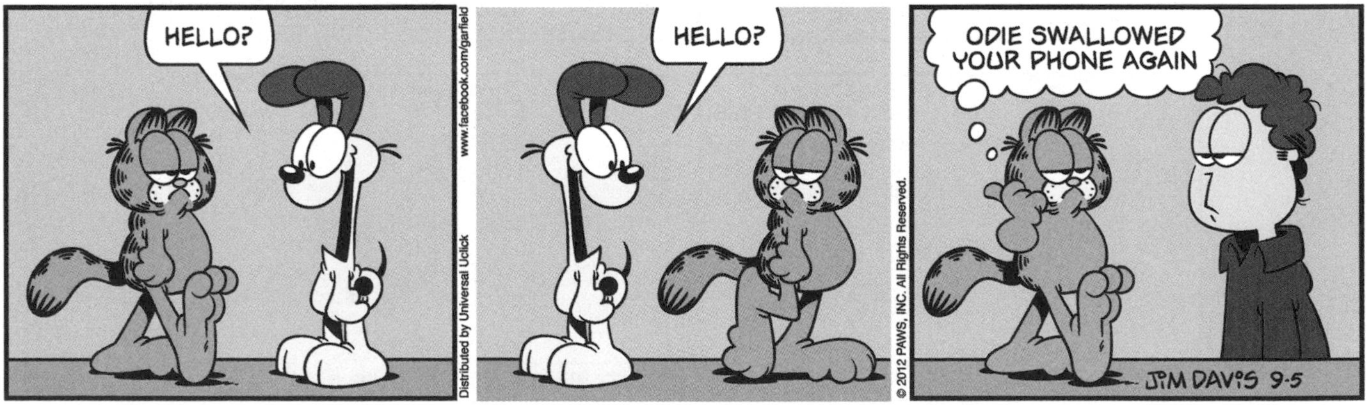
HELLO?
www.facebook.com/garfield
Distributed by Universal Uclick
HELLO?
© 2012 PAWS, INC. All Rights Reserved.
ODIE SWALLOWED YOUR PHONE AGAIN
JIM DAVIS 9-5

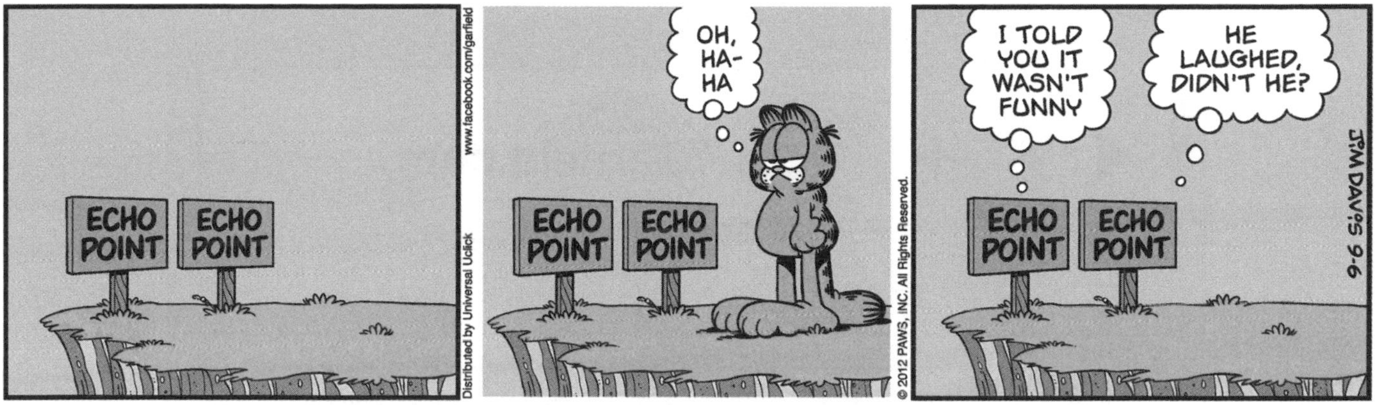
ECHO POINT
ECHO POINT
www.facebook.com/garfield
Distributed by Universal Uclick
OH, HA-HA
© 2012 PAWS, INC. All Rights Reserved.
I TOLD YOU IT WASN'T FUNNY
HE LAUGHED, DIDN'T HE?
JIM DAVIS 9-6

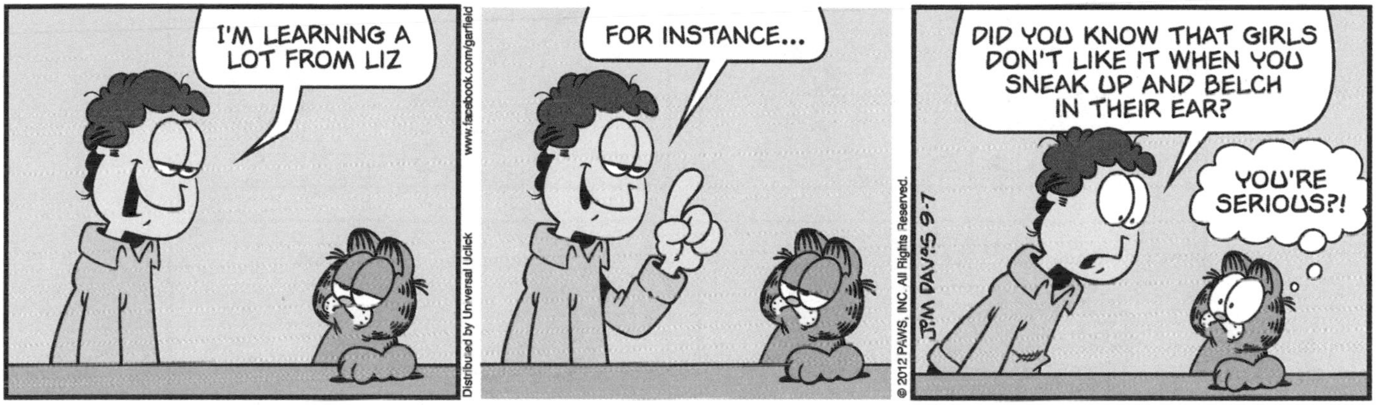
I'M LEARNING A LOT FROM LIZ
www.facebook.com/garfield
Distributed by Universal Uclick
FOR INSTANCE...
© 2012 PAWS, INC. All Rights Reserved.
JIM DAVIS 9-7
DID YOU KNOW THAT GIRLS DON'T LIKE IT WHEN YOU SNEAK UP AND BELCH IN THEIR EAR?
YOU'RE SERIOUS?!

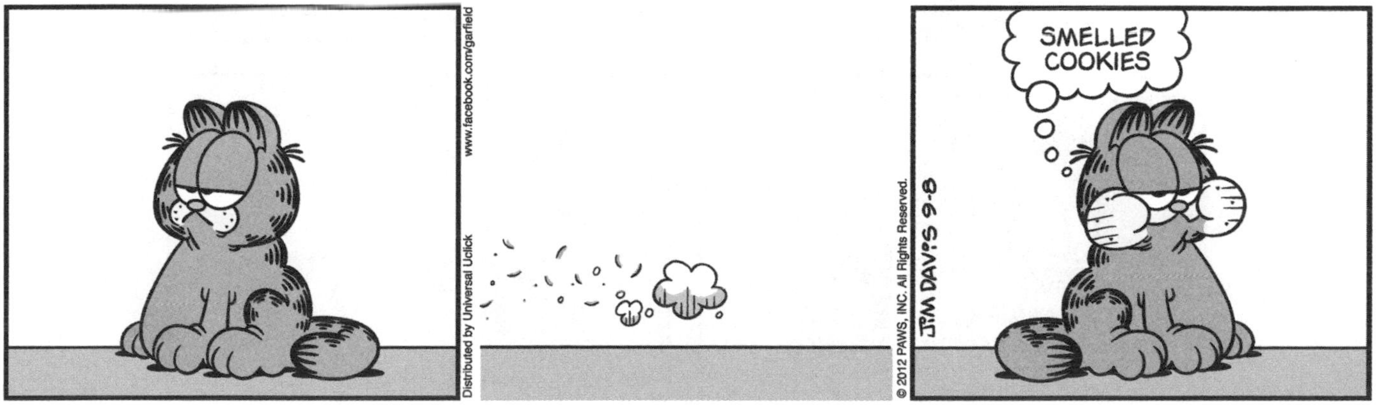
www.facebook.com/garfield
Distributed by Universal Uclick
© 2012 PAWS, INC. All Rights Reserved.
JIM DAVIS 9-8
SMELLED COOKIES

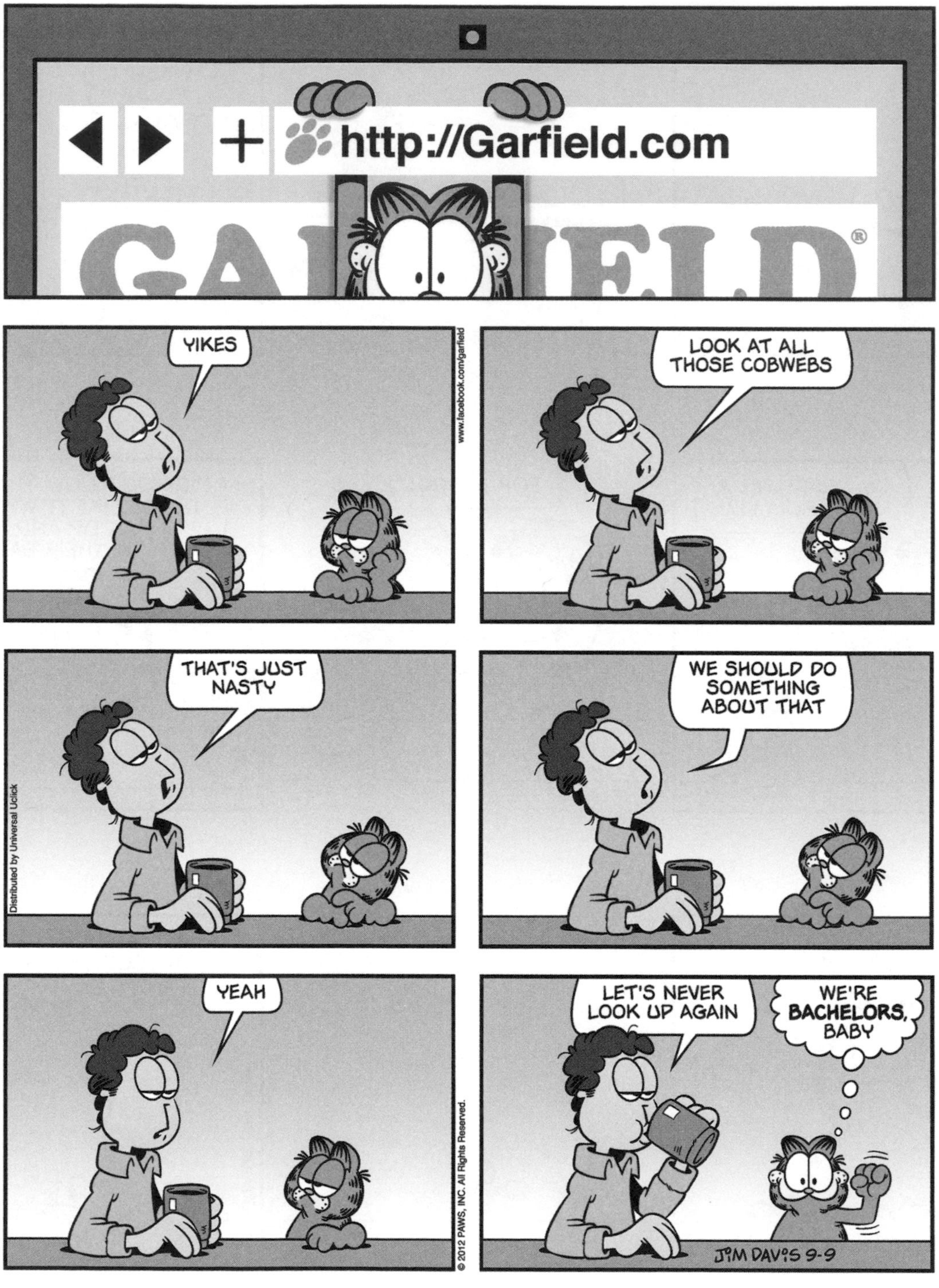
http://Garfield.com
GARFIELD®
YIKES
www.facebook.com/garfield
LOOK AT ALL THOSE COBWEBS
THAT'S JUST NASTY
Distributed by Universal Uclick
WE SHOULD DO SOMETHING ABOUT THAT
YEAH
© 2012 PAWS, INC. All Rights Reserved.
LET'S NEVER LOOK UP AGAIN
WE'RE **BACHELORS**, BABY
JIM DAVIS 9-9

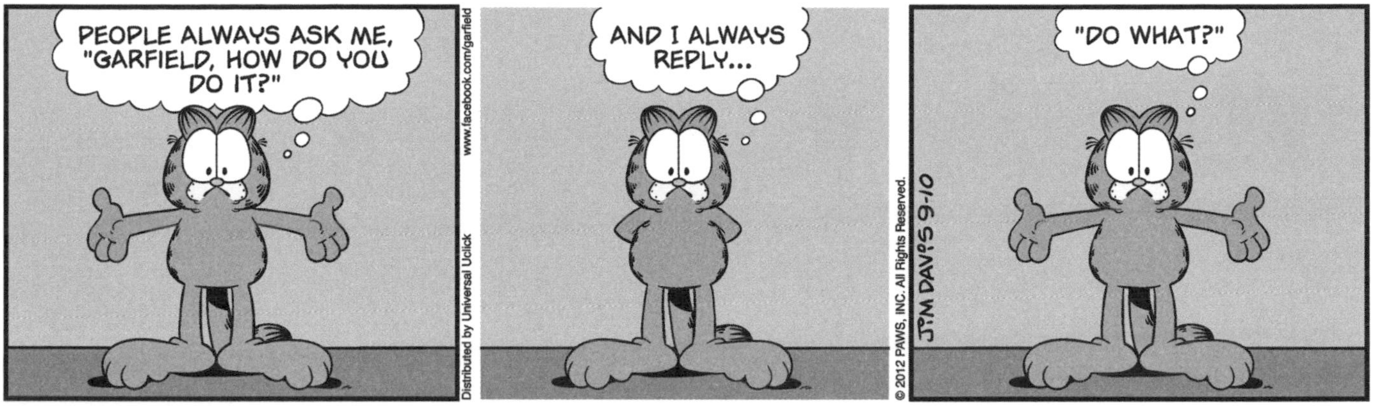
PEOPLE ALWAYS ASK ME, "GARFIELD, HOW DO YOU DO IT?"
Distributed by Universal Uclick
www.facebook.com/garfield
AND I ALWAYS REPLY...
© 2012 PAWS, INC. All Rights Reserved.
JIM DAVIS 9-10
"DO WHAT?"

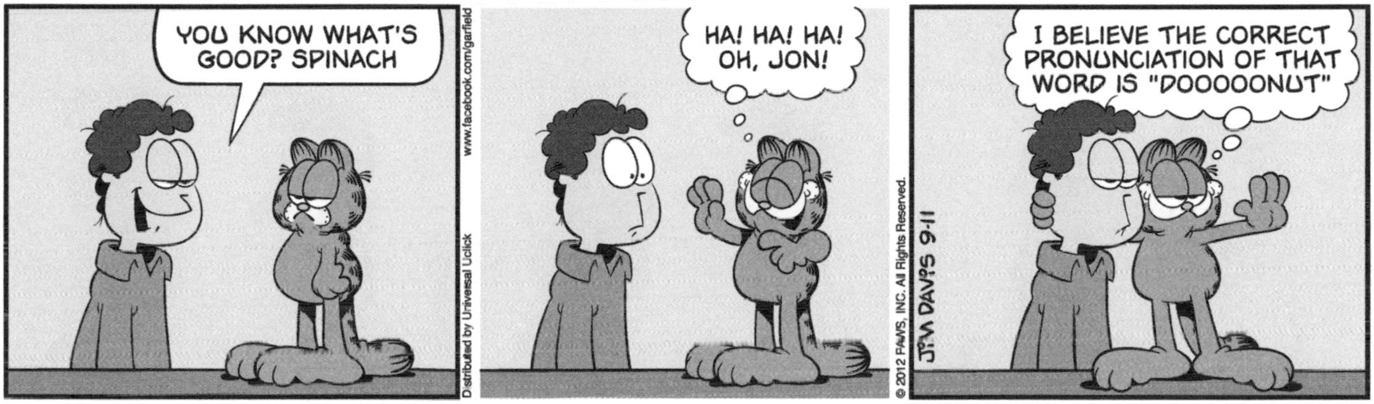
YOU KNOW WHAT'S GOOD? SPINACH
Distributed by Universal Uclick
www.facebook.com/garfield
HA! HA! HA! OH, JON!
© 2012 PAWS, INC. All Rights Reserved.
JIM DAVIS 9-11
I BELIEVE THE CORRECT PRONUNCIATION OF THAT WORD IS "DOOOOONUT"

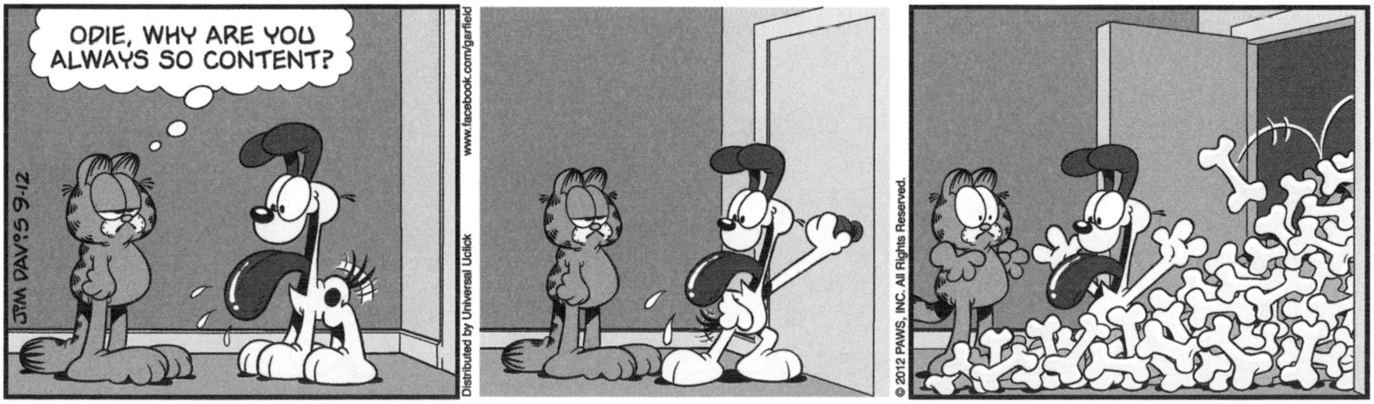
ODIE, WHY ARE YOU ALWAYS SO CONTENT?
JIM DAVIS 9-12
Distributed by Universal Uclick
www.facebook.com/garfield
© 2012 PAWS, INC. All Rights Reserved.

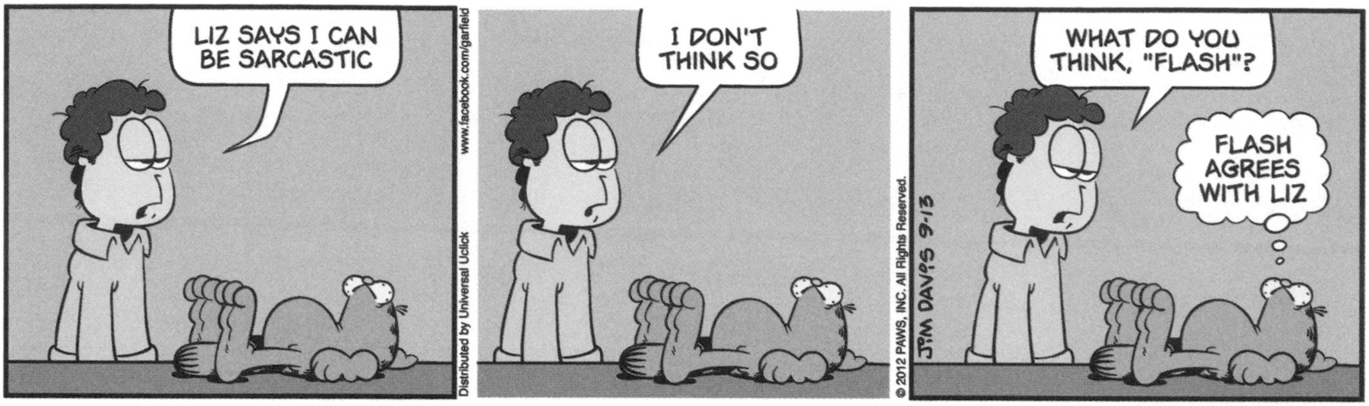
LIZ SAYS I CAN BE SARCASTIC
www.facebook.com/garfield
Distributed by Universal Uclick
I DON'T THINK SO
© 2012 PAWS, INC. All Rights Reserved.
JIM DAVIS 9-13
WHAT DO YOU THINK, "FLASH"?
FLASH AGREES WITH LIZ

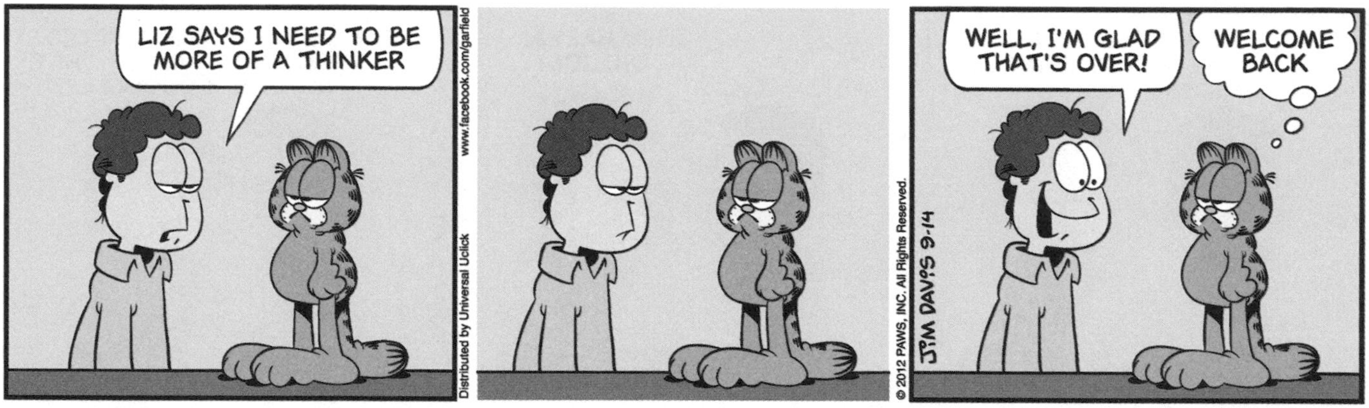
LIZ SAYS I NEED TO BE MORE OF A THINKER
www.facebook.com/garfield
Distributed by Universal Uclick
© 2012 PAWS, INC. All Rights Reserved.
JIM DAVIS 9-14
WELL, I'M GLAD THAT'S OVER!
WELCOME BACK

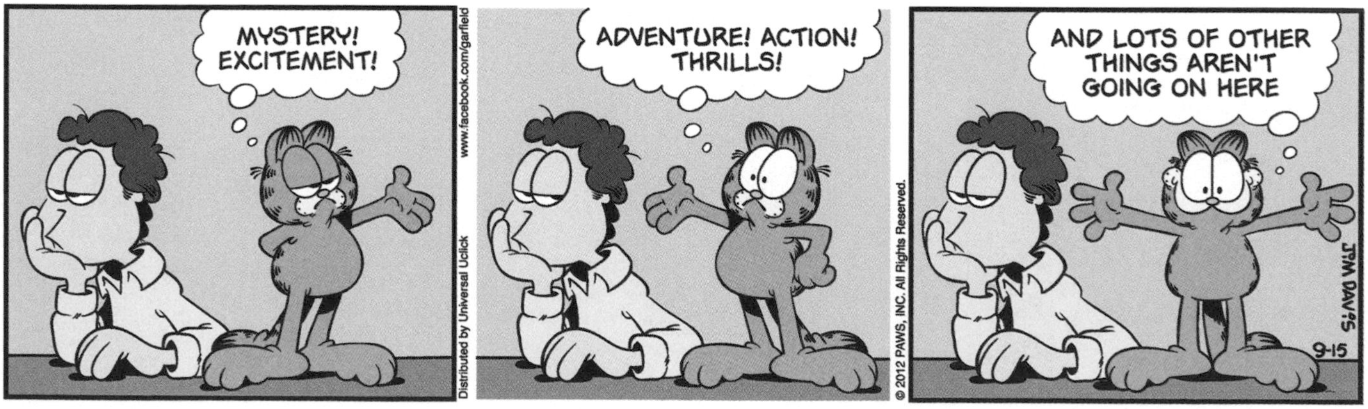
MYSTERY! EXCITEMENT!
www.facebook.com/garfield
Distributed by Universal Uclick
ADVENTURE! ACTION! THRILLS!
© 2012 PAWS, INC. All Rights Reserved.
AND LOTS OF OTHER THINGS AREN'T GOING ON HERE
JIM DAVIS
9-15

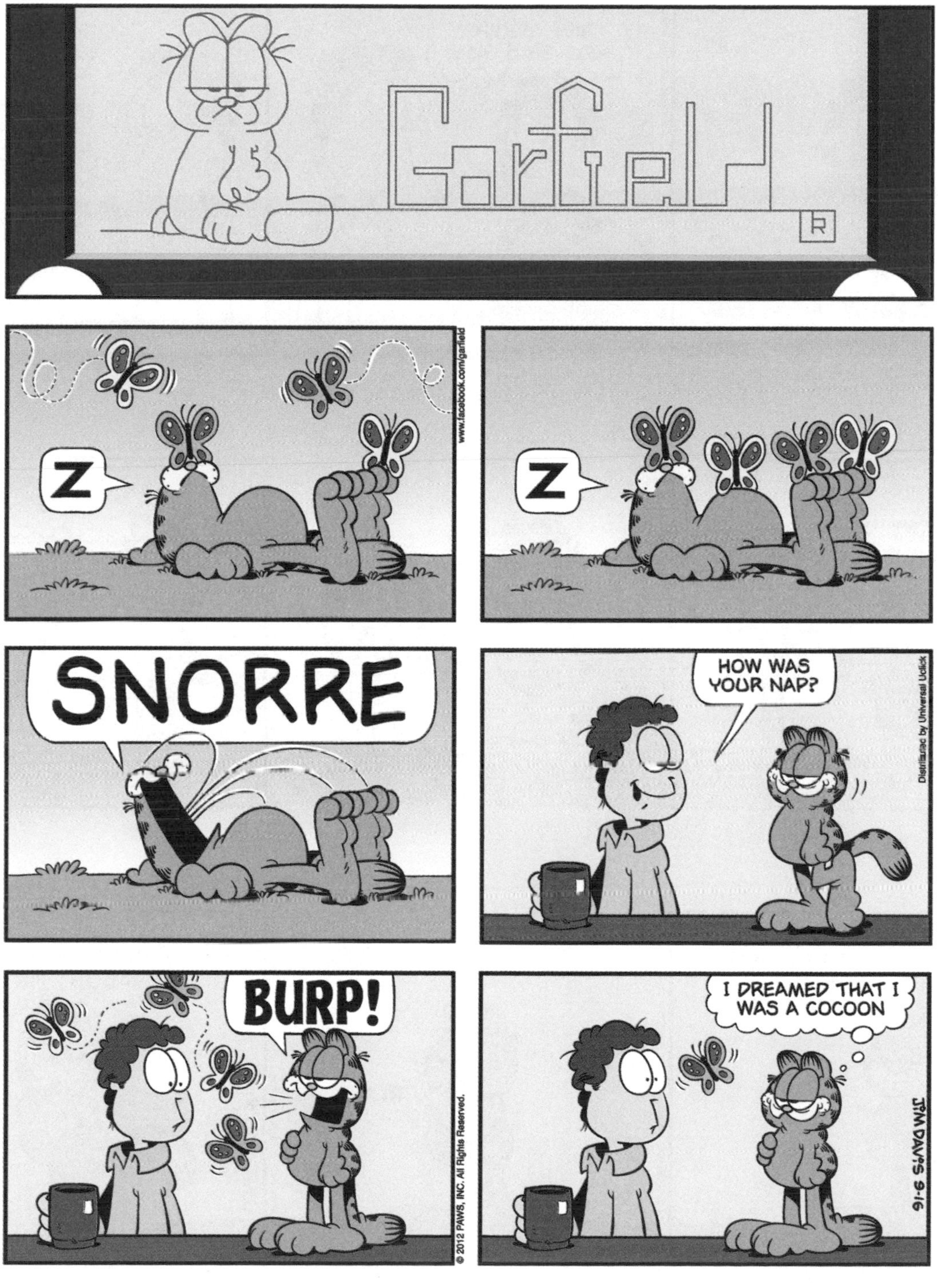

Garfield
Z
Z
SNORRE
HOW WAS YOUR NAP?
BURP!
I DREAMED THAT I WAS A COCOON
www.facebook.com/garfield
Distributed by Universal Uclick
© 2012 PAWS, INC. All Rights Reserved.
JIM DAVIS 9-16

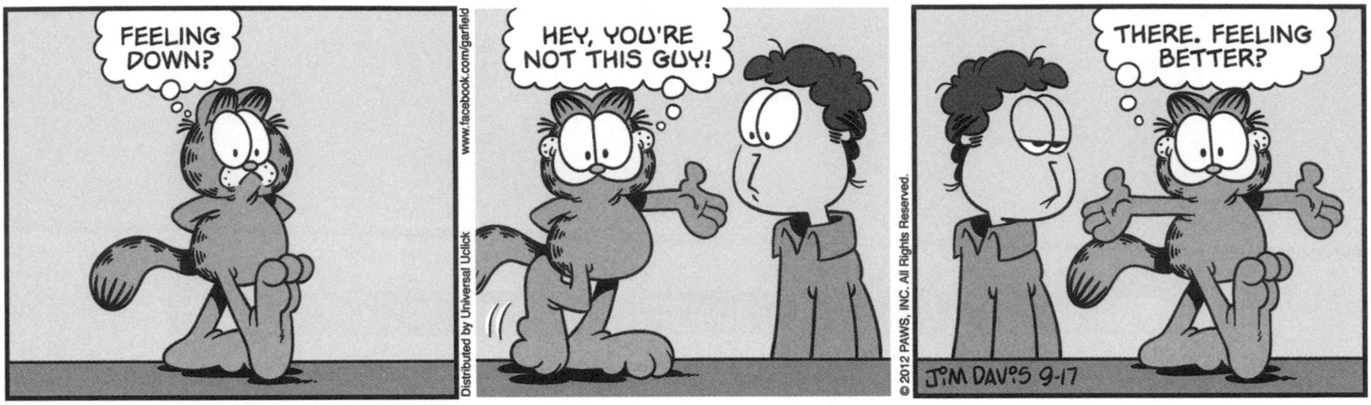
FEELING DOWN?
HEY, YOU'RE NOT THIS GUY!
THERE. FEELING BETTER?
JIM DAVIS 9-17
Distributed by Universal Uclick www.facebook.com/garfield
© 2012 PAWS, INC. All Rights Reserved.

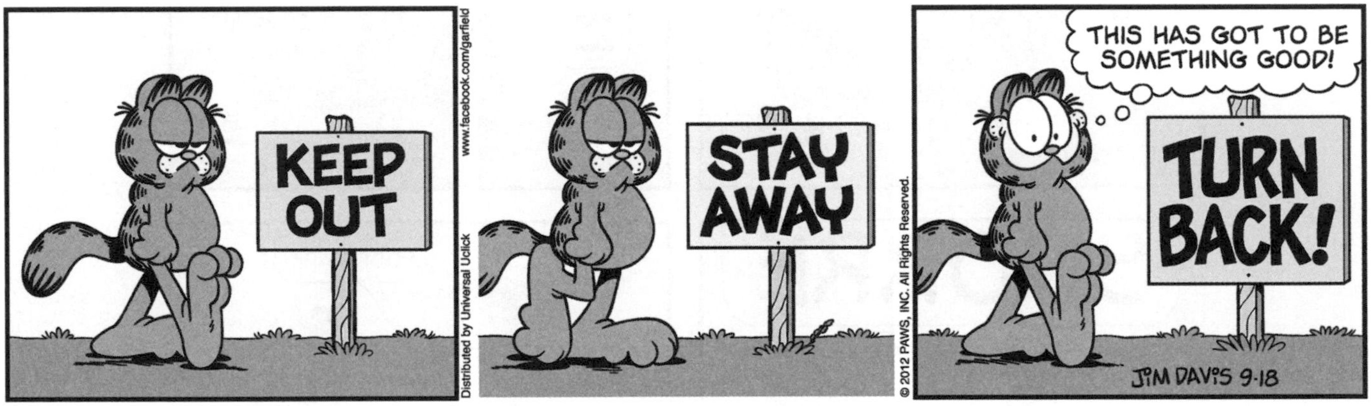
KEEP OUT
STAY AWAY
THIS HAS GOT TO BE SOMETHING GOOD!
TURN BACK!
JIM DAVIS 9-18
Distributed by Universal Uclick www.facebook.com/garfield
© 2012 PAWS, INC. All Rights Reserved.

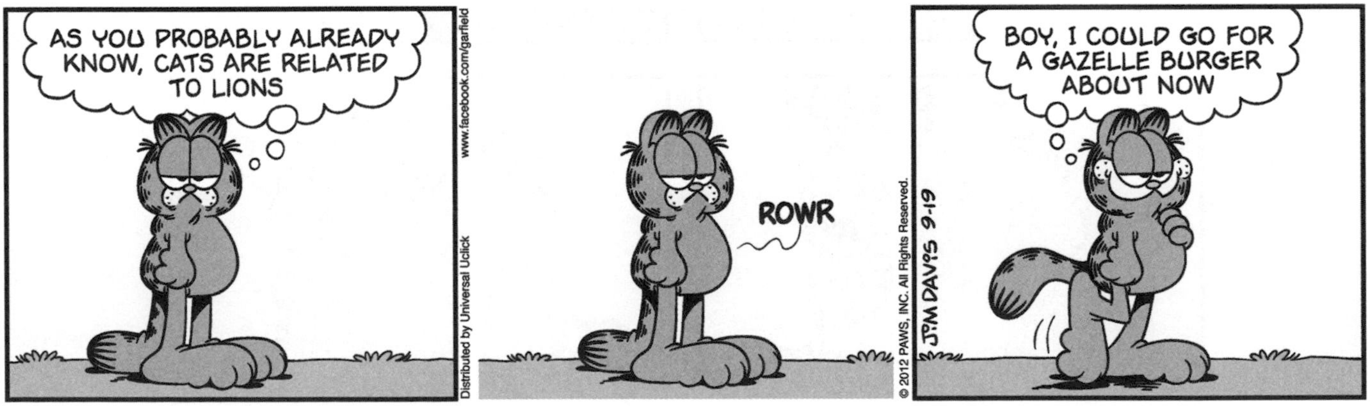
AS YOU PROBABLY ALREADY KNOW, CATS ARE RELATED TO LIONS
ROWR
BOY, I COULD GO FOR A GAZELLE BURGER ABOUT NOW
JIM DAVIS 9-19
Distributed by Universal Uclick www.facebook.com/garfield
© 2012 PAWS, INC. All Rights Reserved.

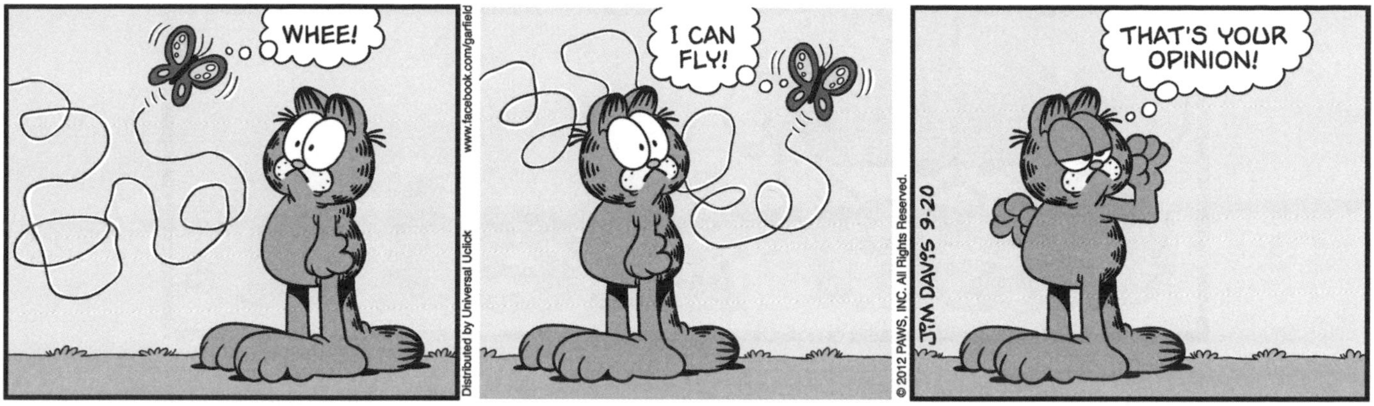
WHEE!
I CAN FLY!
THAT'S YOUR OPINION!
www.facebook.com/garfield
Distributed by Universal Uclick
© 2012 PAWS, INC. All Rights Reserved.
JIM DAVIS 9-20

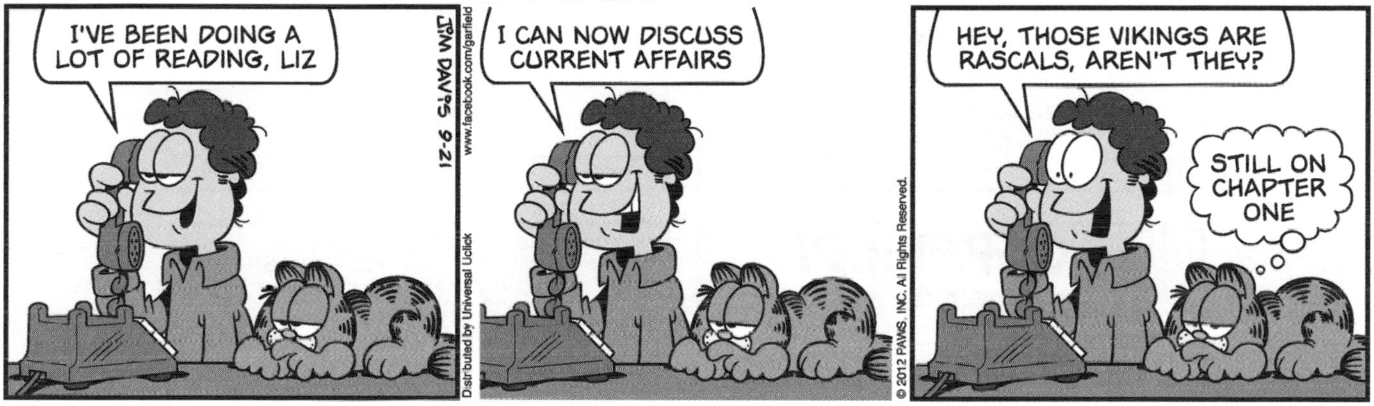
I'VE BEEN DOING A LOT OF READING, LIZ
JIM DAVIS 9-21
www.facebook.com/garfield
Distributed by Universal Uclick
I CAN NOW DISCUSS CURRENT AFFAIRS
© 2012 PAWS, INC. All Rights Reserved.
HEY, THOSE VIKINGS ARE RASCALS, AREN'T THEY?
STILL ON CHAPTER ONE

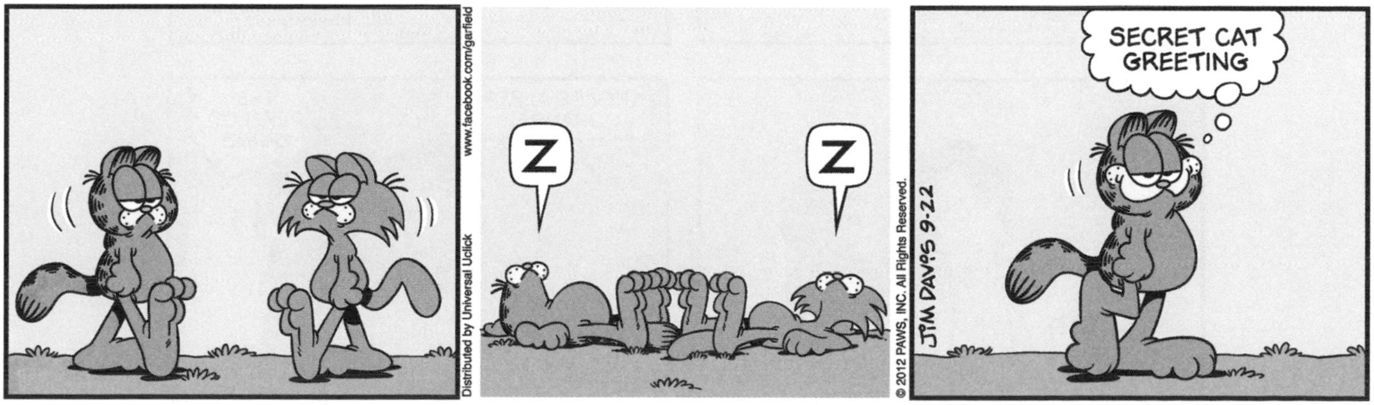
www.facebook.com/garfield
Distributed by Universal Uclick
Z
Z
© 2012 PAWS, INC. All Rights Reserved.
JIM DAVIS 9-22
SECRET CAT GREETING

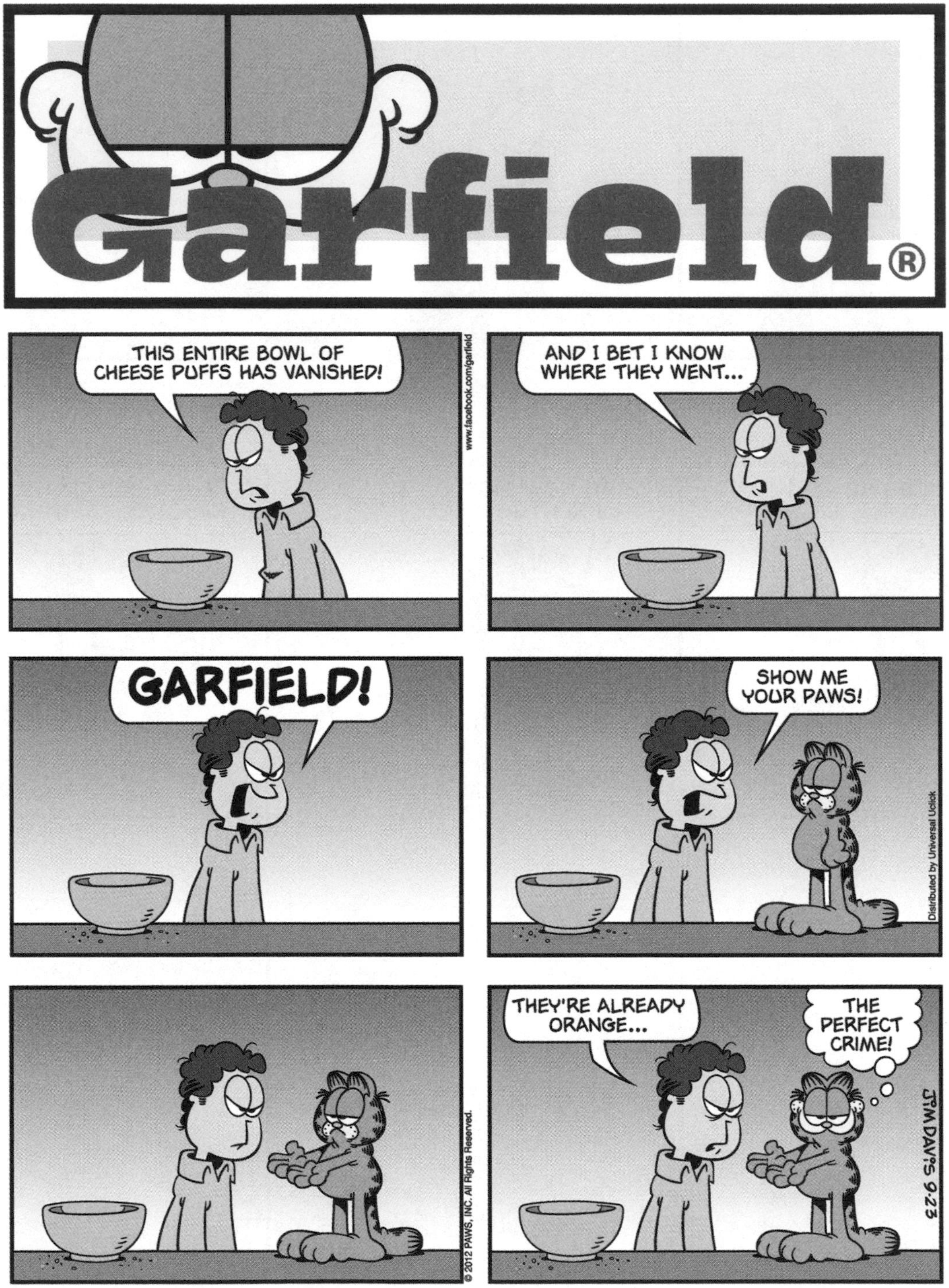
Garfield®
THIS ENTIRE BOWL OF CHEESE PUFFS HAS VANISHED!
www.facebook.com/garfield
AND I BET I KNOW WHERE THEY WENT...
GARFIELD!
SHOW ME YOUR PAWS!
Distributed by Universal Uclick
© 2012 PAWS, INC. All Rights Reserved.
THEY'RE ALREADY ORANGE...
THE PERFECT CRIME!
JIM DAVIS 9-23

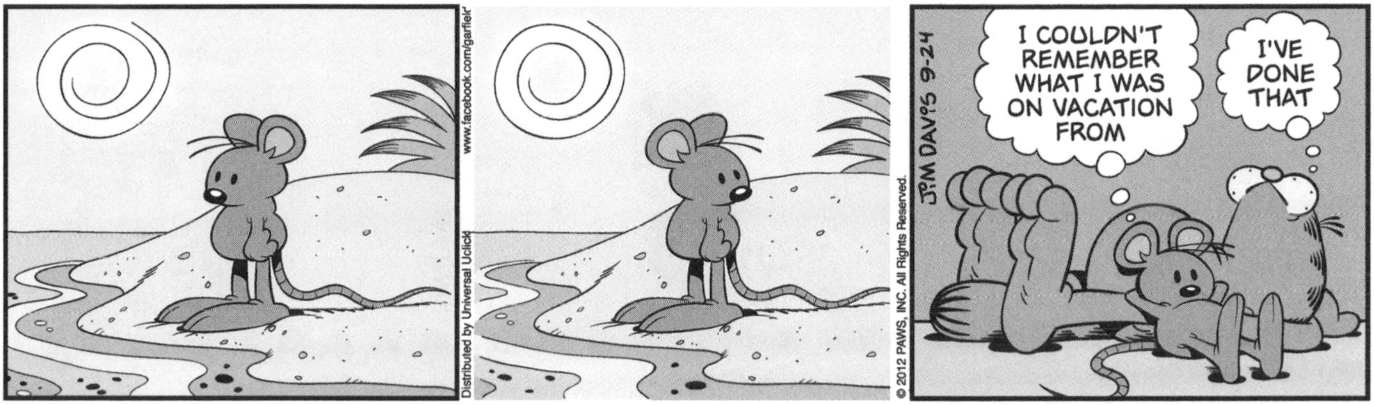
I COULDN'T REMEMBER WHAT I WAS ON VACATION FROM
I'VE DONE THAT
JIM DAVIS 9-24
www.facebook.com/garfield
Distributed by Universal Uclick
© 2012 PAWS, INC. All Rights Reserved.

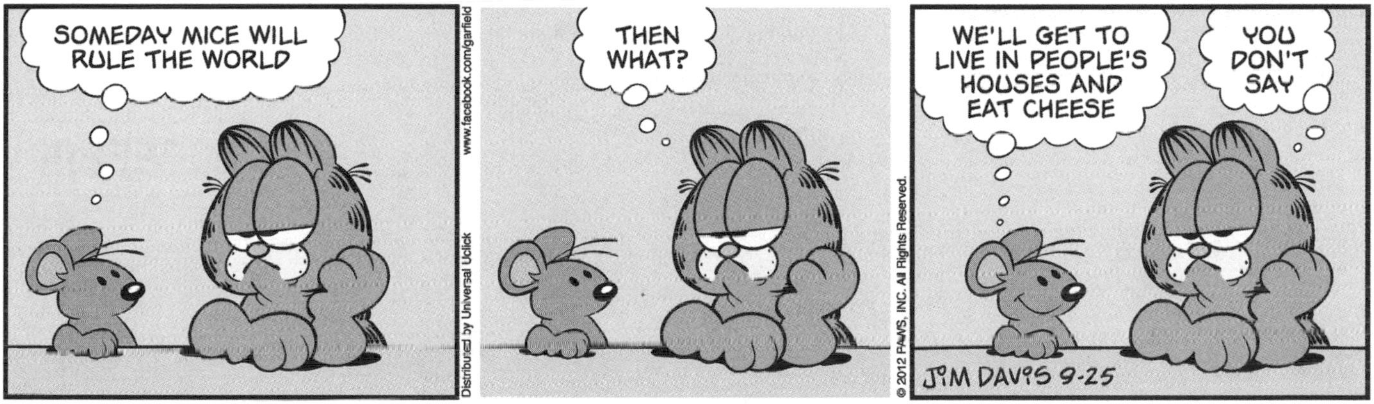
SOMEDAY MICE WILL RULE THE WORLD
THEN WHAT?
WE'LL GET TO LIVE IN PEOPLE'S HOUSES AND EAT CHEESE
YOU DON'T SAY
JIM DAVIS 9-25
www.facebook.com/garfield
Distributed by Universal Uclick
© 2012 PAWS, INC. All Rights Reserved.

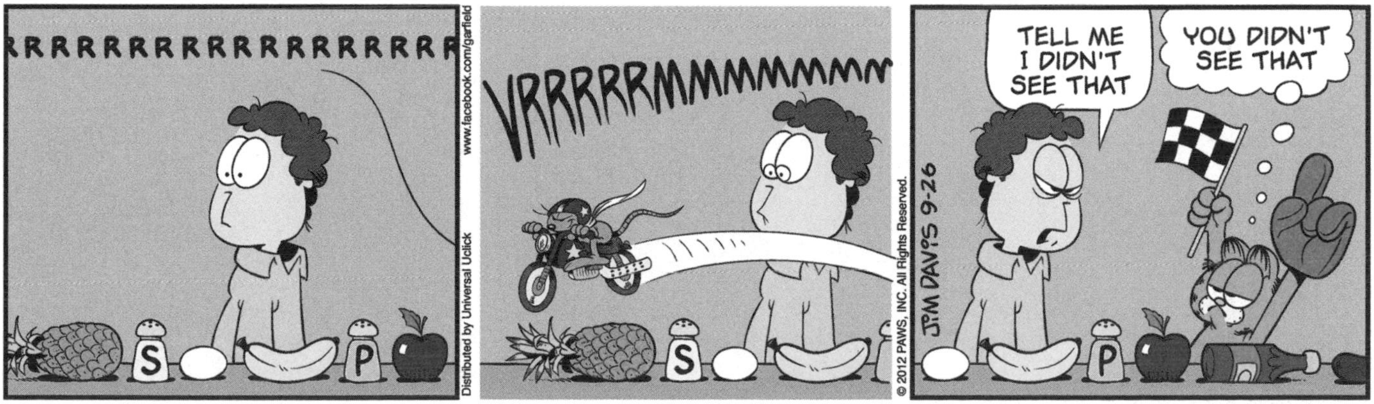
RRRRRRRRRRRRRRRRRRR
VRRRRRMMMMMMMM
TELL ME I DIDN'T SEE THAT
YOU DIDN'T SEE THAT
JIM DAVIS 9-26
www.facebook.com/garfield
Distributed by Universal Uclick
© 2012 PAWS, INC. All Rights Reserved.

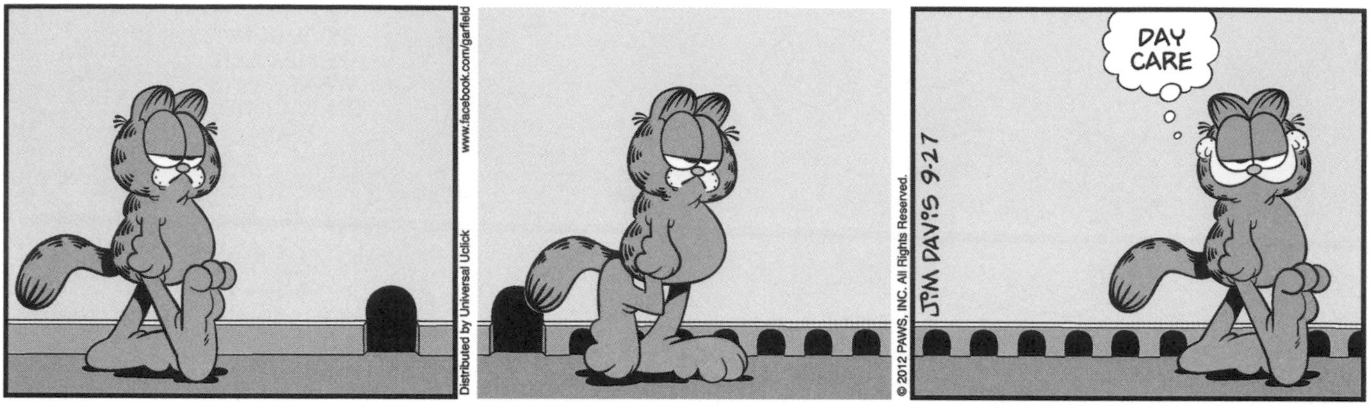
Distributed by Universal Uclick
www.facebook.com/garfield
© 2012 PAWS, INC. All Rights Reserved.
JIM DAVIS 9-27
DAY CARE

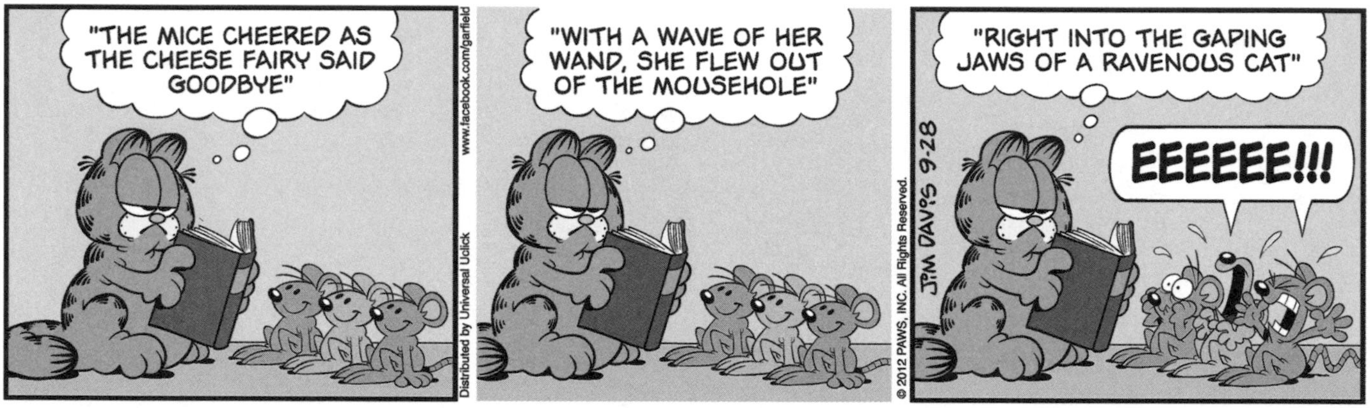
"THE MICE CHEERED AS THE CHEESE FAIRY SAID GOODBYE"
Distributed by Universal Uclick
www.facebook.com/garfield
"WITH A WAVE OF HER WAND, SHE FLEW OUT OF THE MOUSEHOLE"
© 2012 PAWS, INC. All Rights Reserved.
JIM DAVIS 9-28
"RIGHT INTO THE GAPING JAWS OF A RAVENOUS CAT"
EEEEEE!!!

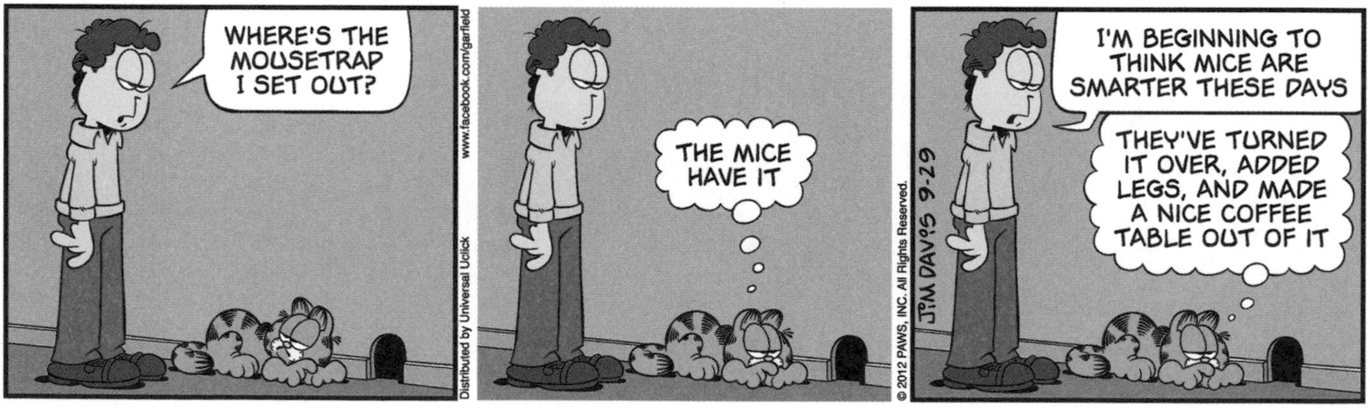
WHERE'S THE MOUSETRAP I SET OUT?
Distributed by Universal Uclick
www.facebook.com/garfield
THE MICE HAVE IT
© 2012 PAWS, INC. All Rights Reserved.
JIM DAVIS 9-29
I'M BEGINNING TO THINK MICE ARE SMARTER THESE DAYS
THEY'VE TURNED IT OVER, ADDED LEGS, AND MADE A NICE COFFEE TABLE OUT OF IT

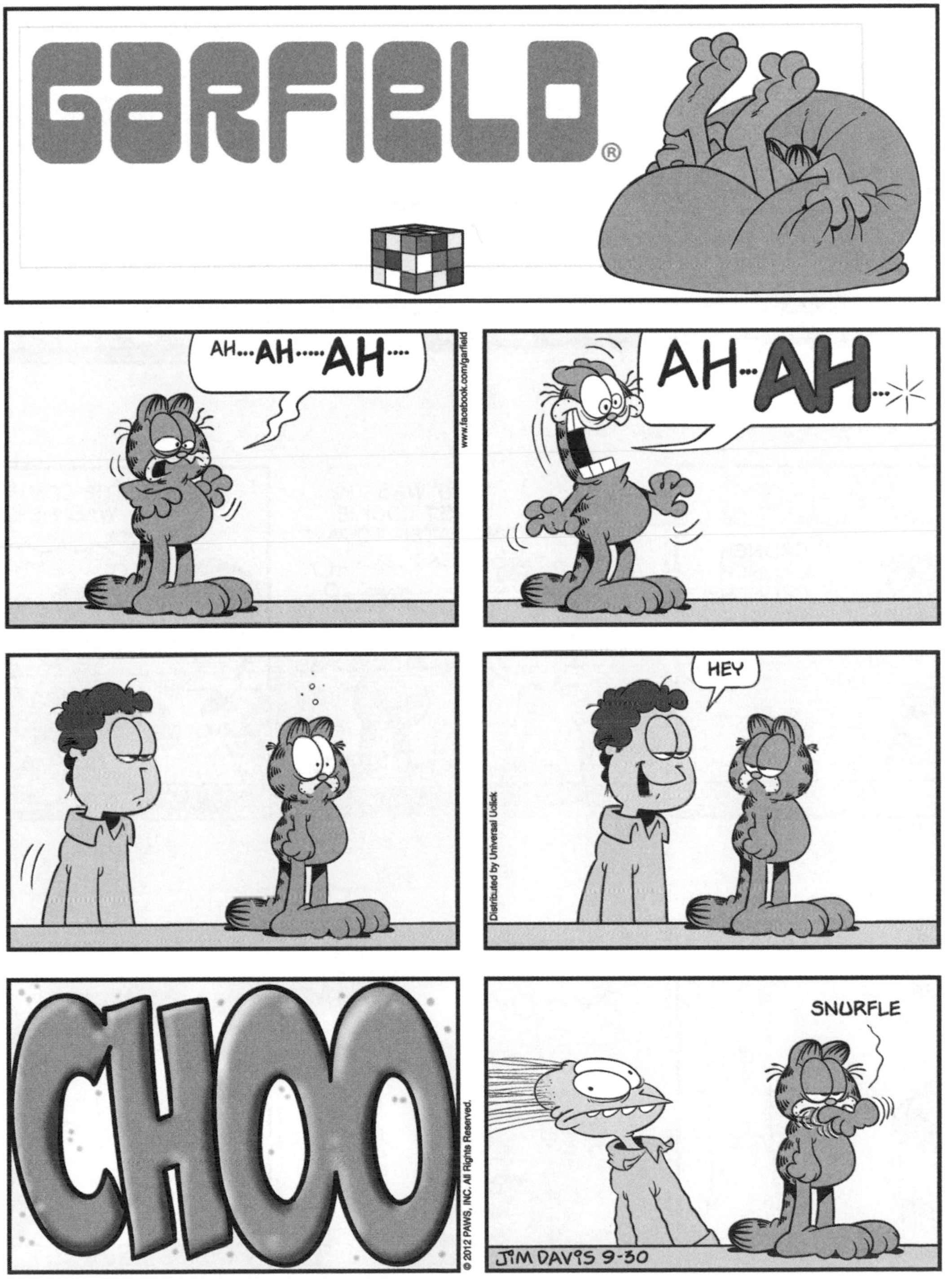
GARFIELD®
AH... AH..... AH....
AH... AH...
HEY
CHOO
SNURFLE
JIM DAVIS 9-30
www.facebook.com/garfield
Distributed by Universal Uclick
© 2012 PAWS, INC. All Rights Reserved.

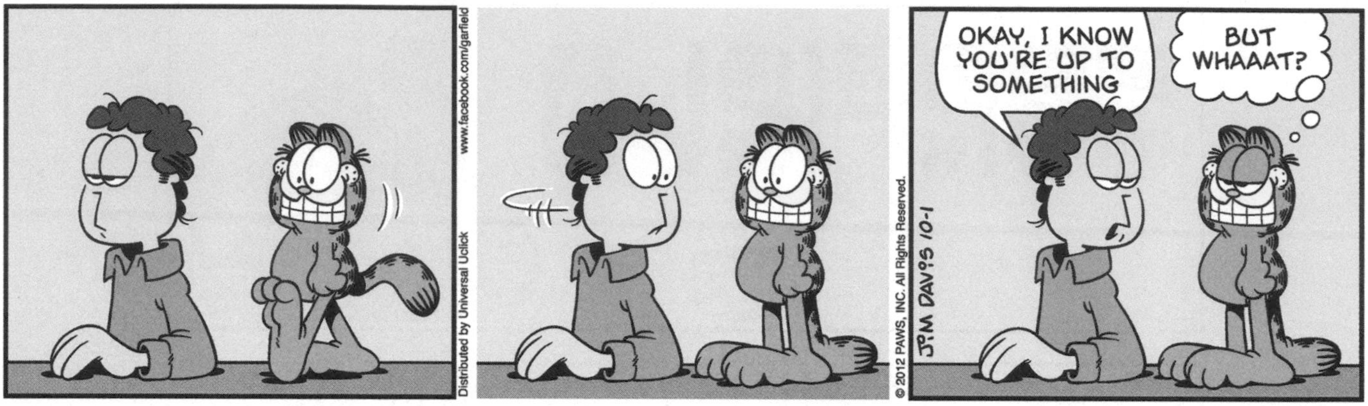
Distributed by Universal Uclick www.facebook.com/garfield
OKAY, I KNOW YOU'RE UP TO SOMETHING
BUT WHAAAT?
© 2012 PAWS, INC. All Rights Reserved.
JIM DAVIS 10-1

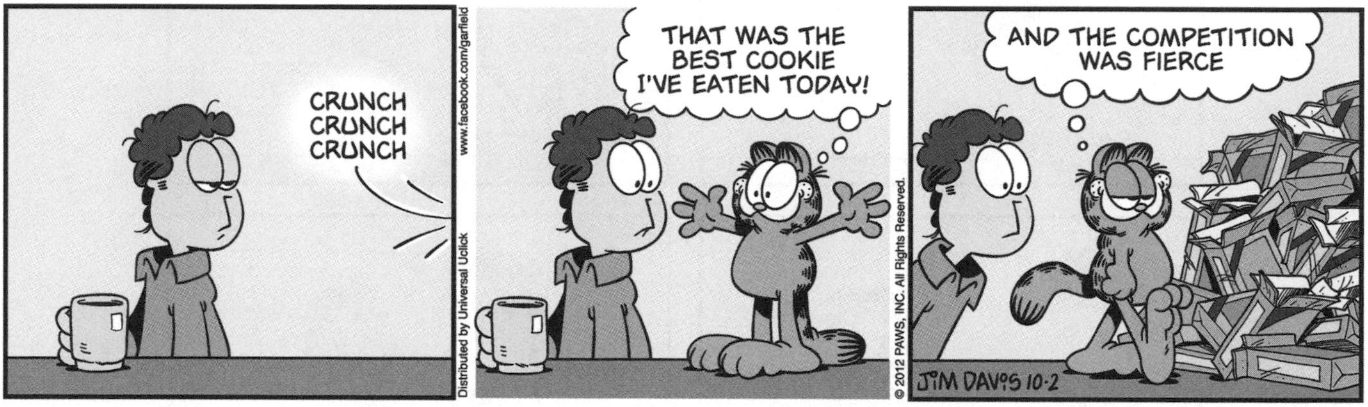
CRUNCH CRUNCH CRUNCH
Distributed by Universal Uclick www.facebook.com/garfield
THAT WAS THE BEST COOKIE I'VE EATEN TODAY!
AND THE COMPETITION WAS FIERCE
© 2012 PAWS, INC. All Rights Reserved.
JIM DAVIS 10-2

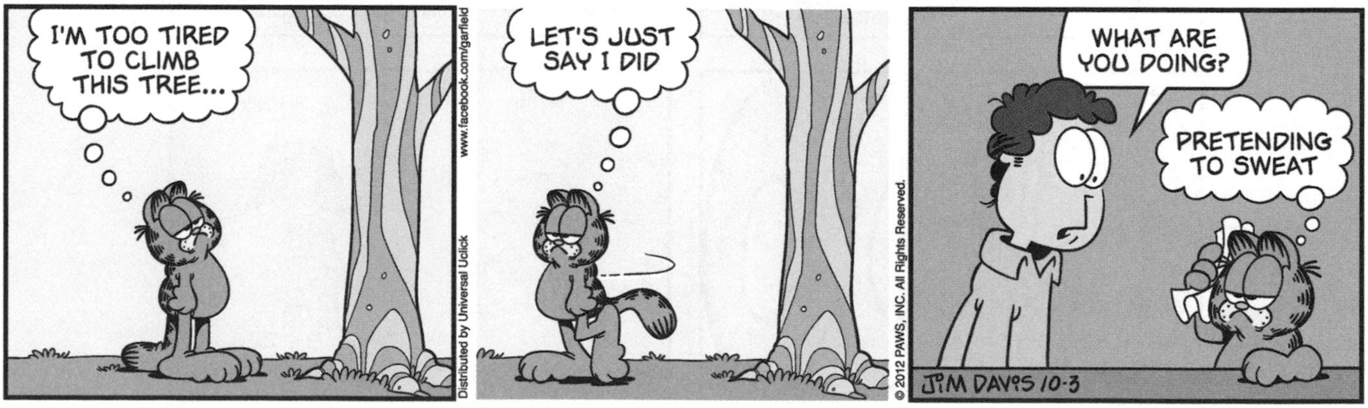
I'M TOO TIRED TO CLIMB THIS TREE...
Distributed by Universal Uclick www.facebook.com/garfield
LET'S JUST SAY I DID
WHAT ARE YOU DOING?
PRETENDING TO SWEAT
© 2012 PAWS, INC. All Rights Reserved.
JIM DAVIS 10-3

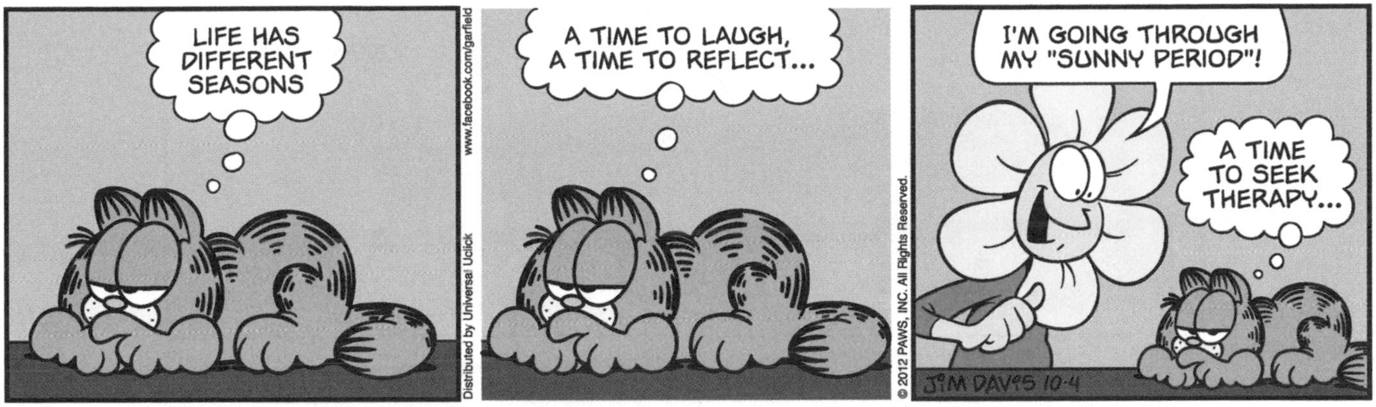
LIFE HAS DIFFERENT SEASONS
A TIME TO LAUGH, A TIME TO REFLECT...
I'M GOING THROUGH MY "SUNNY PERIOD"!
A TIME TO SEEK THERAPY...
www.facebook.com/garfield
Distributed by Universal Uclick
© 2012 PAWS, INC. All Rights Reserved.
JIM DAVIS 10-4

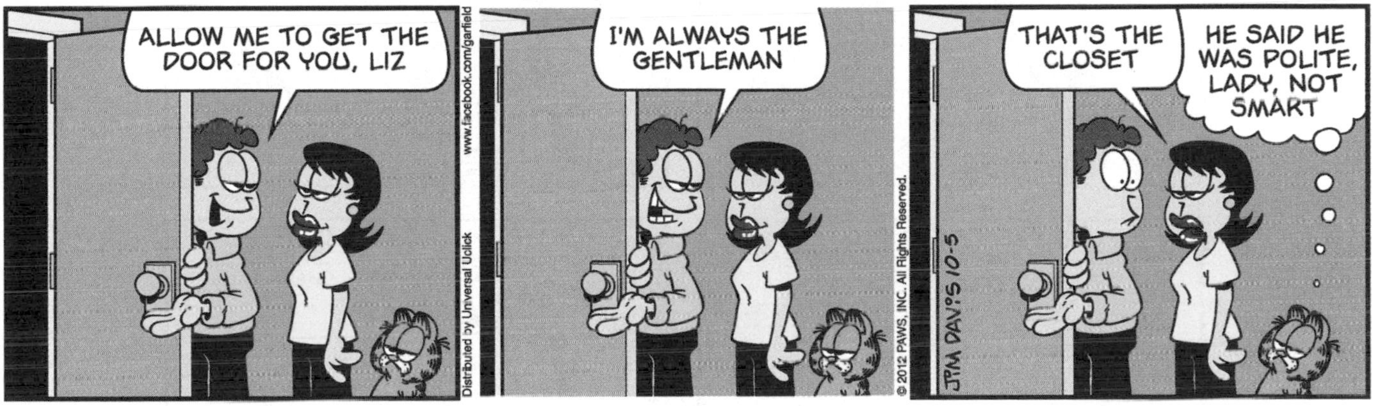
ALLOW ME TO GET THE DOOR FOR YOU, LIZ
I'M ALWAYS THE GENTLEMAN
THAT'S THE CLOSET
HE SAID HE WAS POLITE, LADY, NOT SMART
www.facebook.com/garfield
Distributed by Universal Uclick
© 2012 PAWS, INC. All Rights Reserved.
JIM DAVIS 10-5

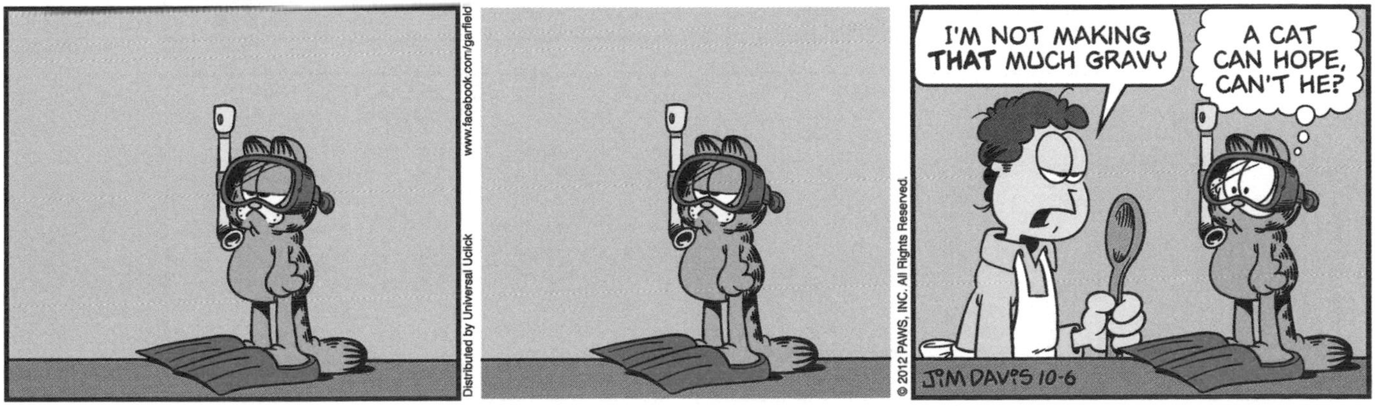
I'M NOT MAKING **THAT** MUCH GRAVY
A CAT CAN HOPE, CAN'T HE?
www.facebook.com/garfield
Distributed by Universal Uclick
© 2012 PAWS, INC. All Rights Reserved.
JIM DAVIS 10-6

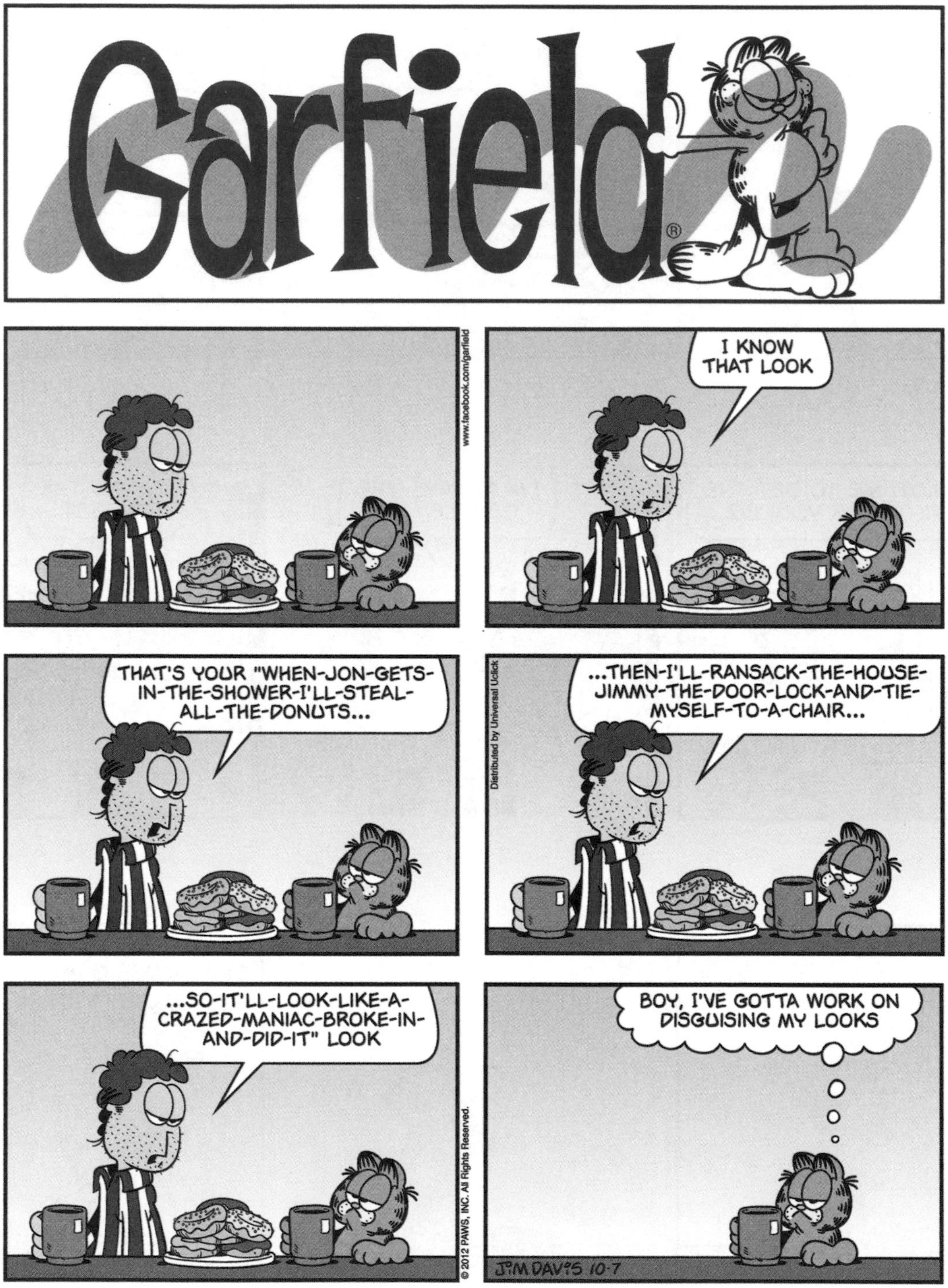
Garfield®
www.facebook.com/garfield
I KNOW THAT LOOK
THAT'S YOUR "WHEN-JON-GETS-IN-THE-SHOWER-I'LL-STEAL-ALL-THE-DONUTS...
Distributed by Universal Uclick
...THEN-I'LL-RANSACK-THE-HOUSE-JIMMY-THE-DOOR-LOCK-AND-TIE-MYSELF-TO-A-CHAIR...
...SO-IT'LL-LOOK-LIKE-A-CRAZED-MANIAC-BROKE-IN-AND-DID-IT" LOOK
© 2012 PAWS, INC. All Rights Reserved.
BOY, I'VE GOTTA WORK ON DISGUISING MY LOOKS
JIM DAVIS 10-7

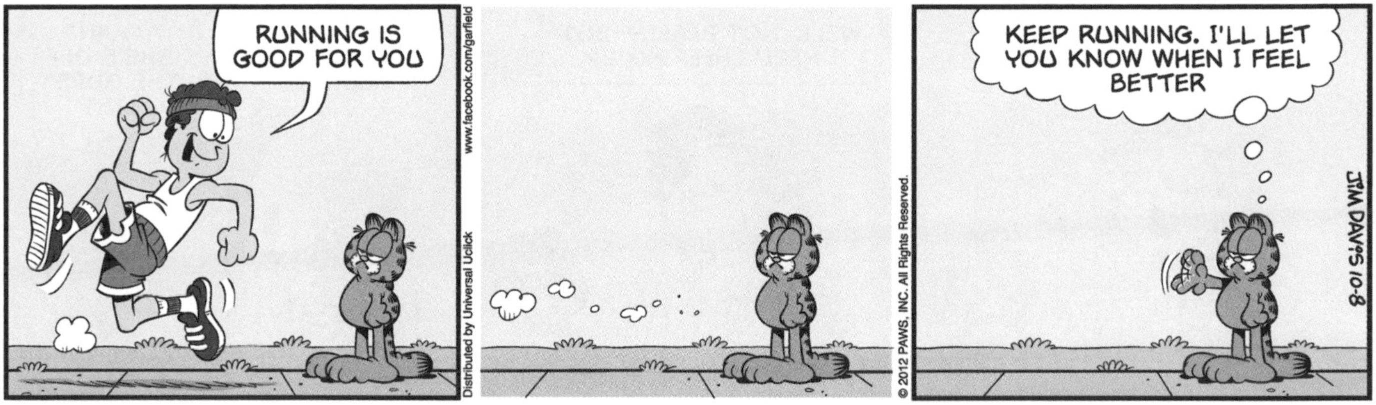
RUNNING IS GOOD FOR YOU
www.facebook.com/garfield
Distributed by Universal Uclick
© 2012 PAWS, INC. All Rights Reserved.
KEEP RUNNING. I'LL LET YOU KNOW WHEN I FEEL BETTER
JIM DAVIS 10-8

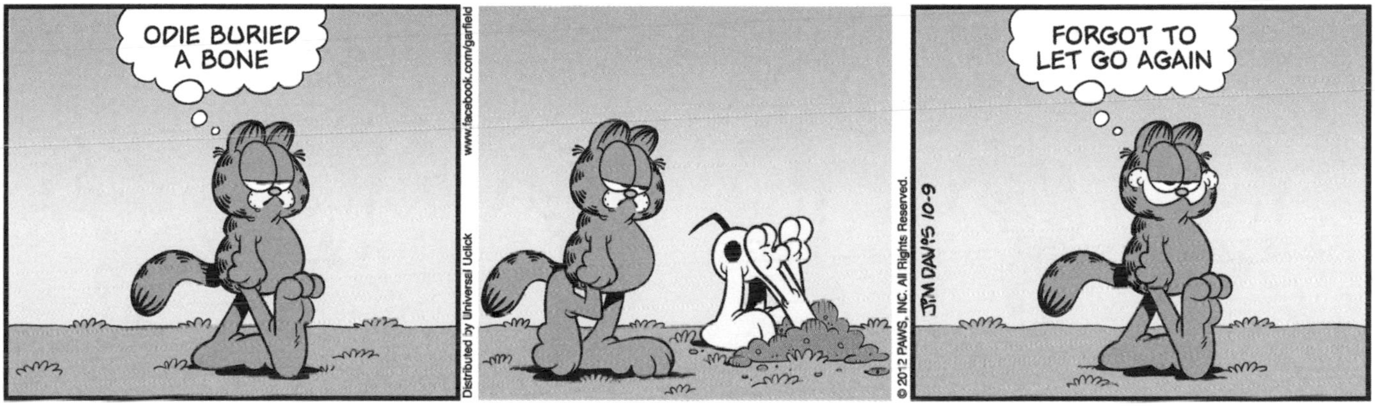
ODIE BURIED A BONE
www.facebook.com/garfield
Distributed by Universal Uclick
© 2012 PAWS, INC. All Rights Reserved.
JIM DAVIS 10-9
FORGOT TO LET GO AGAIN

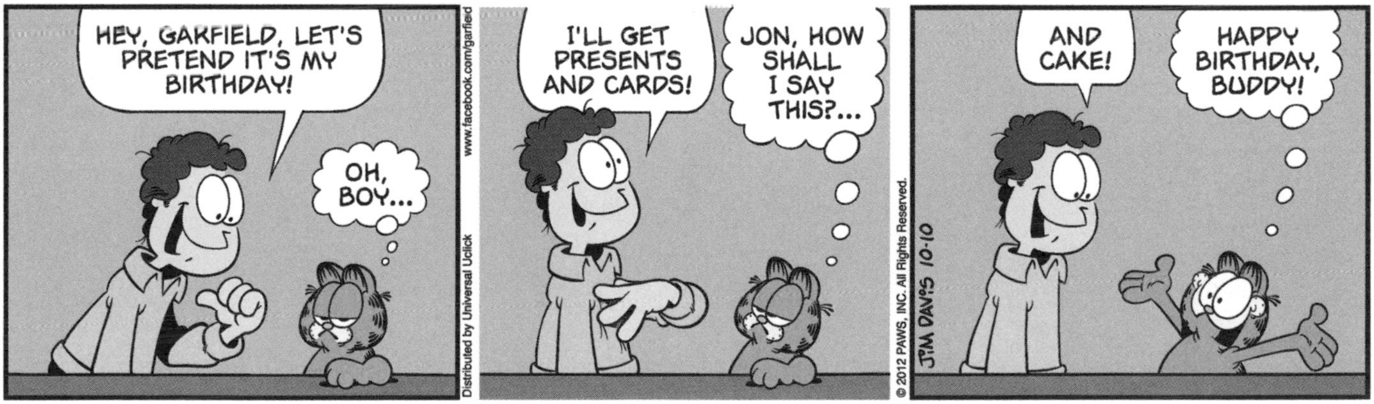
HEY, GARFIELD, LET'S PRETEND IT'S MY BIRTHDAY!
OH, BOY...
www.facebook.com/garfield
Distributed by Universal Uclick
I'LL GET PRESENTS AND CARDS!
JON, HOW SHALL I SAY THIS?...
© 2012 PAWS, INC. All Rights Reserved.
JIM DAVIS 10-10
AND CAKE!
HAPPY BIRTHDAY, BUDDY!

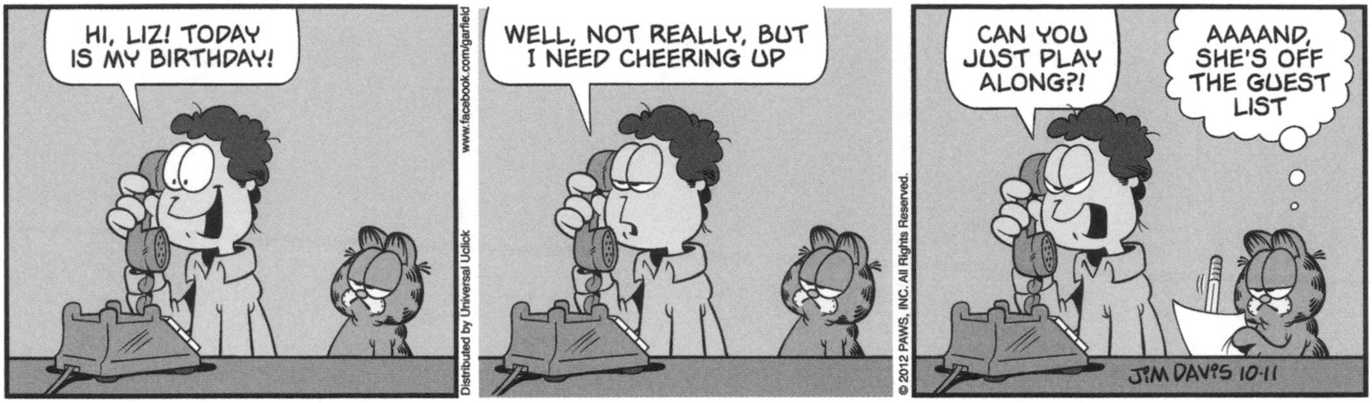
HI, LIZ! TODAY IS MY BIRTHDAY!
WELL, NOT REALLY, BUT I NEED CHEERING UP
CAN YOU JUST PLAY ALONG?!
AAAAND, SHE'S OFF THE GUEST LIST
JIM DAVIS 10-11
Distributed by Universal Uclick
www.facebook.com/garfield
© 2012 PAWS, INC. All Rights Reserved.

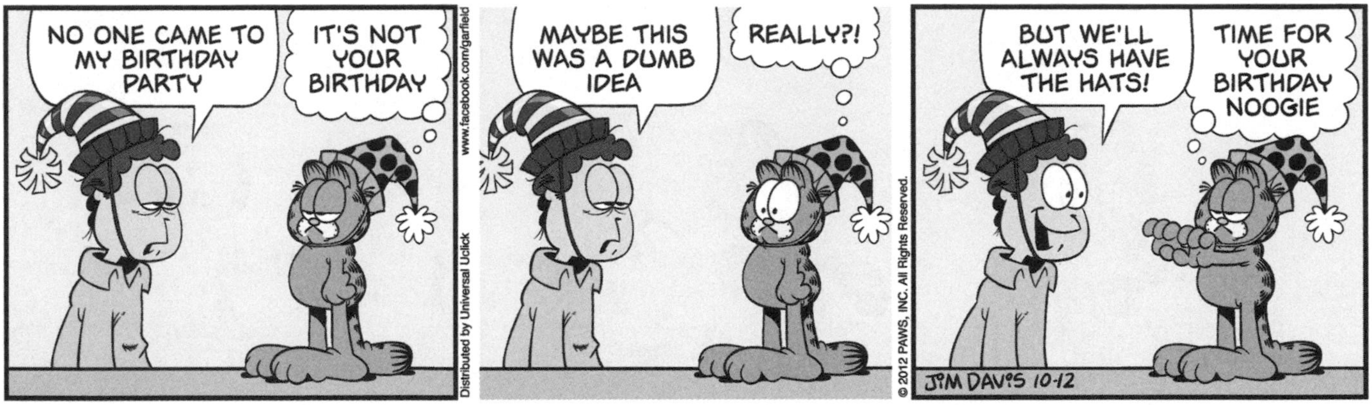
NO ONE CAME TO MY BIRTHDAY PARTY
IT'S NOT YOUR BIRTHDAY
MAYBE THIS WAS A DUMB IDEA
REALLY?!
BUT WE'LL ALWAYS HAVE THE HATS!
TIME FOR YOUR BIRTHDAY NOOGIE
JIM DAVIS 10-12
Distributed by Universal Uclick
www.facebook.com/garfield
© 2012 PAWS, INC. All Rights Reserved.

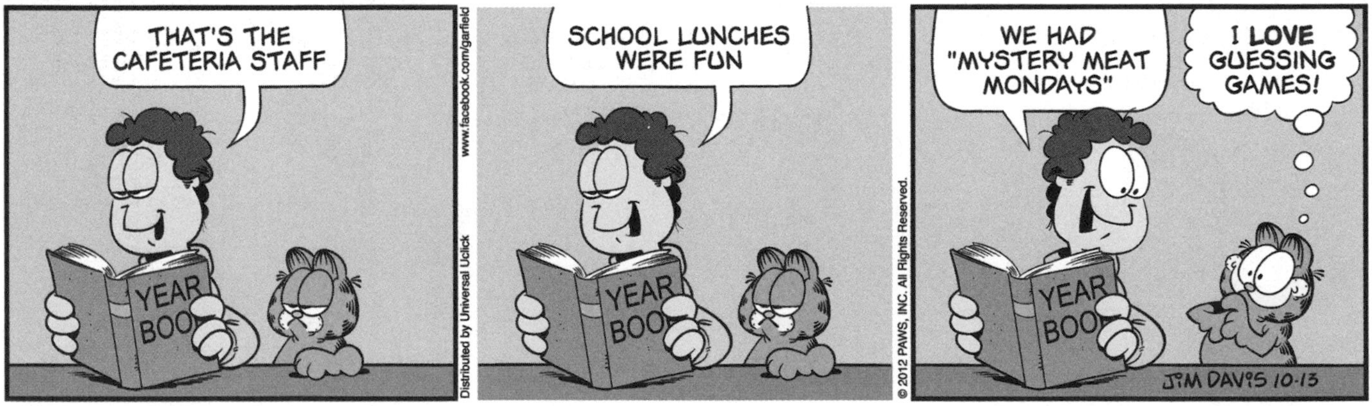
THAT'S THE CAFETERIA STAFF
YEAR BOO
SCHOOL LUNCHES WERE FUN
WE HAD "MYSTERY MEAT MONDAYS"
I **LOVE** GUESSING GAMES!
JIM DAVIS 10-13
Distributed by Universal Uclick
www.facebook.com/garfield
© 2012 PAWS, INC. All Rights Reserved.

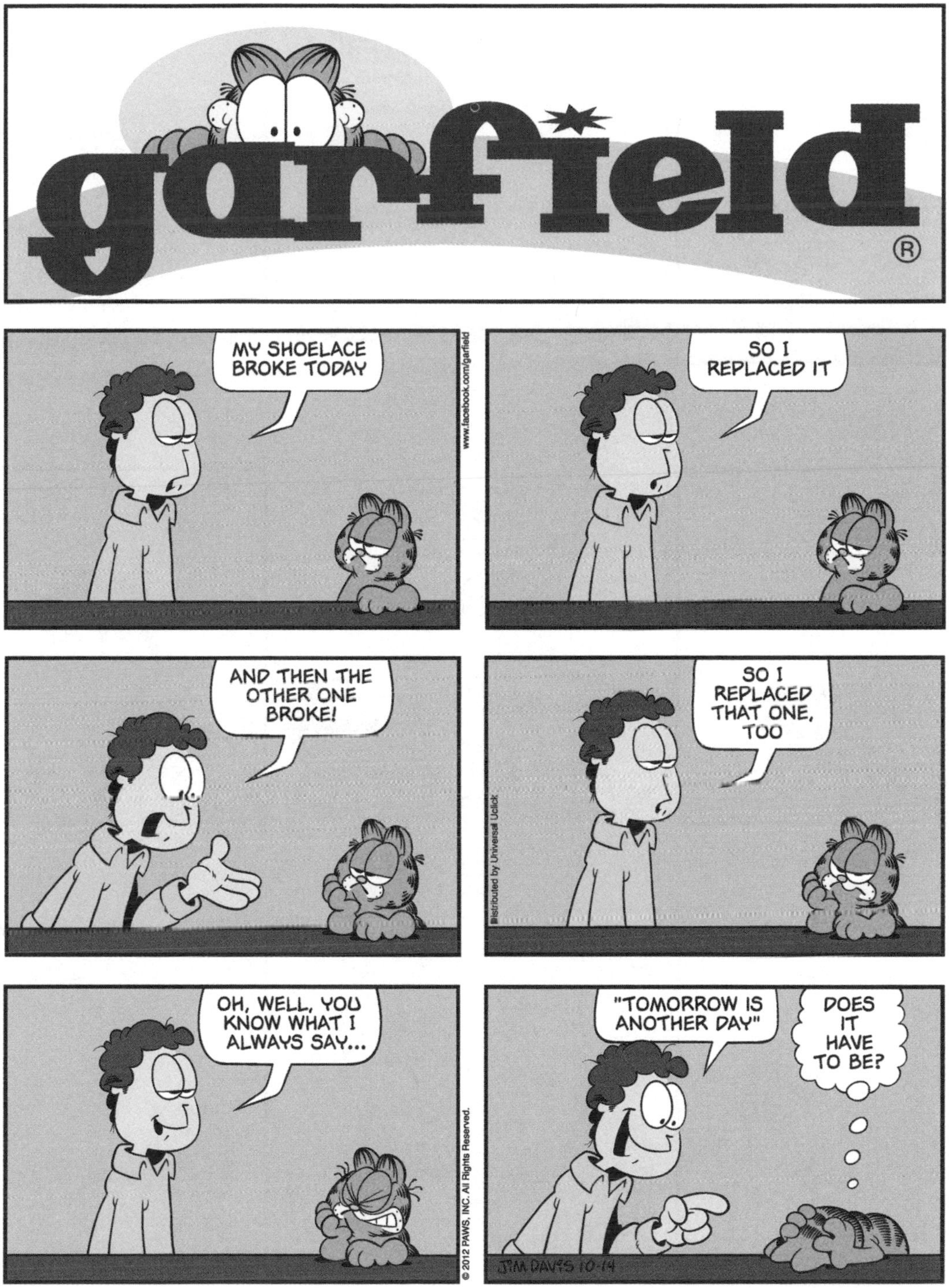
garfield
MY SHOELACE BROKE TODAY
SO I REPLACED IT
AND THEN THE OTHER ONE BROKE!
SO I REPLACED THAT ONE, TOO
OH, WELL, YOU KNOW WHAT I ALWAYS SAY...
"TOMORROW IS ANOTHER DAY"
DOES IT HAVE TO BE?
www.facebook.com/garfield
Distributed by Universal Uclick
© 2012 PAWS, INC. All Rights Reserved.
JIM DAVIS 10-14

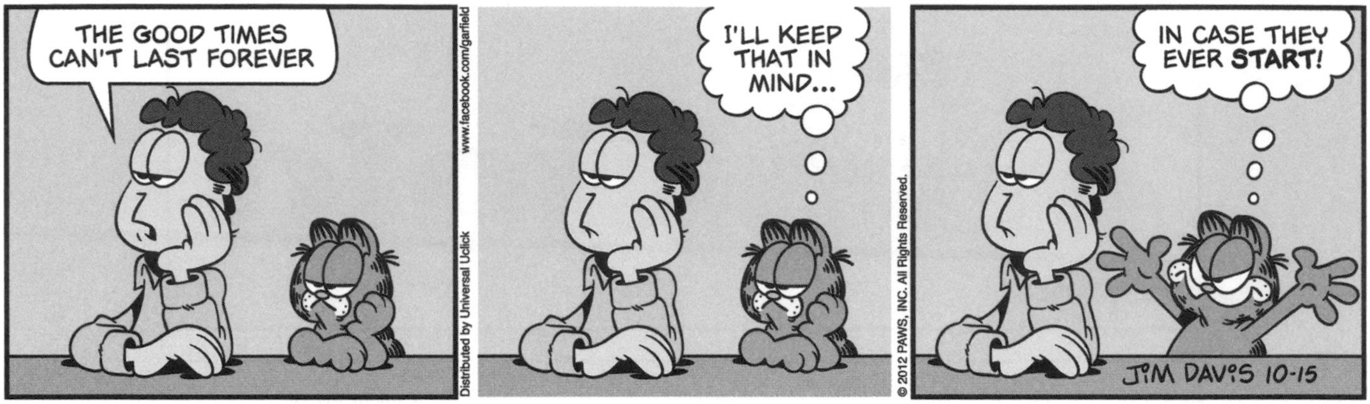
THE GOOD TIMES CAN'T LAST FOREVER
I'LL KEEP THAT IN MIND...
IN CASE THEY EVER **START**!
JIM DAVIS 10-15
Distributed by Universal Uclick www.facebook.com/garfield
© 2012 PAWS, INC. All Rights Reserved.

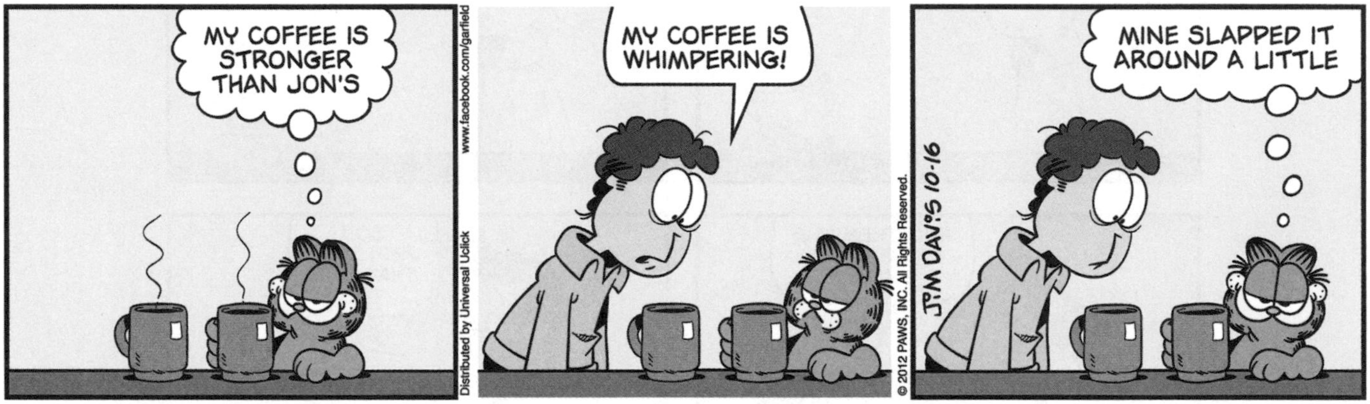
MY COFFEE IS STRONGER THAN JON'S
MY COFFEE IS WHIMPERING!
MINE SLAPPED IT AROUND A LITTLE
JIM DAVIS 10-16
Distributed by Universal Uclick www.facebook.com/garfield
© 2012 PAWS, INC. All Rights Reserved.

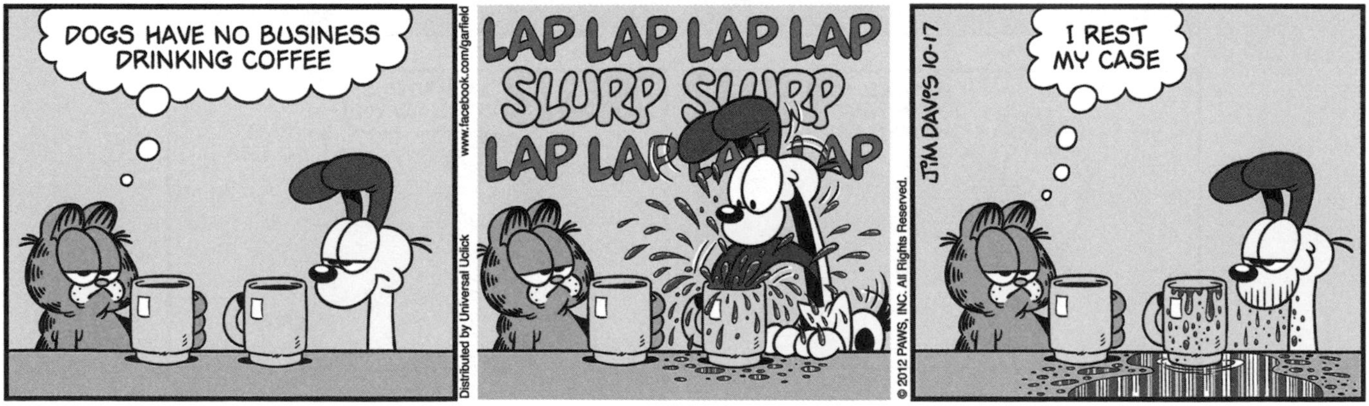
DOGS HAVE NO BUSINESS DRINKING COFFEE
LAP LAP LAP LAP
SLURP SLURP
I REST MY CASE
JIM DAVIS 10-17
Distributed by Universal Uclick www.facebook.com/garfield
© 2012 PAWS, INC. All Rights Reserved.

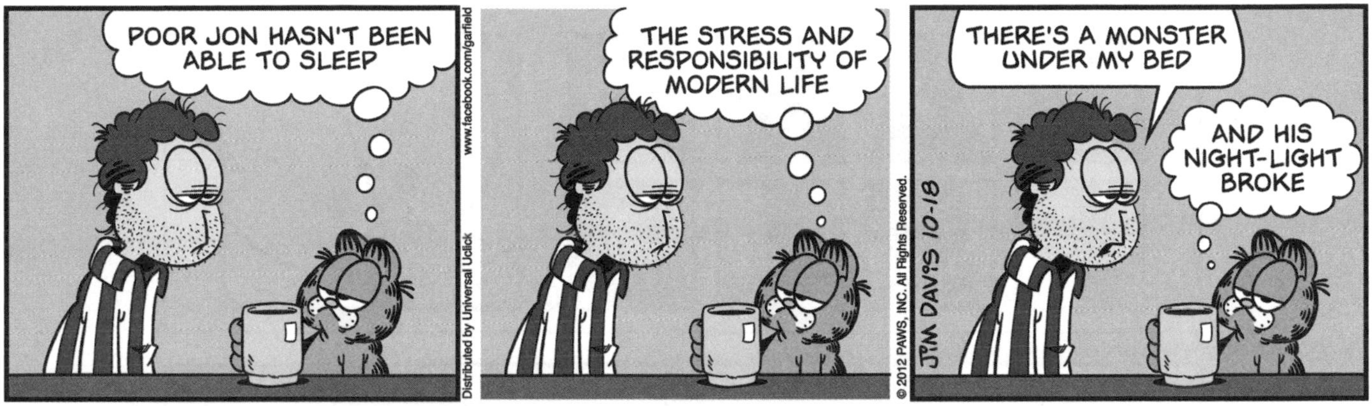
POOR JON HASN'T BEEN ABLE TO SLEEP
Distributed by Universal Uclick www.facebook.com/garfield
THE STRESS AND RESPONSIBILITY OF MODERN LIFE
© 2012 PAWS, INC. All Rights Reserved.
JIM DAVIS 10-18
THERE'S A MONSTER UNDER MY BED
AND HIS NIGHT-LIGHT BROKE

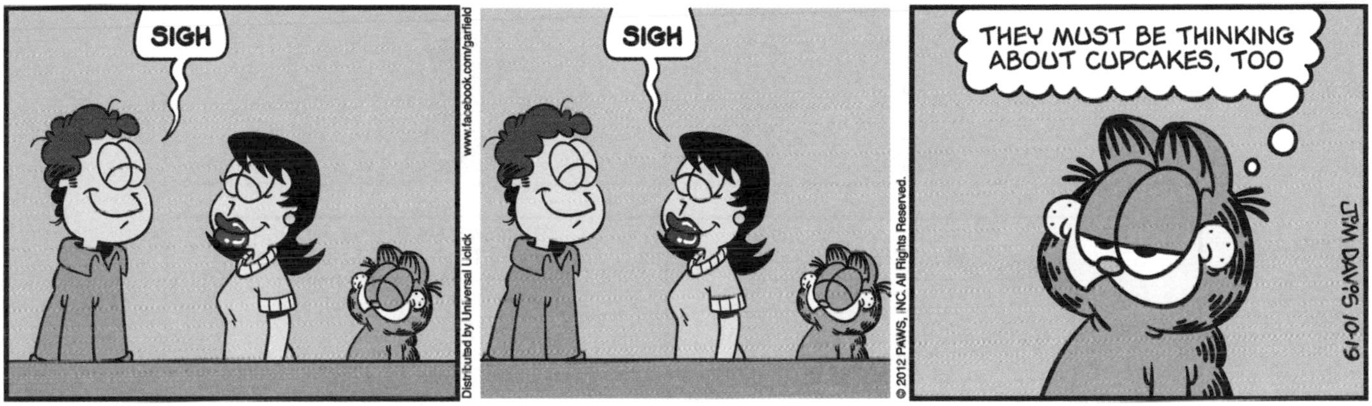
SIGH
Distributed by Universal Uclick www.facebook.com/garfield
SIGH
© 2012 PAWS, INC. All Rights Reserved.
THEY MUST BE THINKING ABOUT CUPCAKES, TOO
JIM DAVIS 10-19

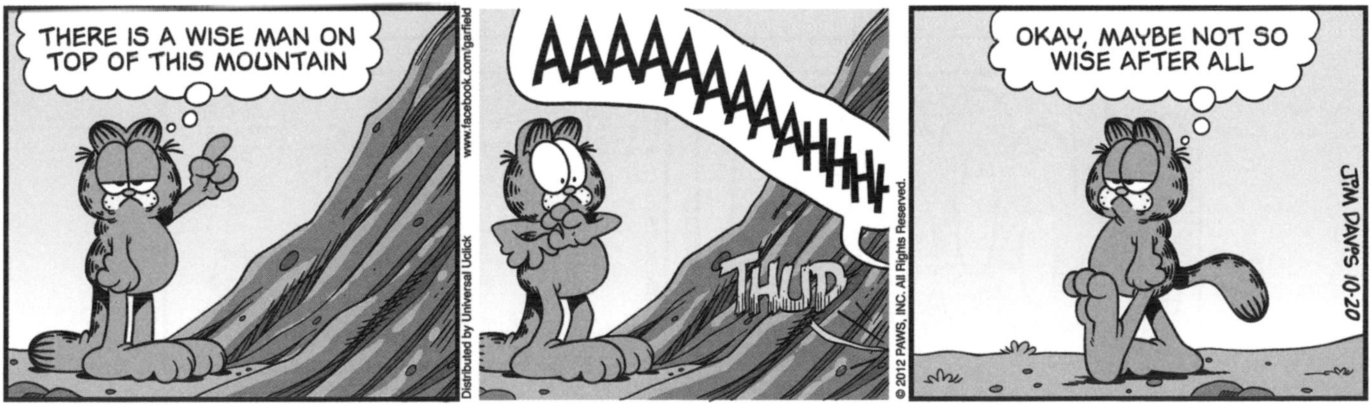
THERE IS A WISE MAN ON TOP OF THIS MOUNTAIN
Distributed by Universal Uclick www.facebook.com/garfield
AAAAAAAAAAAHHHH
THUD
© 2012 PAWS, INC. All Rights Reserved.
OKAY, MAYBE NOT SO WISE AFTER ALL
JIM DAVIS 10-20

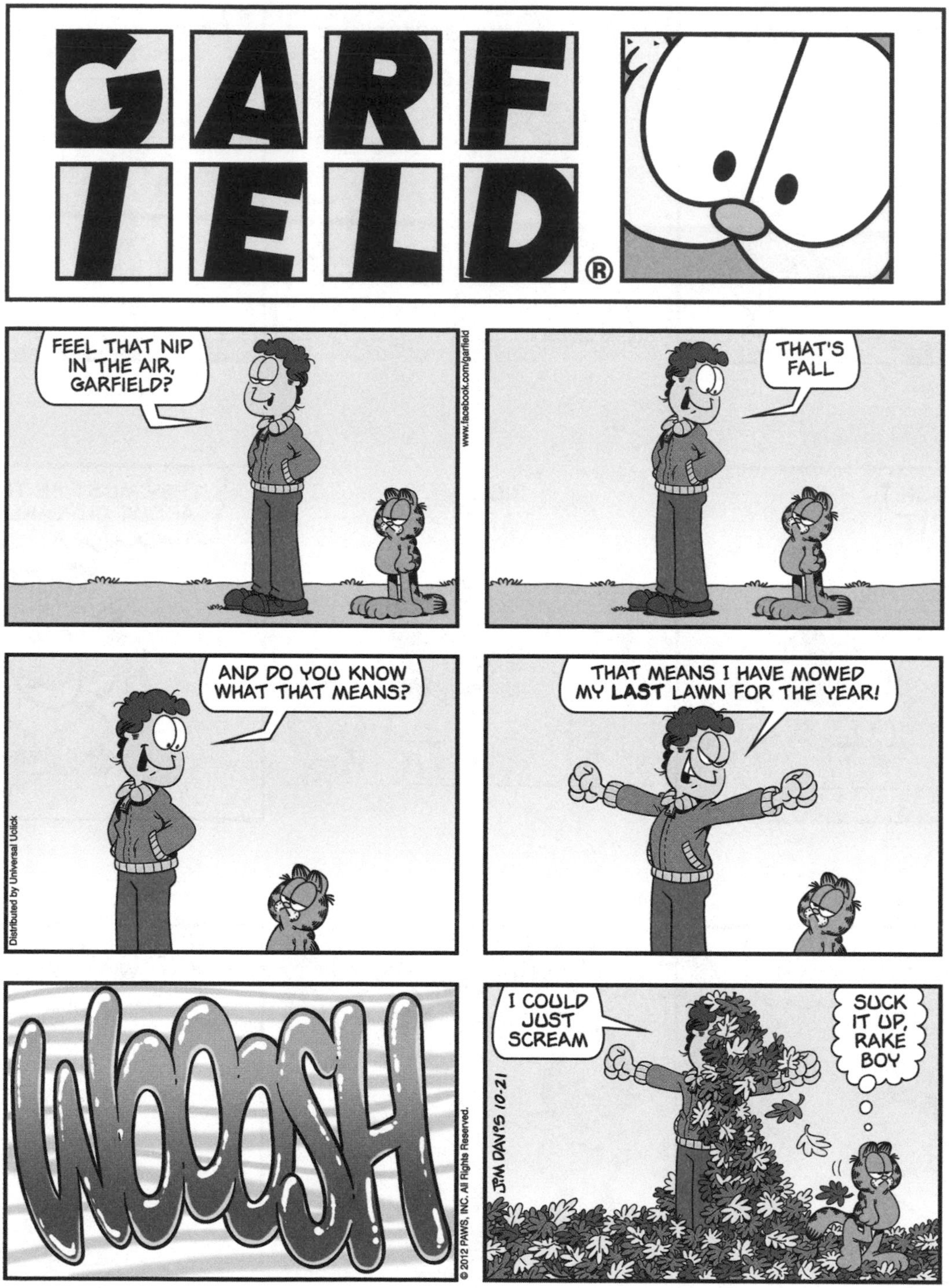
GARFIELD®
FEEL THAT NIP IN THE AIR, GARFIELD?
www.facebook.com/garfield
THAT'S FALL
AND DO YOU KNOW WHAT THAT MEANS?
Distributed by Universal Uclick
THAT MEANS I HAVE MOWED MY **LAST** LAWN FOR THE YEAR!
WOOOSH
© 2012 PAWS, INC. All Rights Reserved.
JIM DAVIS 10-21
I COULD JUST SCREAM
SUCK IT UP, RAKE BOY

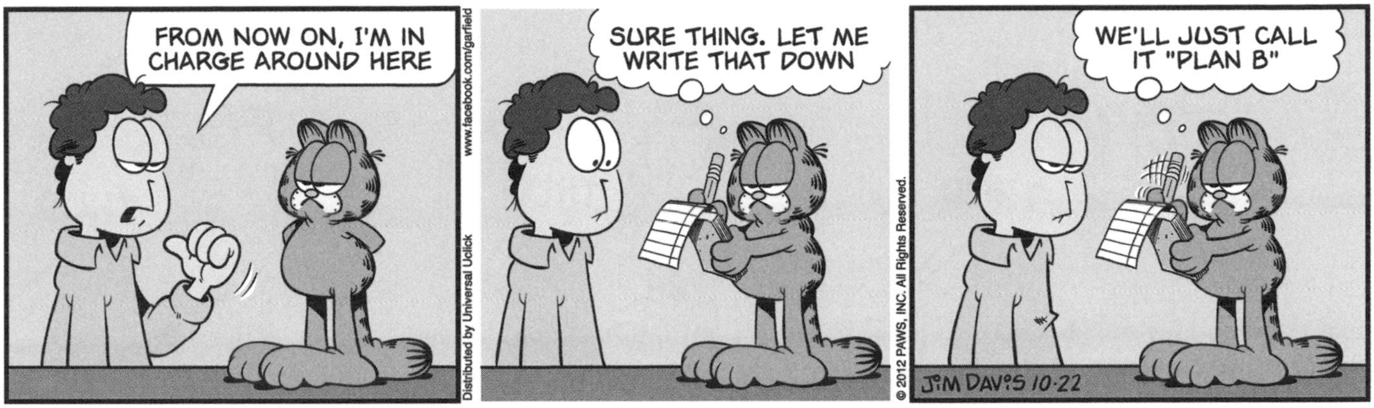
FROM NOW ON, I'M IN CHARGE AROUND HERE
www.facebook.com/garfield
Distributed by Universal Uclick
SURE THING. LET ME WRITE THAT DOWN
© 2012 PAWS, INC. All Rights Reserved.
WE'LL JUST CALL IT "PLAN B"
JIM DAVIS 10-22

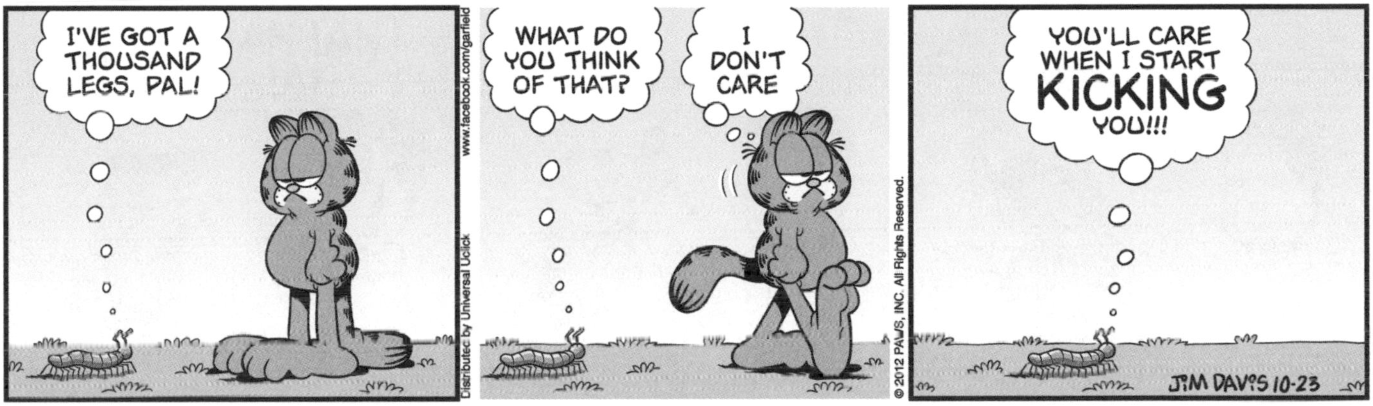
I'VE GOT A THOUSAND LEGS, PAL!
www.facebook.com/garfield
Distributed by Universal Uclick
WHAT DO YOU THINK OF THAT?
I DON'T CARE
© 2012 PAWS, INC. All Rights Reserved.
YOU'LL CARE WHEN I START KICKING YOU!!!
JIM DAVIS 10-23

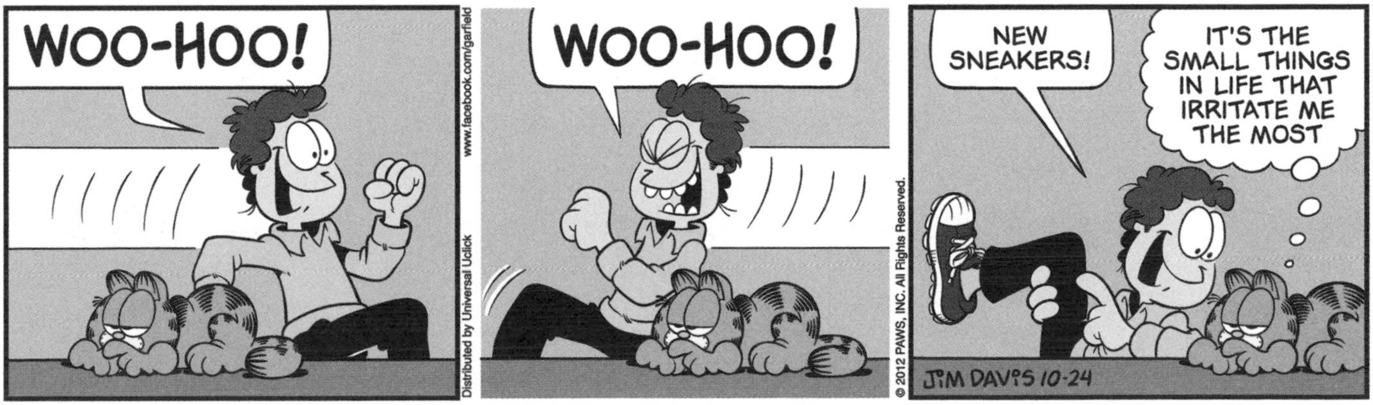
WOO-HOO!
www.facebook.com/garfield
Distributed by Universal Uclick
WOO-HOO!
© 2012 PAWS, INC. All Rights Reserved.
NEW SNEAKERS!
IT'S THE SMALL THINGS IN LIFE THAT IRRITATE ME THE MOST
JIM DAVIS 10-24

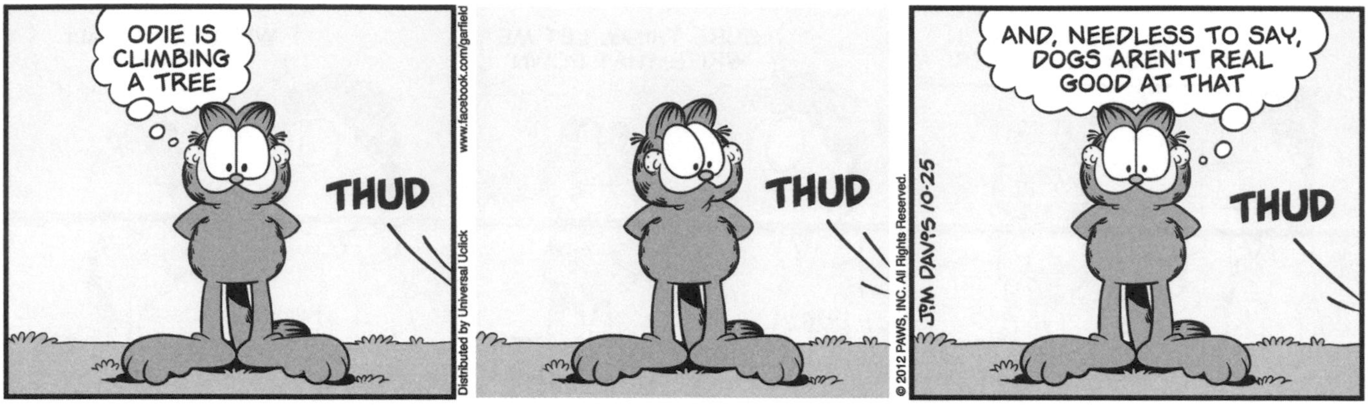
ODIE IS CLIMBING A TREE
THUD
THUD
AND, NEEDLESS TO SAY, DOGS AREN'T REAL GOOD AT THAT
THUD
Distributed by Universal Uclick www.facebook.com/garfield
© 2012 PAWS, INC. All Rights Reserved.
JIM DAVIS 10-25

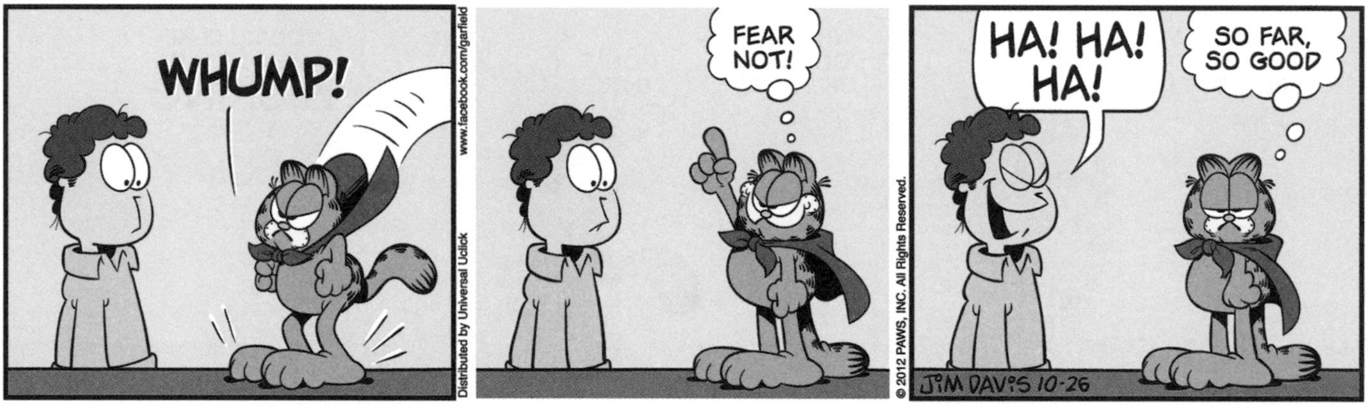
WHUMP!
FEAR NOT!
HA! HA! HA!
SO FAR, SO GOOD
Distributed by Universal Uclick www.facebook.com/garfield
© 2012 PAWS, INC. All Rights Reserved.
JIM DAVIS 10-26

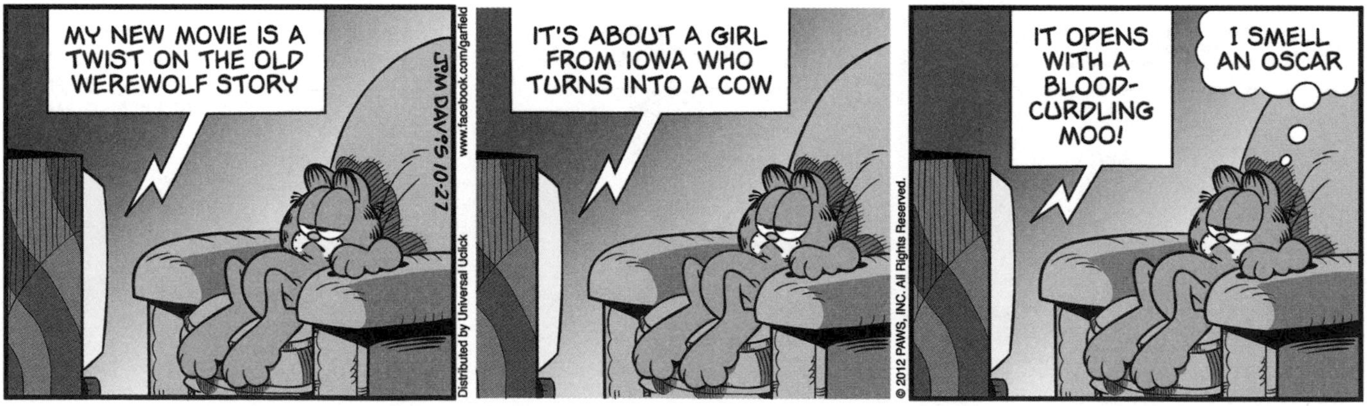
MY NEW MOVIE IS A TWIST ON THE OLD WEREWOLF STORY
JIM DAVIS 10-27
IT'S ABOUT A GIRL FROM IOWA WHO TURNS INTO A COW
IT OPENS WITH A BLOOD-CURDLING MOO!
I SMELL AN OSCAR
Distributed by Universal Uclick www.facebook.com/garfield
© 2012 PAWS, INC. All Rights Reserved.

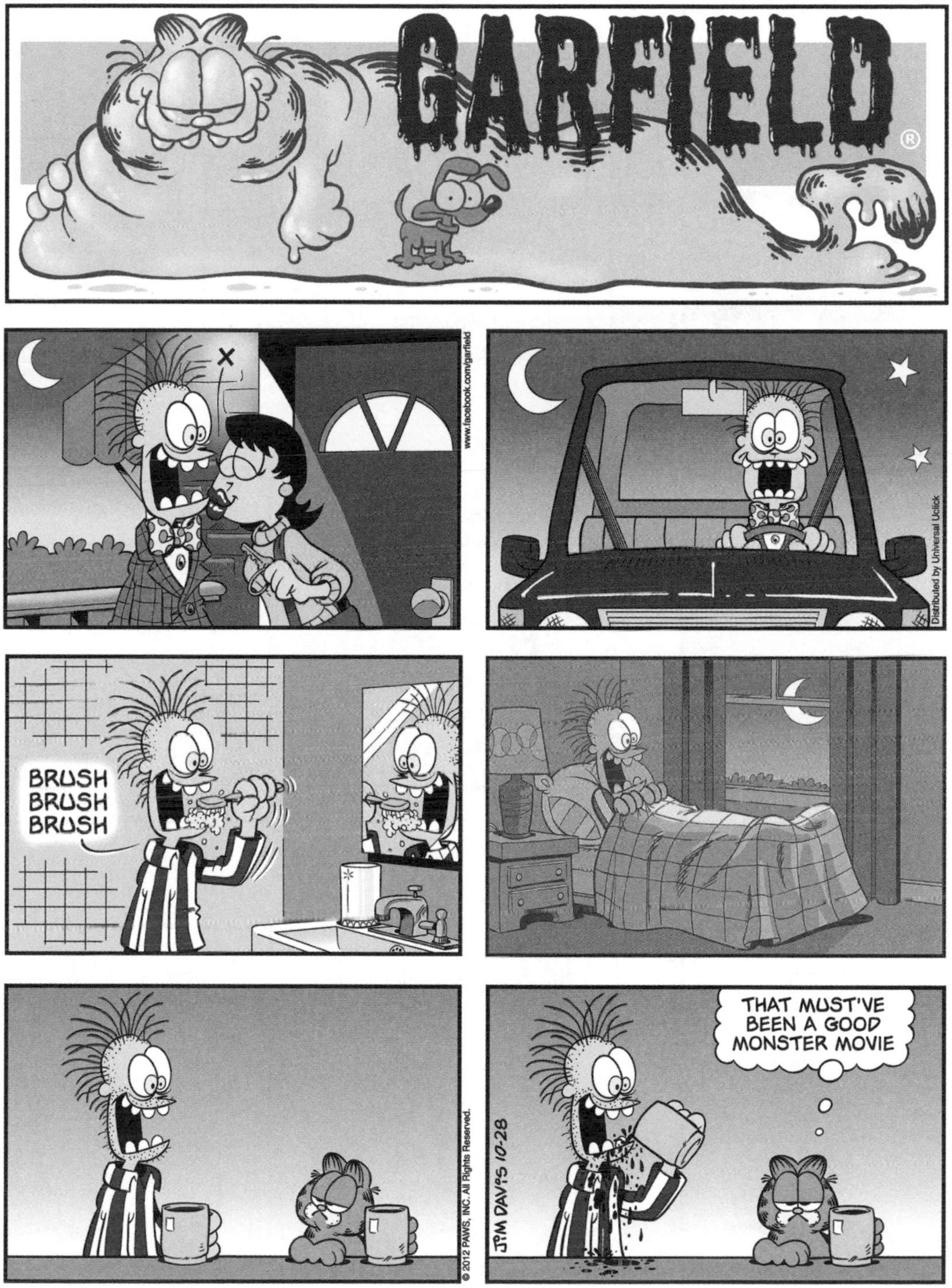
GARFIELD®
www.facebook.com/garfield
Distributed by Universal Uclick
BRUSH
BRUSH
BRUSH
© 2012 PAWS, INC. All Rights Reserved.
JIM DAVIS 10-28
THAT MUST'VE BEEN A GOOD MONSTER MOVIE

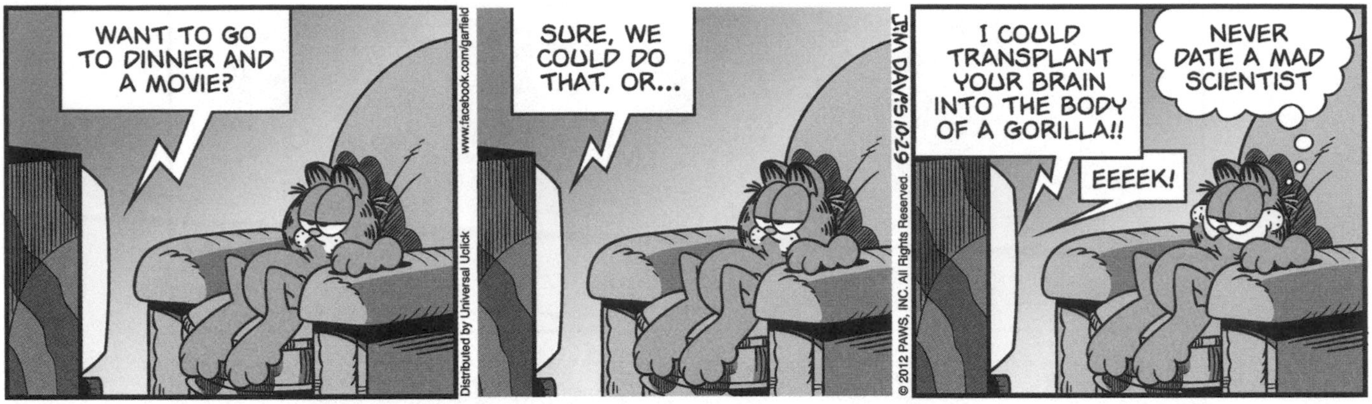
WANT TO GO TO DINNER AND A MOVIE?
SURE, WE COULD DO THAT, OR...
I COULD TRANSPLANT YOUR BRAIN INTO THE BODY OF A GORILLA!!
EEEEK!
NEVER DATE A MAD SCIENTIST
JIM DAVIS 10-29
Distributed by Universal Uclick
www.facebook.com/garfield
© 2012 PAWS, INC. All Rights Reserved.

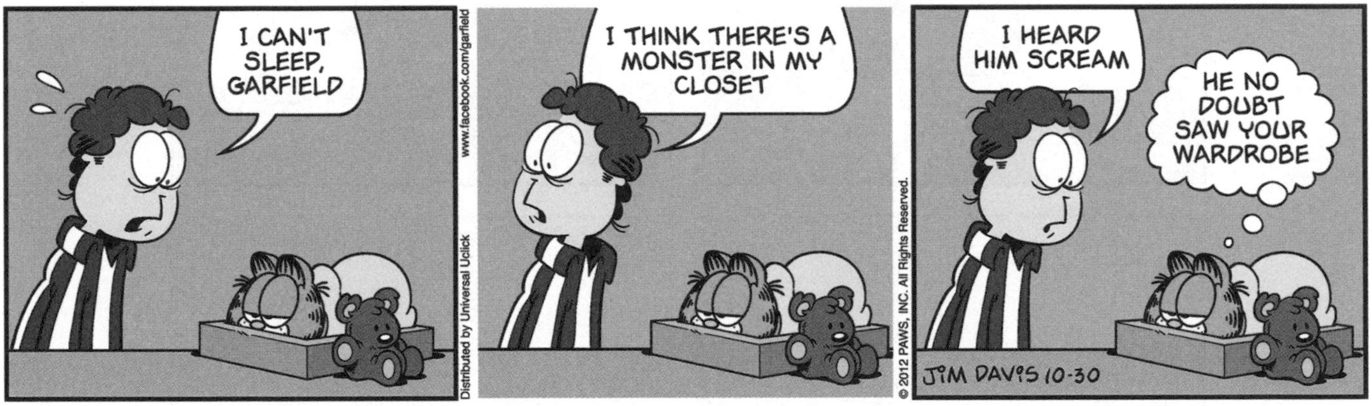
I CAN'T SLEEP, GARFIELD
I THINK THERE'S A MONSTER IN MY CLOSET
I HEARD HIM SCREAM
HE NO DOUBT SAW YOUR WARDROBE
JIM DAVIS 10-30
Distributed by Universal Uclick
www.facebook.com/garfield
© 2012 PAWS, INC. All Rights Reserved.

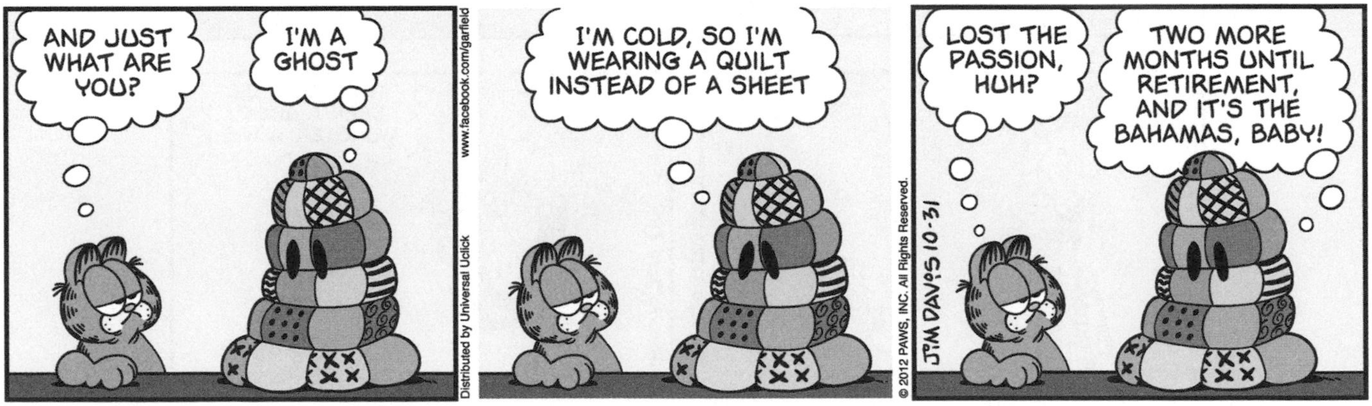
AND JUST WHAT ARE YOU?
I'M A GHOST
I'M COLD, SO I'M WEARING A QUILT INSTEAD OF A SHEET
LOST THE PASSION, HUH?
TWO MORE MONTHS UNTIL RETIREMENT, AND IT'S THE BAHAMAS, BABY!
JIM DAVIS 10-31
Distributed by Universal Uclick
www.facebook.com/garfield
© 2012 PAWS, INC. All Rights Reserved.

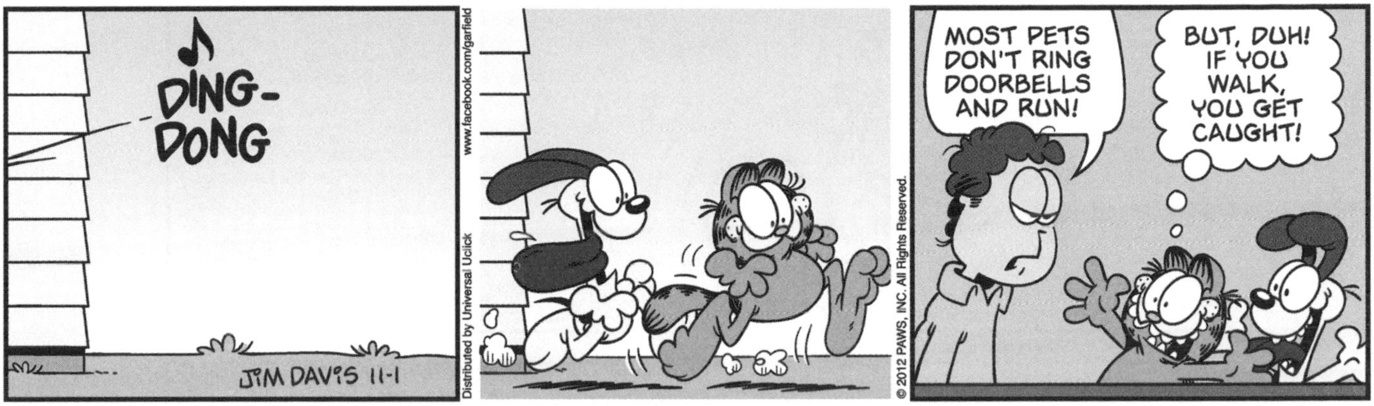
DING-DONG
JIM DAVIS 11-1
www.facebook.com/garfield
Distributed by Universal Uclick
MOST PETS DON'T RING DOORBELLS AND RUN!
BUT, DUH! IF YOU WALK, YOU GET CAUGHT!
© 2012 PAWS, INC. All Rights Reserved.

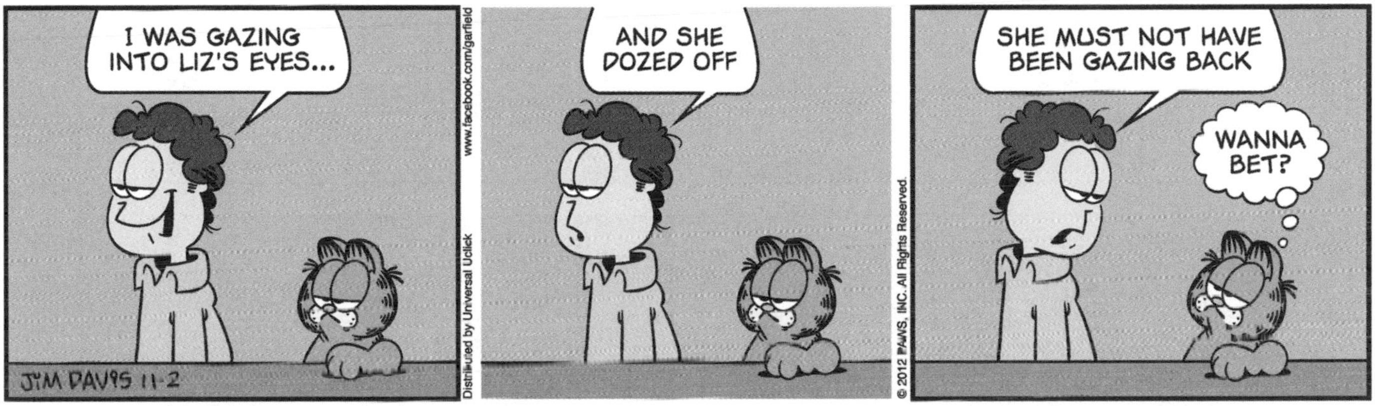
I WAS GAZING INTO LIZ'S EYES...
JIM DAVIS 11-2
www.facebook.com/garfield
Distributed by Universal Uclick
AND SHE DOZED OFF
SHE MUST NOT HAVE BEEN GAZING BACK
WANNA BET?
© 2012 PAWS, INC. All Rights Reserved.

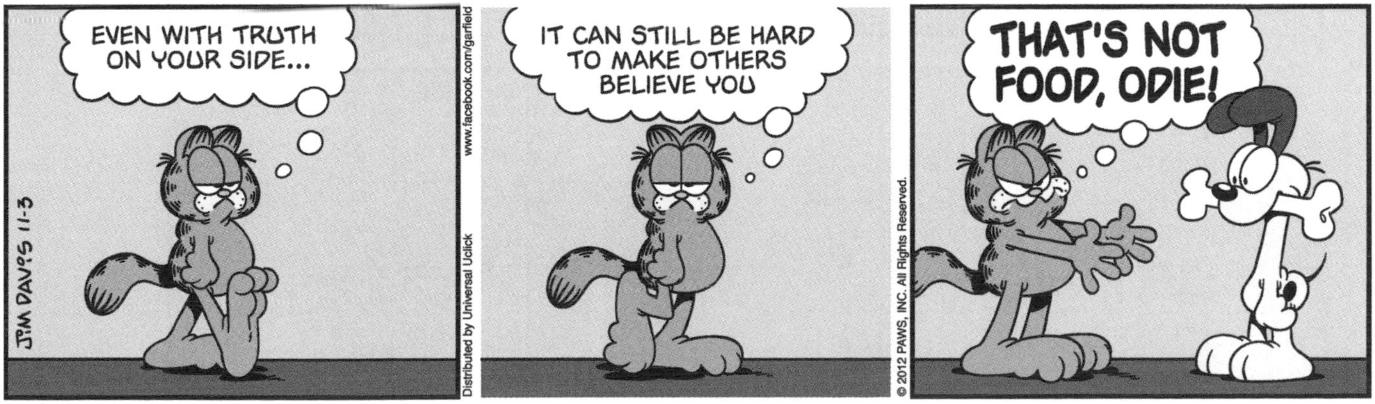
EVEN WITH TRUTH ON YOUR SIDE...
JIM DAVIS 11-3
www.facebook.com/garfield
Distributed by Universal Uclick
IT CAN STILL BE HARD TO MAKE OTHERS BELIEVE YOU
THAT'S NOT FOOD, ODIE!
© 2012 PAWS, INC. All Rights Reserved.

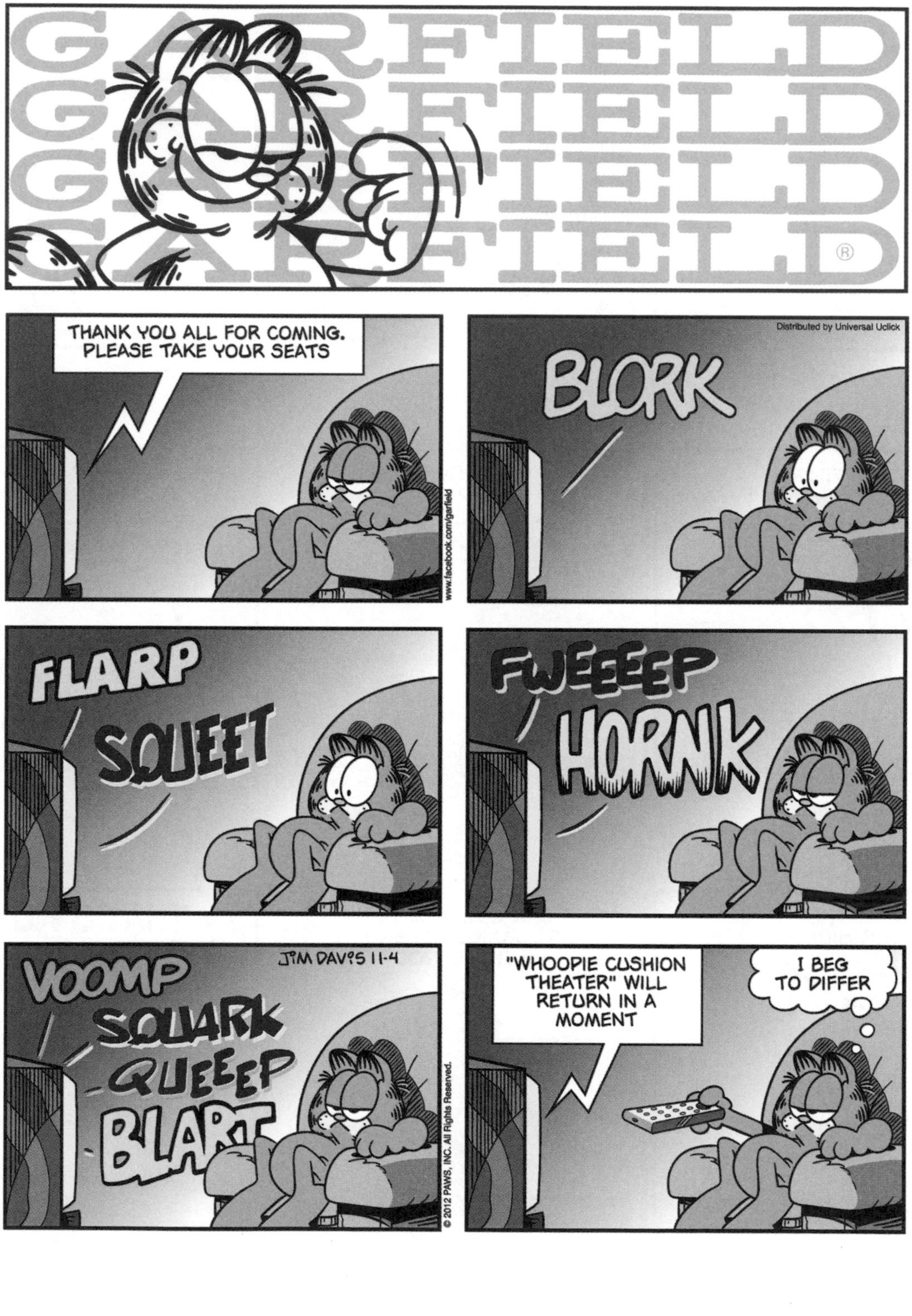
GARFIELD
GARFIELD
GARFIELD
GARFIELD®
THANK YOU ALL FOR COMING. PLEASE TAKE YOUR SEATS
www.facebook.com/garfield
Distributed by Universal Uclick
BLORK
FLARP
SQUEET
FWEEEEP
HORNK
VOOMP
SQUARK
QUEEEP
BLART
JIM DAVIS 11-4
© 2012 PAWS, INC. All Rights Reserved.
"WHOOPIE CUSHION THEATER" WILL RETURN IN A MOMENT
I BEG TO DIFFER

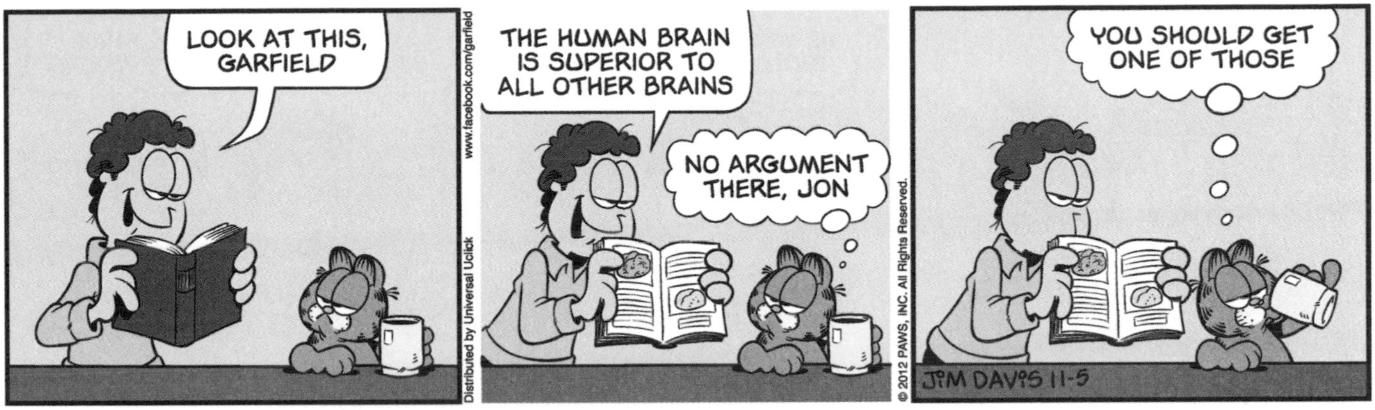
LOOK AT THIS, GARFIELD
Distributed by Universal Uclick
www.facebook.com/garfield
THE HUMAN BRAIN IS SUPERIOR TO ALL OTHER BRAINS
NO ARGUMENT THERE, JON
© 2012 PAWS, INC. All Rights Reserved.
YOU SHOULD GET ONE OF THOSE
JIM DAVIS 11-5

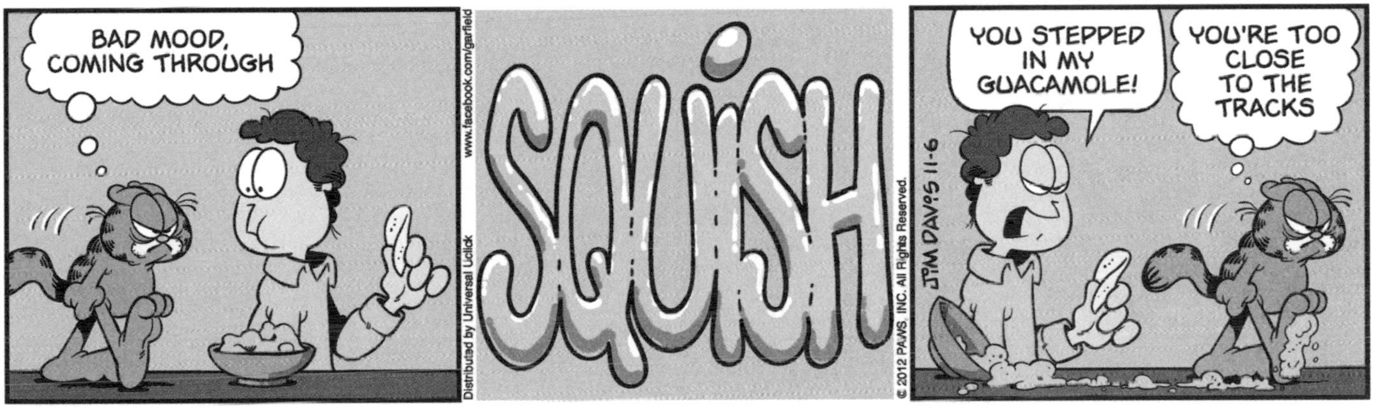
BAD MOOD, COMING THROUGH
Distributed by Universal Uclick
www.facebook.com/garfield
SQUISH
© 2012 PAWS, INC. All Rights Reserved.
JIM DAVIS 11-6
YOU STEPPED IN MY GUACAMOLE!
YOU'RE TOO CLOSE TO THE TRACKS

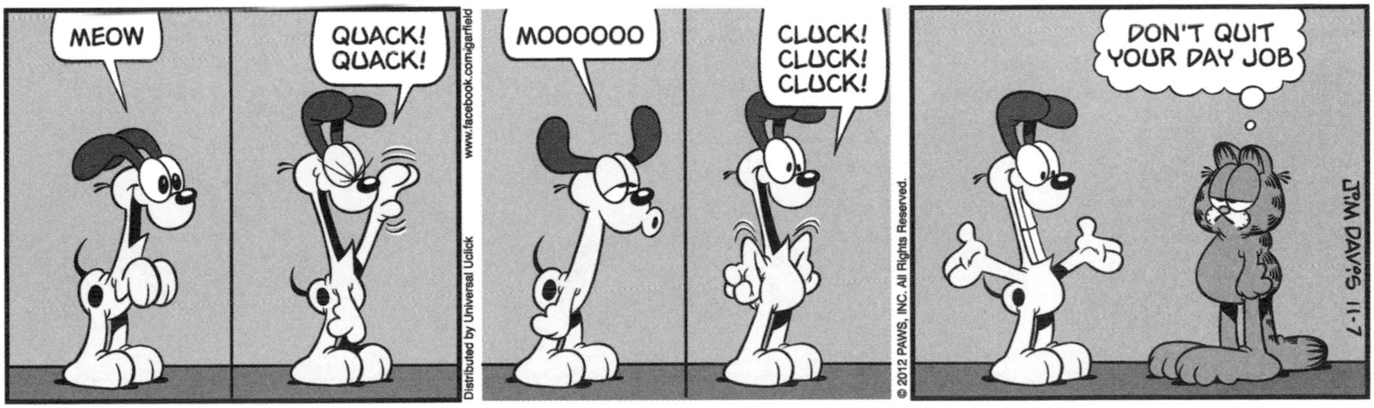
MEOW
QUACK! QUACK!
Distributed by Universal Uclick
www.facebook.com/garfield
MOOOOOO
CLUCK! CLUCK! CLUCK!
© 2012 PAWS, INC. All Rights Reserved.
DON'T QUIT YOUR DAY JOB
JIM DAVIS 11-7

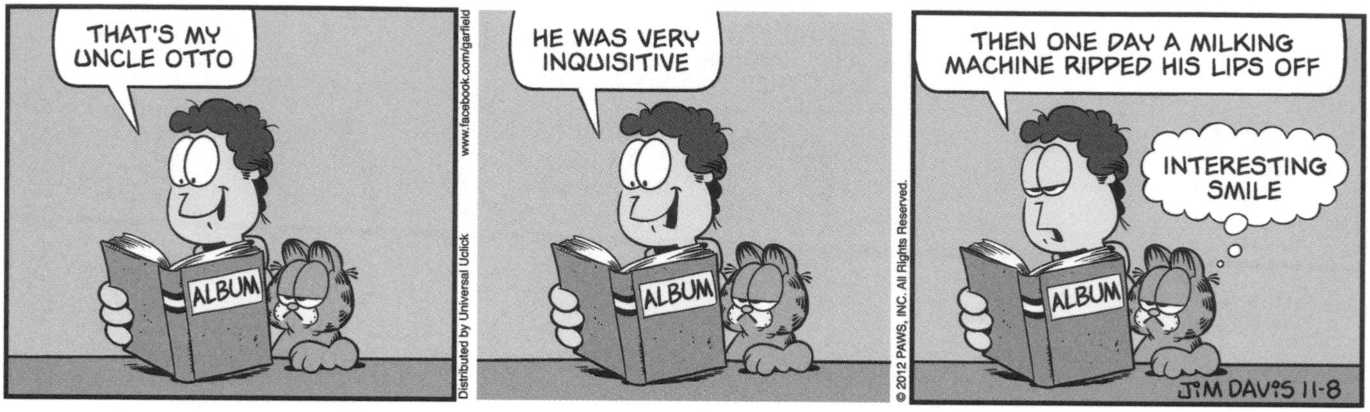
THAT'S MY UNCLE OTTO
Distributed by Universal Uclick www.facebook.com/garfield
HE WAS VERY INQUISITIVE
© 2012 PAWS, INC. All Rights Reserved.
THEN ONE DAY A MILKING MACHINE RIPPED HIS LIPS OFF
INTERESTING SMILE
ALBUM
JIM DAVIS 11-8

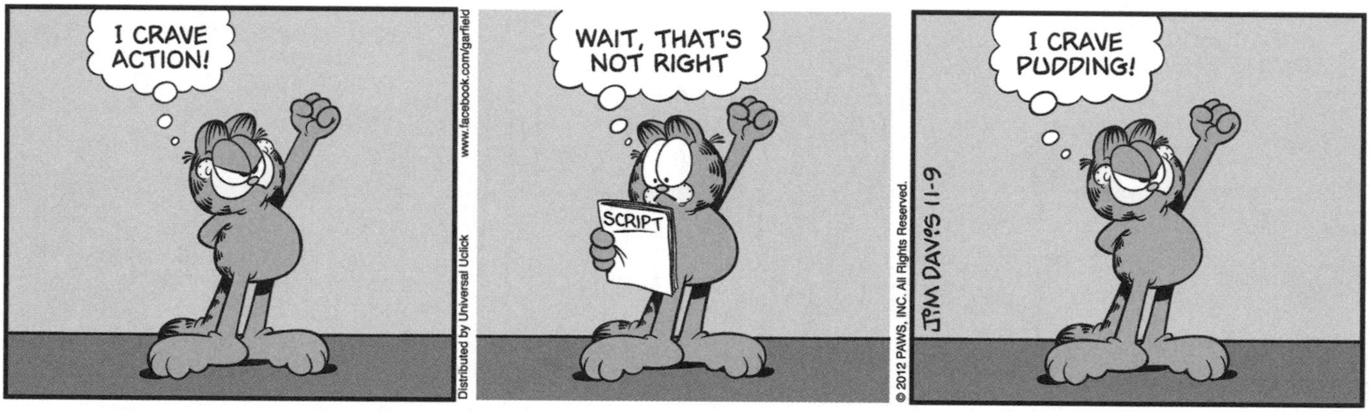
I CRAVE ACTION!
Distributed by Universal Uclick www.facebook.com/garfield
WAIT, THAT'S NOT RIGHT
SCRIPT
© 2012 PAWS, INC. All Rights Reserved.
JIM DAVIS 11-9
I CRAVE PUDDING!

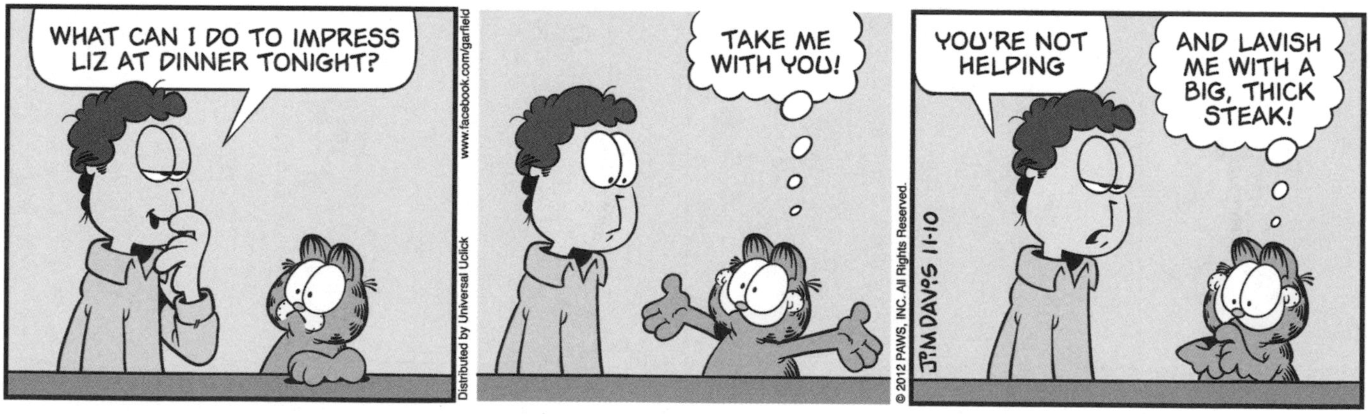
WHAT CAN I DO TO IMPRESS LIZ AT DINNER TONIGHT?
Distributed by Universal Uclick www.facebook.com/garfield
TAKE ME WITH YOU!
© 2012 PAWS, INC. All Rights Reserved.
JIM DAVIS 11-10
YOU'RE NOT HELPING
AND LAVISH ME WITH A BIG, THICK STEAK!

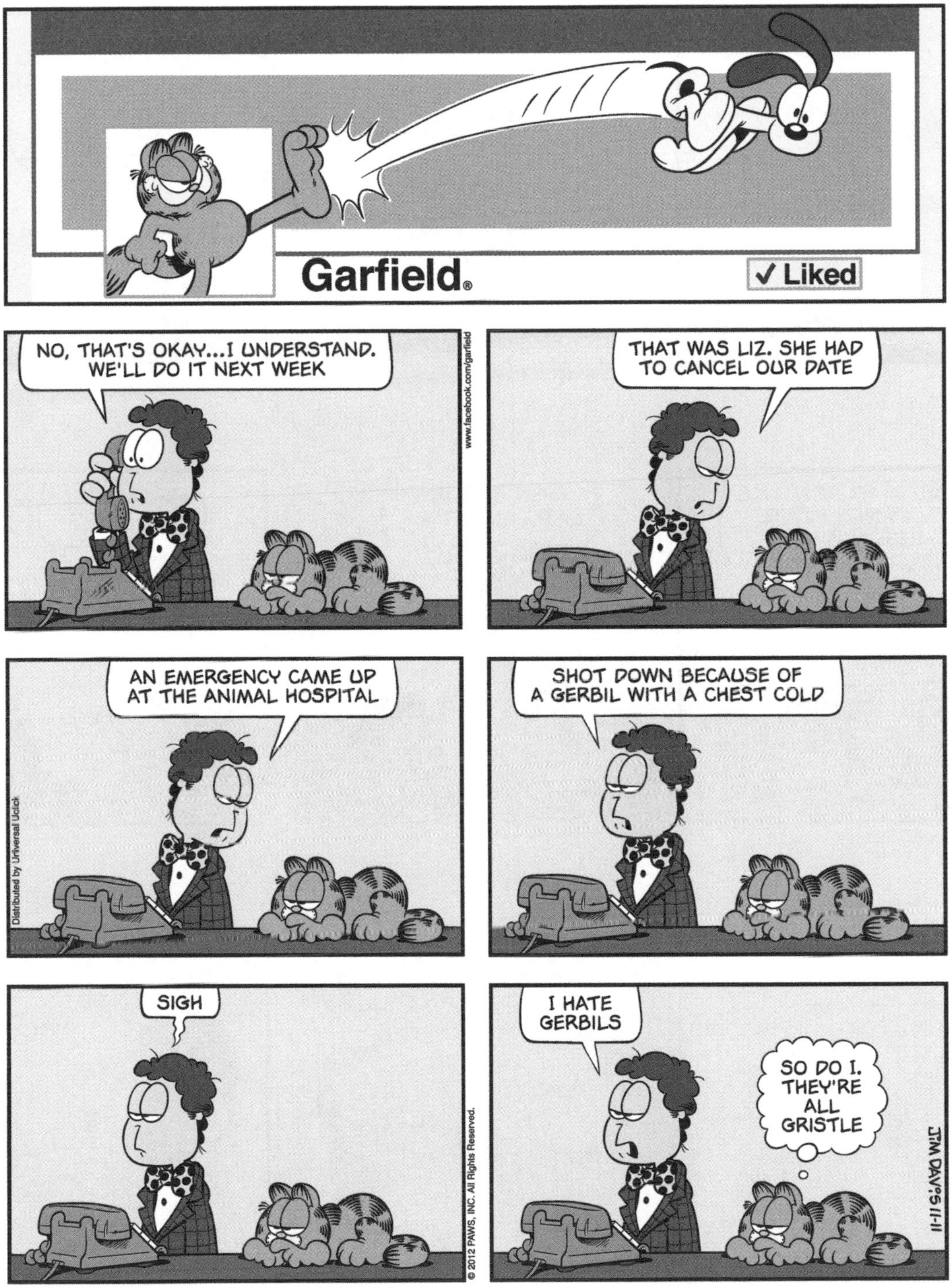
Garfield®
✓ Liked
NO, THAT'S OKAY...I UNDERSTAND. WE'LL DO IT NEXT WEEK
www.facebook.com/garfield
THAT WAS LIZ. SHE HAD TO CANCEL OUR DATE
AN EMERGENCY CAME UP AT THE ANIMAL HOSPITAL
Distributed by Universal Uclick
SHOT DOWN BECAUSE OF A GERBIL WITH A CHEST COLD
SIGH
© 2012 PAWS, INC. All Rights Reserved.
I HATE GERBILS
SO DO I. THEY'RE ALL GRISTLE
JIM DAVIS 5-1-11

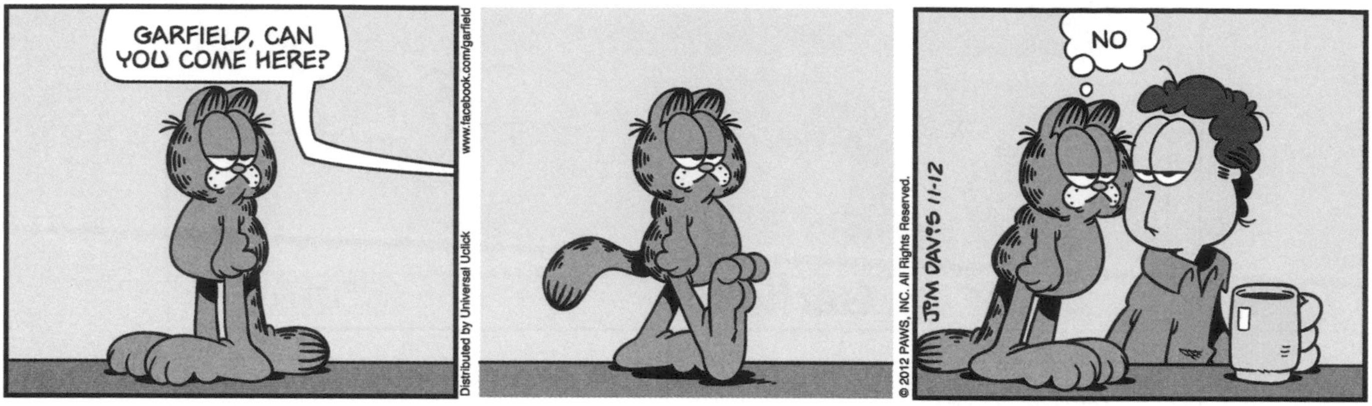
GARFIELD, CAN YOU COME HERE?
Distributed by Universal Uclick www.facebook.com/garfield
NO
© 2012 PAWS, INC. All Rights Reserved.
JIM DAVIS 11-12

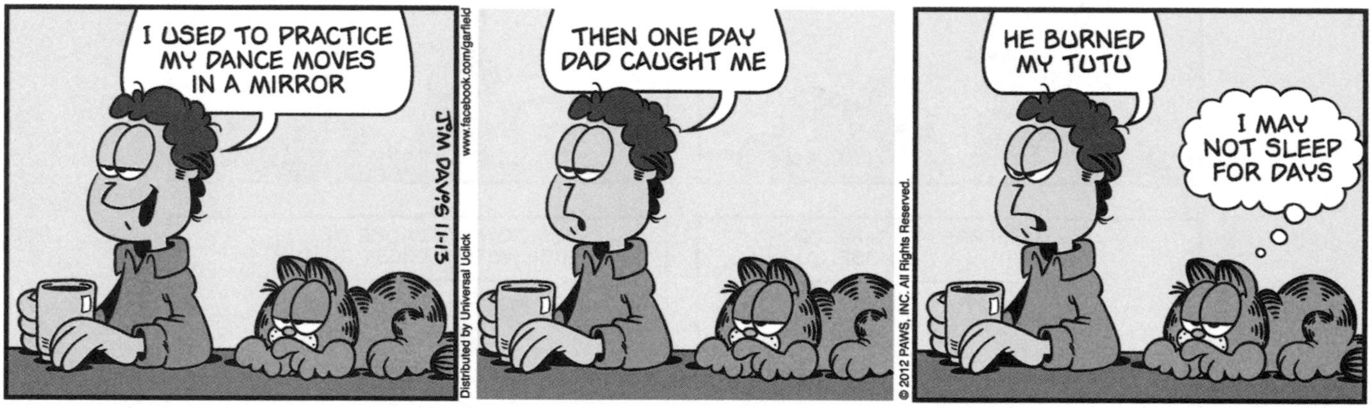
I USED TO PRACTICE MY DANCE MOVES IN A MIRROR
JIM DAVIS 11-13
Distributed by Universal Uclick www.facebook.com/garfield
THEN ONE DAY DAD CAUGHT ME
© 2012 PAWS, INC. All Rights Reserved.
HE BURNED MY TUTU
I MAY NOT SLEEP FOR DAYS

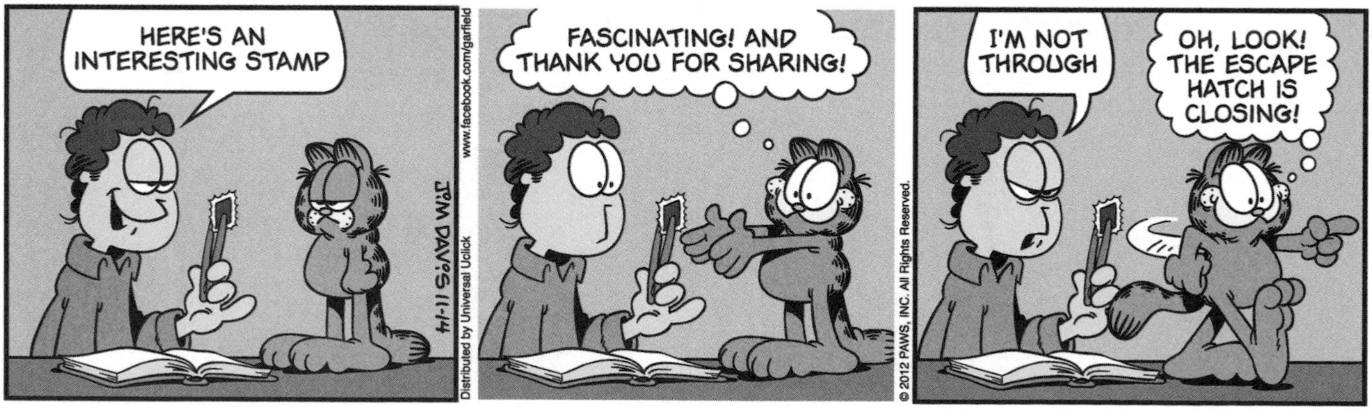
HERE'S AN INTERESTING STAMP
JIM DAVIS 11-14
Distributed by Universal Uclick www.facebook.com/garfield
FASCINATING! AND THANK YOU FOR SHARING!
© 2012 PAWS, INC. All Rights Reserved.
I'M NOT THROUGH
OH, LOOK! THE ESCAPE HATCH IS CLOSING!

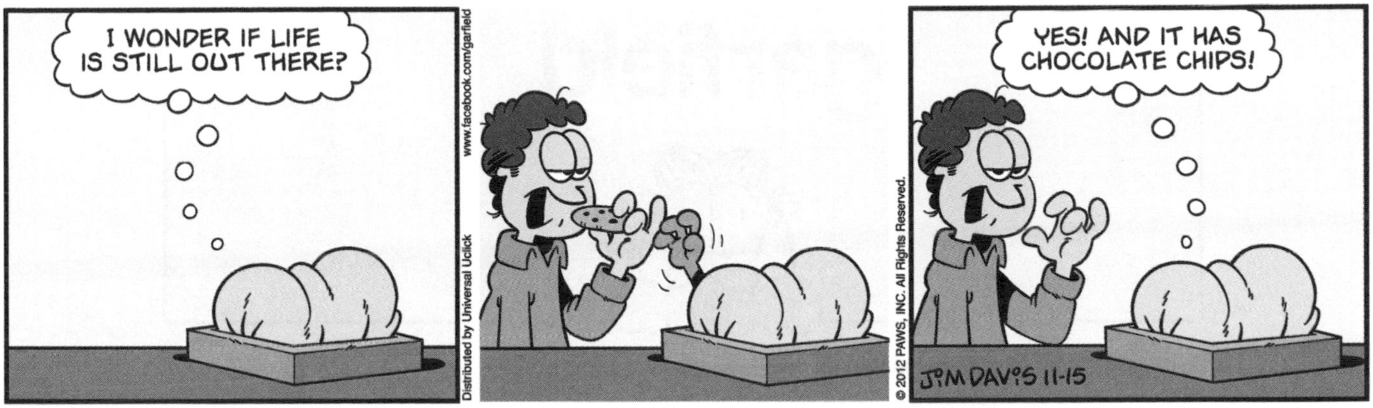
I WONDER IF LIFE IS STILL OUT THERE?
www.facebook.com/garfield
Distributed by Universal Uclick
YES! AND IT HAS CHOCOLATE CHIPS!
© 2012 PAWS, INC. All Rights Reserved.
JIM DAVIS 11-15

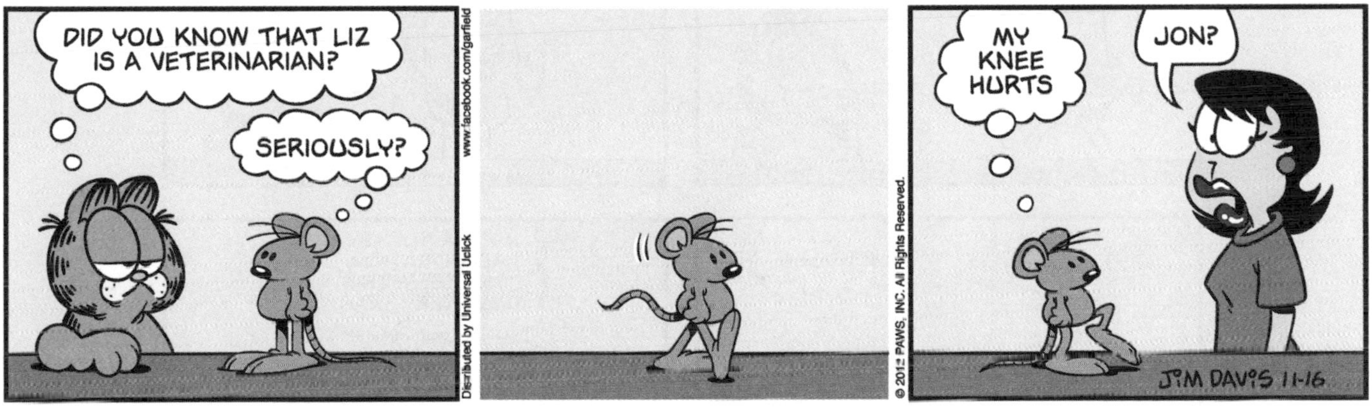
DID YOU KNOW THAT LIZ IS A VETERINARIAN?
SERIOUSLY?
www.facebook.com/garfield
Distributed by Universal Uclick
MY KNEE HURTS
JON?
© 2012 PAWS, INC. All Rights Reserved.
JIM DAVIS 11-16

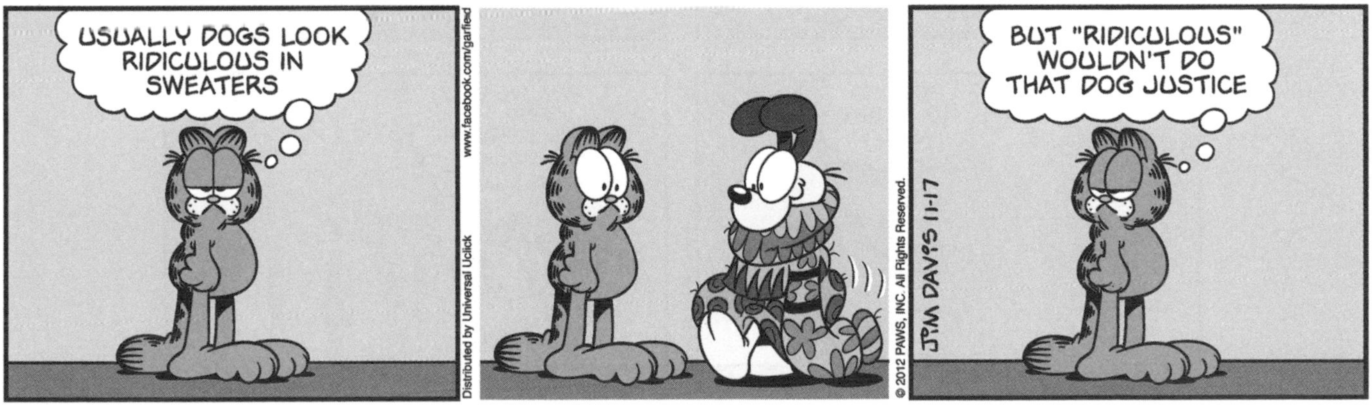
USUALLY DOGS LOOK RIDICULOUS IN SWEATERS
www.facebook.com/garfield
Distributed by Universal Uclick
© 2012 PAWS, INC. All Rights Reserved.
JIM DAVIS 11-17
BUT "RIDICULOUS" WOULDN'T DO THAT DOG JUSTICE

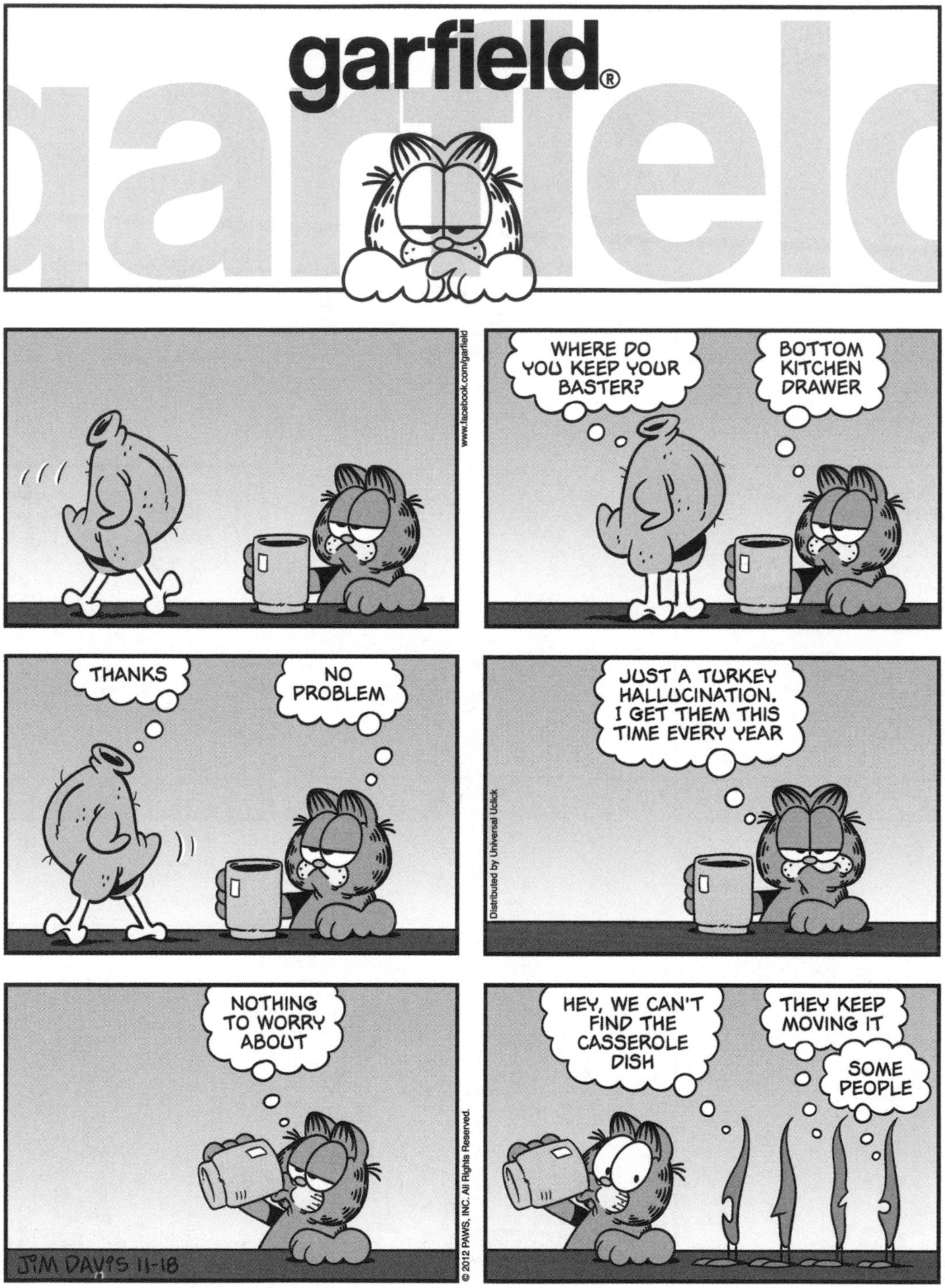
garfield®
www.facebook.com/garfield
WHERE DO YOU KEEP YOUR BASTER?
BOTTOM KITCHEN DRAWER
THANKS
NO PROBLEM
Distributed by Universal Uclick
JUST A TURKEY HALLUCINATION. I GET THEM THIS TIME EVERY YEAR
NOTHING TO WORRY ABOUT
JIM DAVIS 11-18
© 2012 PAWS, INC. All Rights Reserved.
HEY, WE CAN'T FIND THE CASSEROLE DISH
THEY KEEP MOVING IT
SOME PEOPLE

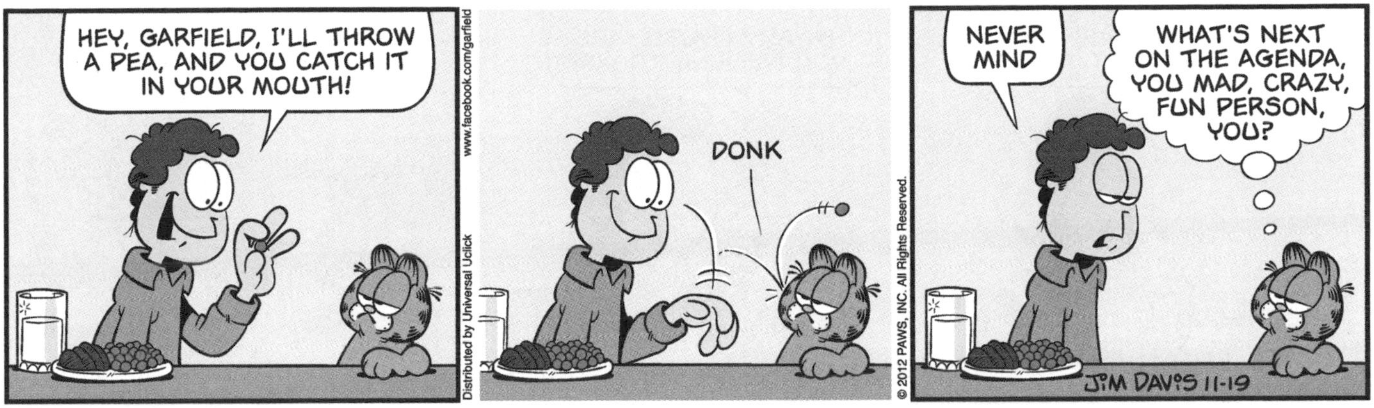
HEY, GARFIELD, I'LL THROW A PEA, AND YOU CATCH IT IN YOUR MOUTH!
DONK
NEVER MIND
WHAT'S NEXT ON THE AGENDA, YOU MAD, CRAZY, FUN PERSON, YOU?
JIM DAVIS 11-19
Distributed by Universal Uclick www.facebook.com/garfield
© 2012 PAWS, INC. All Rights Reserved.

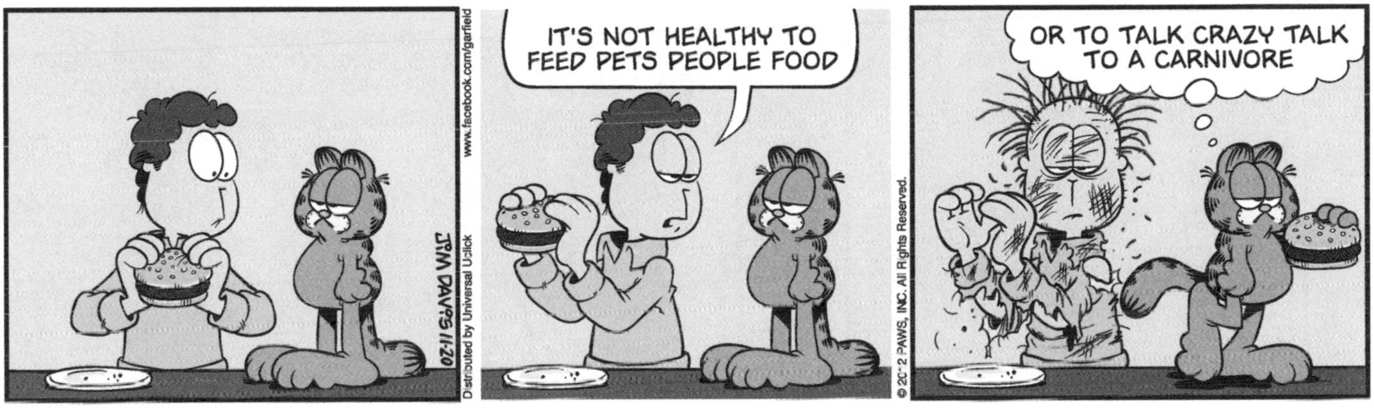
JIM DAVIS 11-20
IT'S NOT HEALTHY TO FEED PETS PEOPLE FOOD
OR TO TALK CRAZY TALK TO A CARNIVORE
Distributed by Universal Uclick www.facebook.com/garfield
© 2012 PAWS, INC. All Rights Reserved.

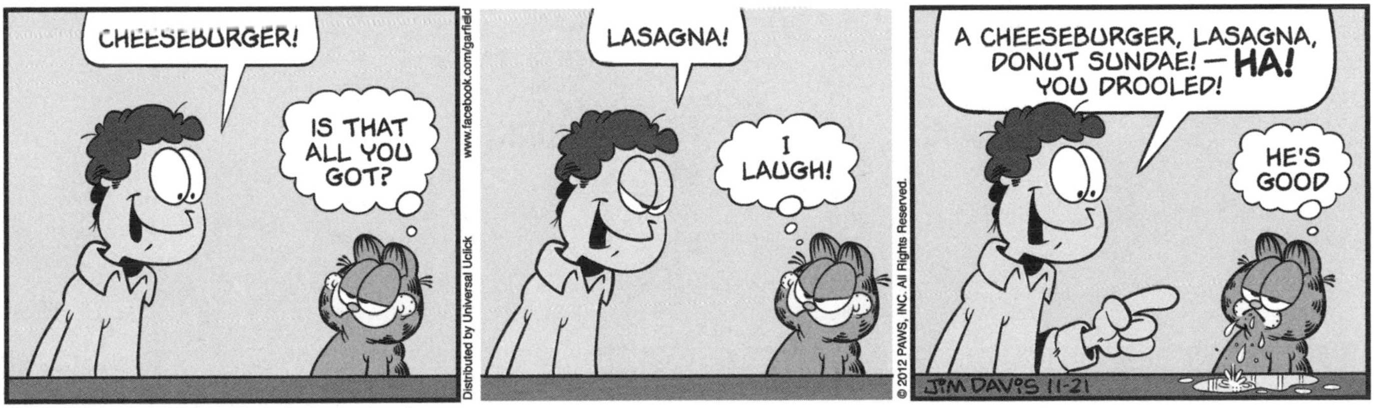
CHEESEBURGER!
IS THAT ALL YOU GOT?
LASAGNA!
I LAUGH!
A CHEESEBURGER, LASAGNA, DONUT SUNDAE! — HA! YOU DROOLED!
HE'S GOOD
JIM DAVIS 11-21
Distributed by Universal Uclick www.facebook.com/garfield
© 2012 PAWS, INC. All Rights Reserved.

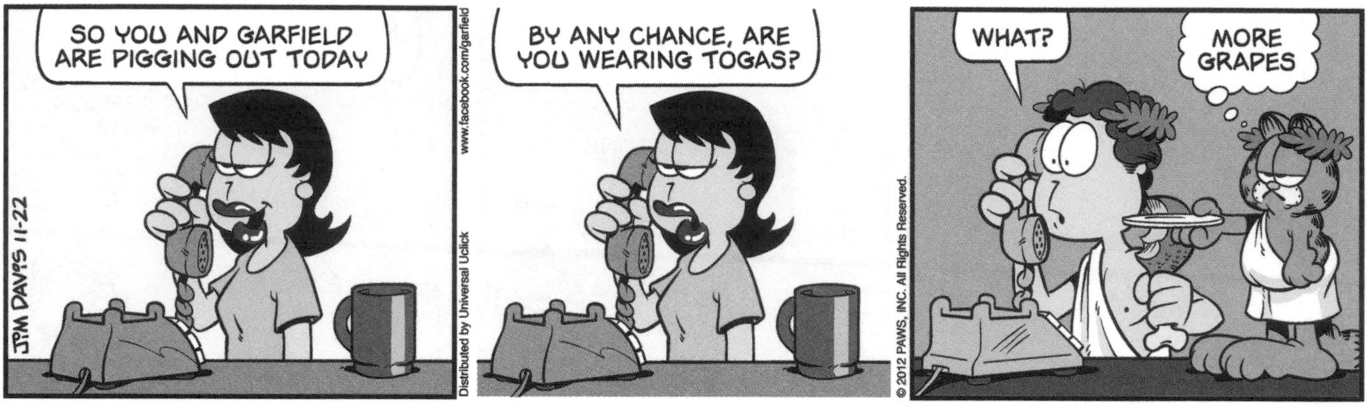
JIM DAVIS 11-22
SO YOU AND GARFIELD ARE PIGGING OUT TODAY
Distributed by Universal Uclick www.facebook.com/garfield
BY ANY CHANCE, ARE YOU WEARING TOGAS?
© 2012 PAWS, INC. All Rights Reserved.
WHAT?
MORE GRAPES

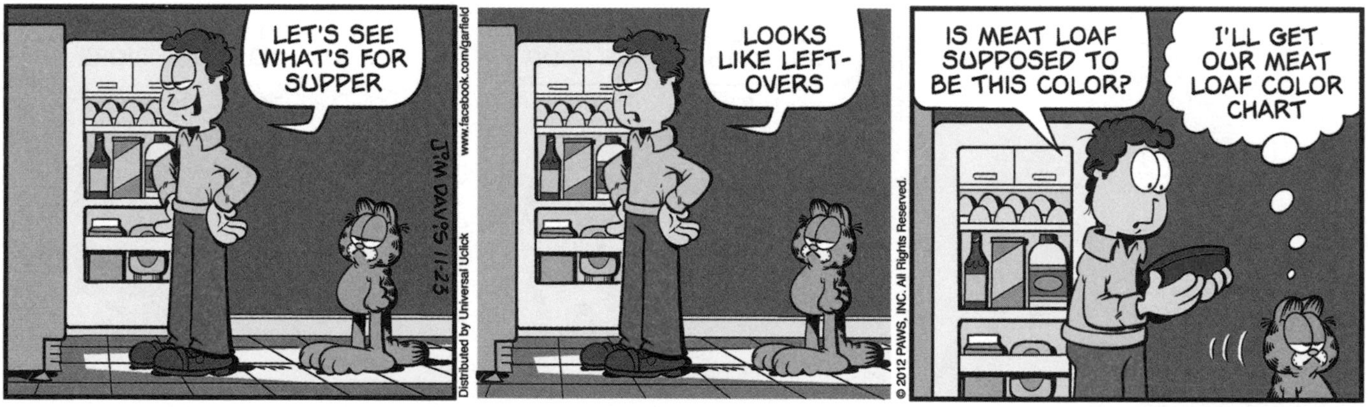
LET'S SEE WHAT'S FOR SUPPER
JIM DAVIS 11-23
Distributed by Universal Uclick www.facebook.com/garfield
LOOKS LIKE LEFT-OVERS
© 2012 PAWS, INC. All Rights Reserved.
IS MEAT LOAF SUPPOSED TO BE THIS COLOR?
I'LL GET OUR MEAT LOAF COLOR CHART

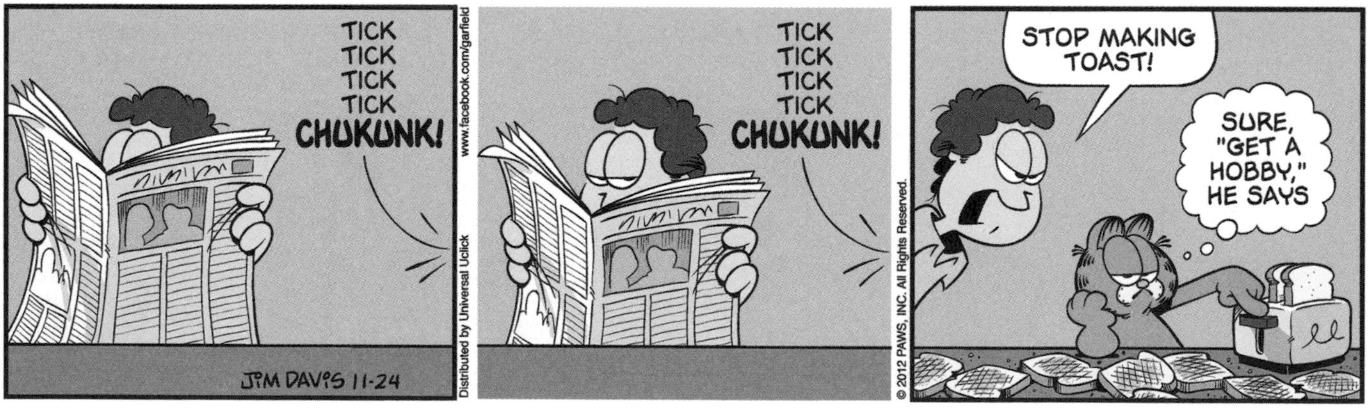
TICK TICK TICK TICK
CHUKUNK!
JIM DAVIS 11-24
Distributed by Universal Uclick www.facebook.com/garfield
TICK TICK TICK TICK
CHUKUNK!
© 2012 PAWS, INC. All Rights Reserved.
STOP MAKING TOAST!
SURE, "GET A HOBBY," HE SAYS

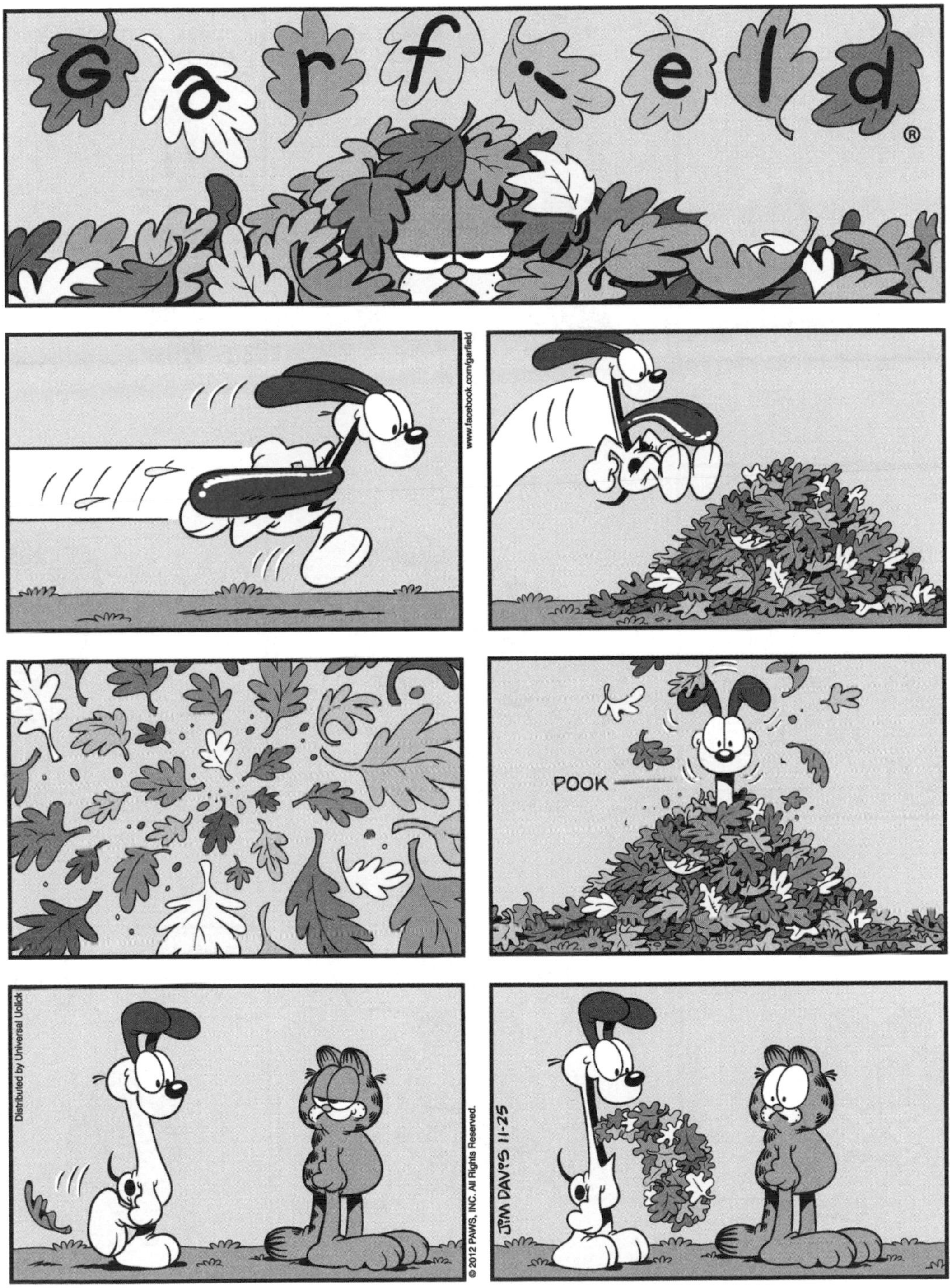
Garfield®
www.facebook.com/garfield
POOK
Distributed by Universal Uclick
© 2012 PAWS, INC. All Rights Reserved.
JIM DAVIS 11-25

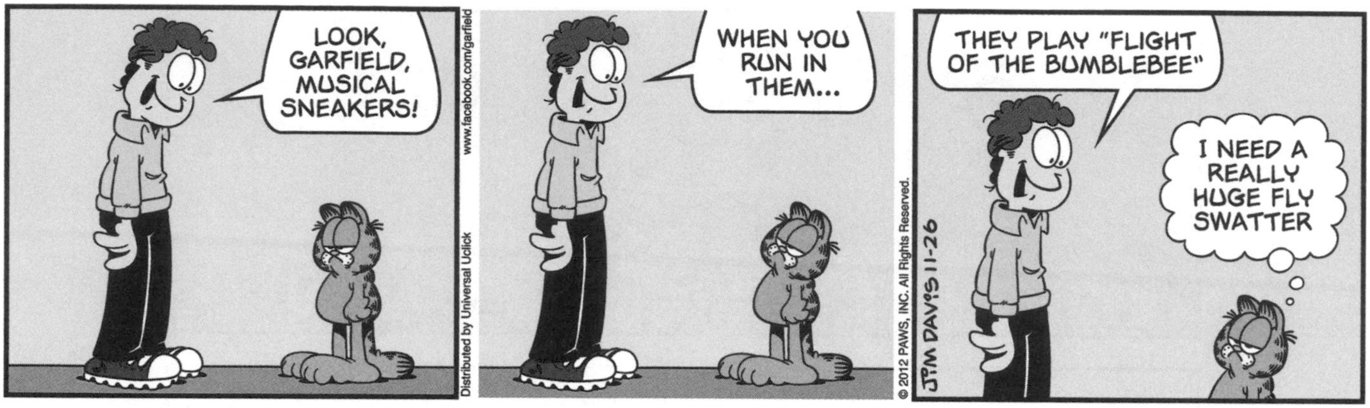
LOOK, GARFIELD, MUSICAL SNEAKERS!
WHEN YOU RUN IN THEM...
THEY PLAY "FLIGHT OF THE BUMBLEBEE"
I NEED A REALLY HUGE FLY SWATTER
Distributed by Universal Uclick www.facebook.com/garfield
© 2012 PAWS, INC. All Rights Reserved.
JIM DAVIS 11-26

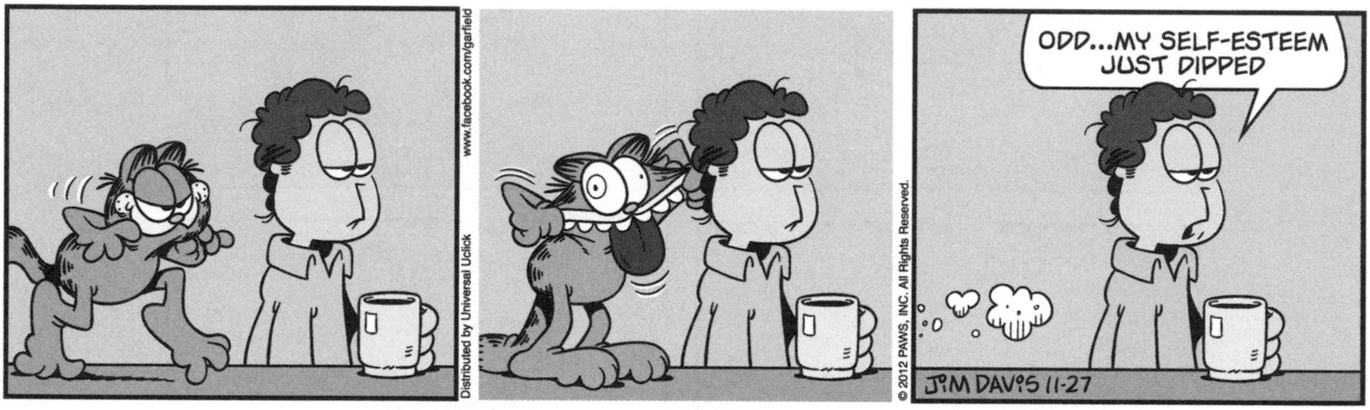
ODD...MY SELF-ESTEEM JUST DIPPED
Distributed by Universal Uclick www.facebook.com/garfield
© 2012 PAWS, INC. All Rights Reserved.
JIM DAVIS 11-27

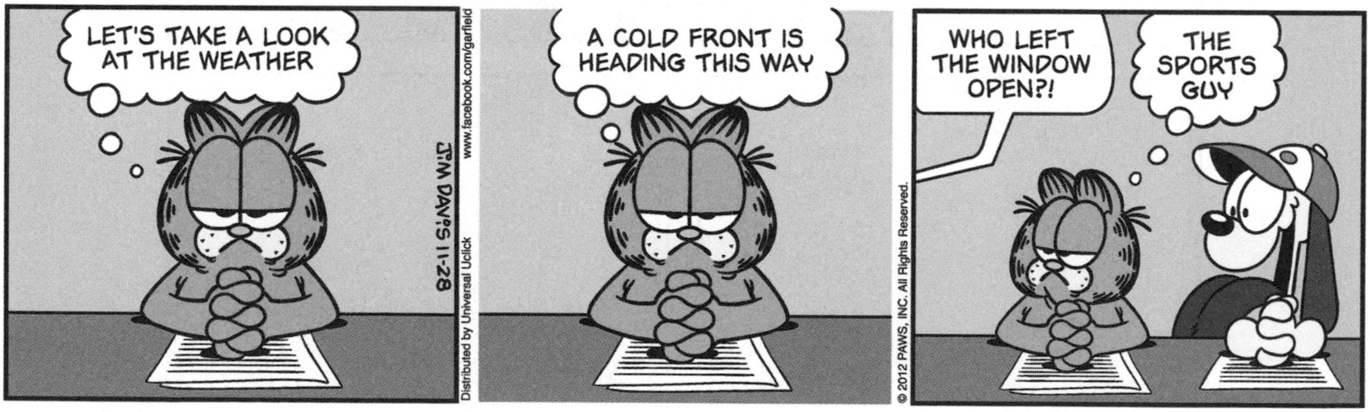
LET'S TAKE A LOOK AT THE WEATHER
A COLD FRONT IS HEADING THIS WAY
WHO LEFT THE WINDOW OPEN?!
THE SPORTS GUY
JIM DAVIS 11-28
Distributed by Universal Uclick www.facebook.com/garfield
© 2012 PAWS, INC. All Rights Reserved.

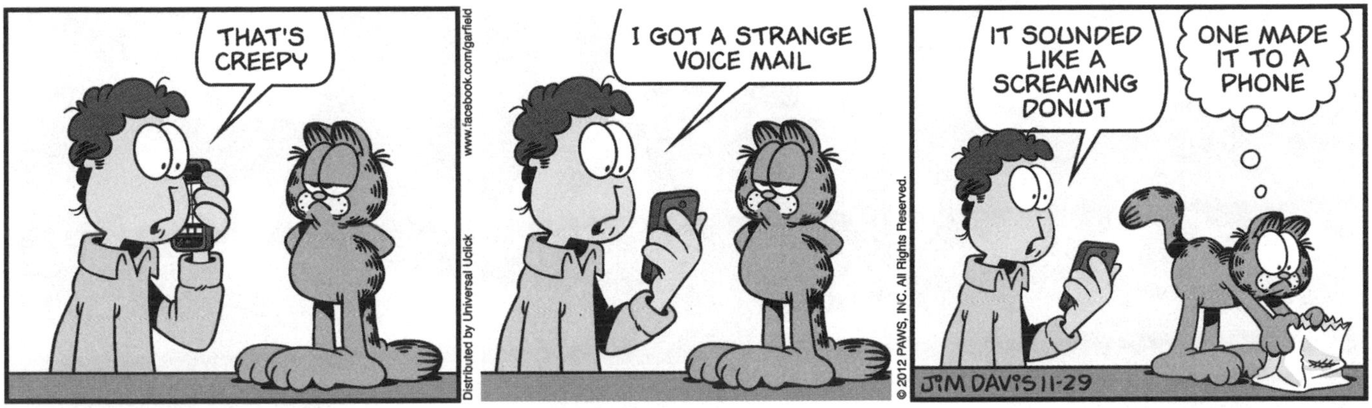
I GOT A STRANGE VOICE MAIL
IT SOUNDED LIKE A SCREAMING DONUT
ONE MADE IT TO A PHONE
THAT'S CREEPY
JIM DAVIS 11-29
www.facebook.com/garfield
Distributed by Universal Uclick
© 2012 PAWS, INC. All Rights Reserved.

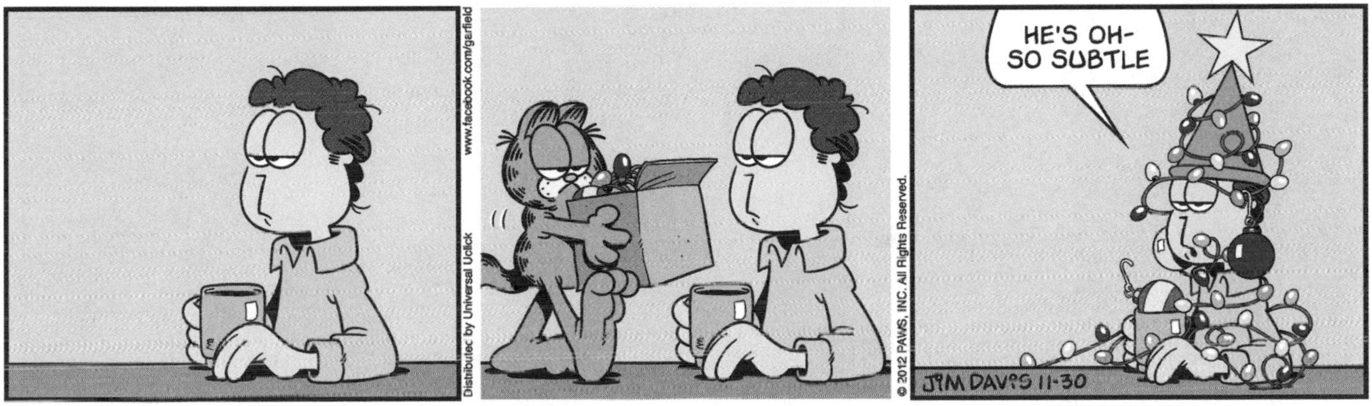
HE'S OH-SO SUBTLE
JIM DAVIS 11-30
www.facebook.com/garfield
Distributed by Universal Uclick
© 2012 PAWS, INC. All Rights Reserved.

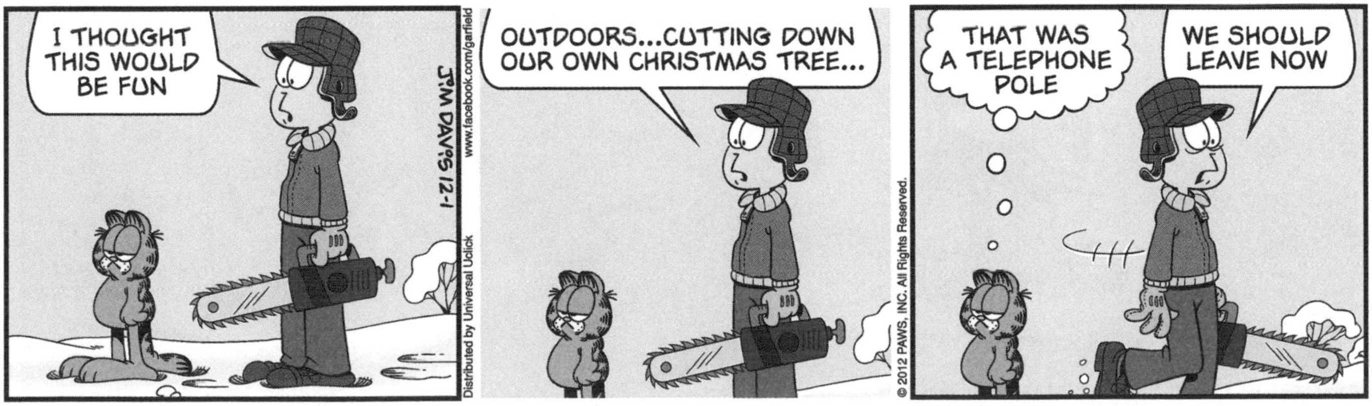
OUTDOORS...CUTTING DOWN OUR OWN CHRISTMAS TREE...
I THOUGHT THIS WOULD BE FUN
THAT WAS A TELEPHONE POLE
WE SHOULD LEAVE NOW
JIM DAVIS 12-1
www.facebook.com/garfield
Distributed by Universal Uclick
© 2012 PAWS, INC. All Rights Reserved.

More Super School Excuses

Why I Had a Bad Game...

A grasshopper hopped up my nose!

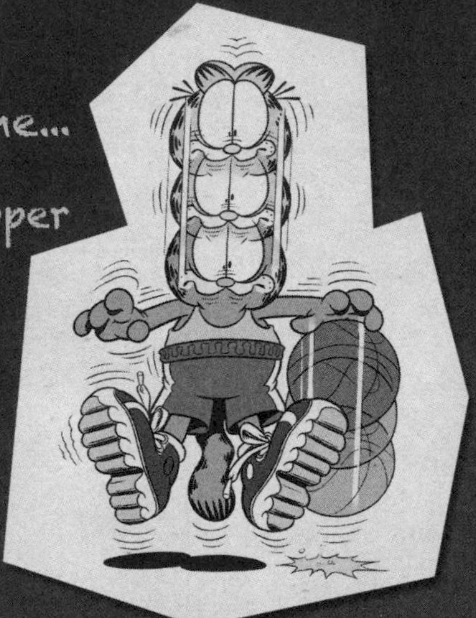

Why I Was Absent...

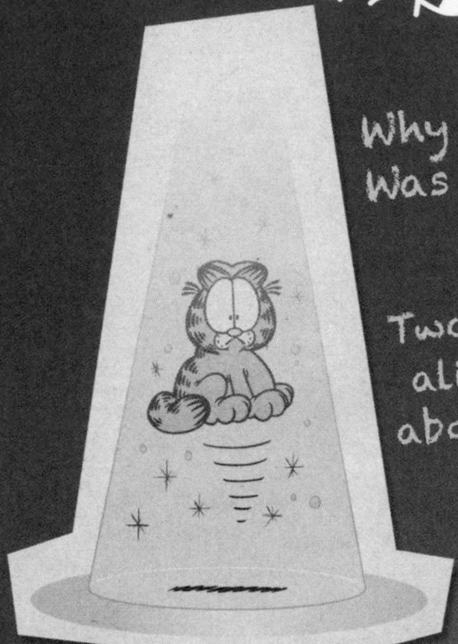

Two words: alien abduction!

Why I Need to See the Nurse...

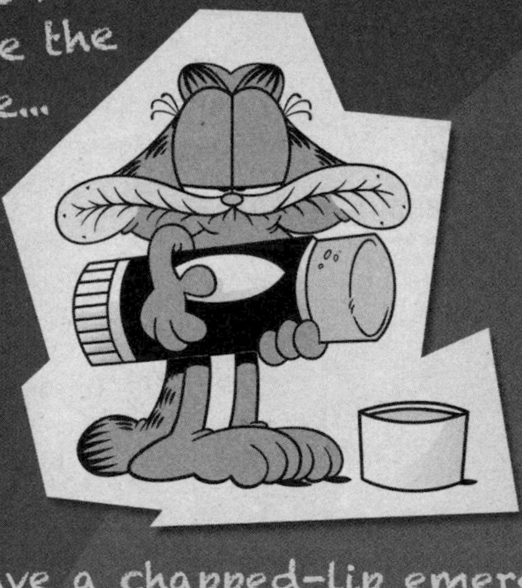

I have a chapped-lip emergency.

Why I Can't Go Out with You...

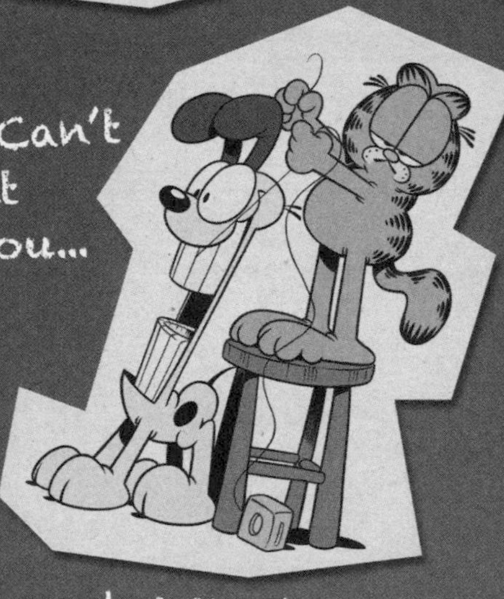

Sorry, but that's my night to floss the dog.

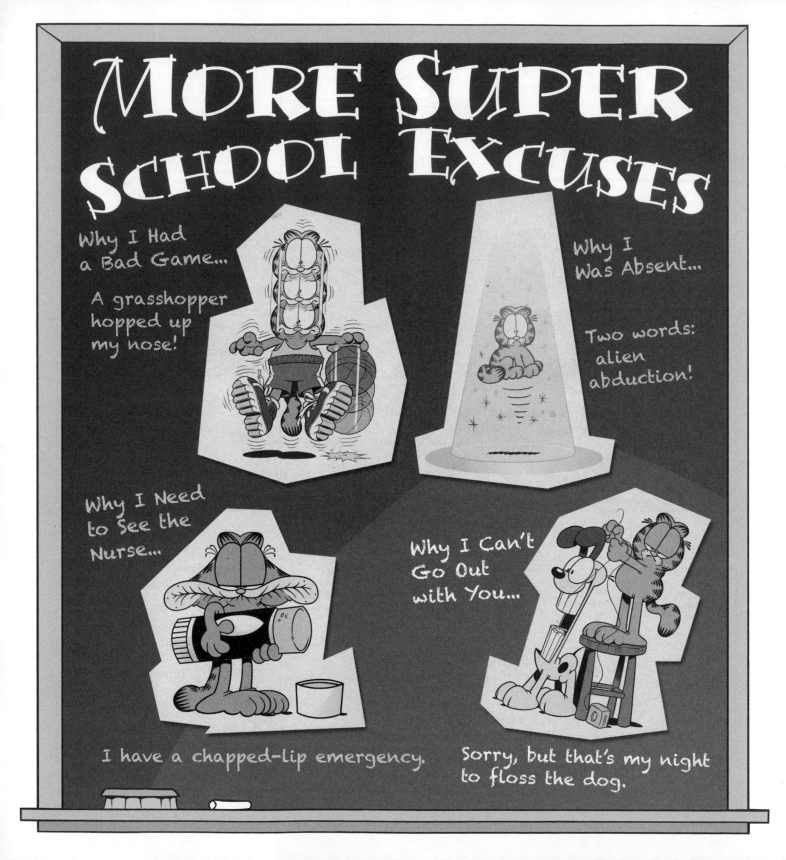

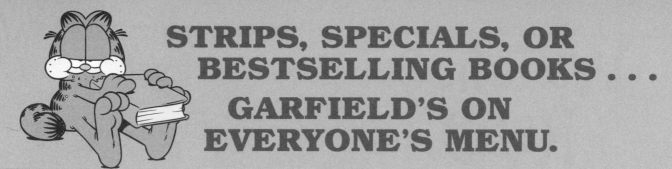

STRIPS, SPECIALS, OR BESTSELLING BOOKS . . .
GARFIELD'S ON EVERYONE'S MENU.

Don't miss even one episode in the Tubby Tabby's hilarious series!

New larger, full-color format!